DISTANT DRUMS

DISTANT DRUMS

IRISH SOLDIERS IN FOREIGN ARMIES

MYLES DUNGAN

Appletree Press

To my mother, Maire, and her uncle, Rifleman John Patrick
O'Reilly,
2 Battalion, Royal Irish Rifles, killed in action in France, 29
September 1916.

And to my late father, William Niall Dungan, and his uncle,
Guardsman Thomas Coonan, 4th Battalion, Guards Machine Gun
Regiment, killed in action in France, 7 May 1918.

Published and printed by
The Appletree Press Ltd
19–21 Alfred Street
Belfast BT2 8DL
1993

British Library Cataloguing-in-Publication Data
A catalogue record for this book is available from the British Library.

ISBN 0 86281 384 0

9 8 7 6 5 3 2 1

Contents

Foreword

A book which grows out of a radio series is, in one sense only, a sound basis for historical research. The imperatives of the broadcaster are not those of the historian. The latter bases little of his work on oral evidence, the former bases most of his on the spoken word. So anyone expecting a definitive and exhaustive work of military history from *Distant Drums* had better continue that search elsewhere. The writer has no great interest in military history *per se*, has never had the slightest desire to fight in a war (or even a modest skirmish for that matter), but is fascinated by those who have done so and by the stories they have to tell. Few works of military history have ever successfully conveyed the 'feel' of what it is like to experience raw fear, hunger, extreme discomfort and sheer misery and loneliness, all of which are as much elements of war as frontal assaults, flanking attacks or regimental colours.

The story of the Irish soldier, the overwhelming majority of whom have fought in foreign armies, has many interesting facets of general historical interest emanating from the divisive and often tortured history of this island. In a volume purely devoted to the study of military history, these could easily be ignored amidst the rumble of cannon and the celebration of the courage of myriad Irish units in battle. The selection of a small number of conflicts for particular attention in this book is entirely arbitrary and accords only with the interests and tastes of the writer. Such is the egotism and fascism of authorship! An opening chapter, like a grasshopper on hot asphalt, jumps around a multiplicity of wars while only briefly alighting on any particular one. What follows tends to concentrate on 'modern' warfare, while still consigning some conflicts to perdition. The emphasis in the radio series was on the spoken word. It relied on living witnesses, those who had participated in warfare themselves and had stories worth telling. This immediately narrowed down the number of available wars. The inclusion of the American Civil and Frontier Wars reflected a personal bias and a belief that not enough attention has been paid in

Ireland to 'emigrant history'. How many Irish school-children know that 100,000 native Irishmen fought in the United States of America's crippling Civil War? How many are aware that thirty-two Irish died along with Colonel George Armstrong Custer at the Little Bighorn?

Because much of the material in this book is based on oral evidence gathered by the author (some areas have been beefed up and supplemented by documentary or secondary written sources), and because of the author's lamentable ignorance of military history, there are probably a number of 'howlers' lurking in the pages of this work for the initiated to drool over. Let me apologise for them in advance. I have made every effort to check out and reconcile the accounts of participants in particular events but, in the end, when in doubt I have opted to trust the memories (and veracity) of those who are quoted.

I owe a debt of gratitude to a number of people, principally the sixty or more interviewees who contributed to the original radio series and those who, additionally, agreed to interviews for this book. Kevin Healy, Director of Radio, and Tom Manning, Head of Information Programmes in RTE, both stoically endured my overweening enthusiasm for the series and are, therefore, partly responsible for the contents of the book. For Appletree Press, Douglas Marshall shocked me one bright day by writing to me and asking me to turn words and music into words on a printed page; since then he has had to tolerate my bewilderingly inconsistent changes of direction, just as my editor Andrea Service has had to endure lapses in grammar and punctuation as well as excessive procrastination. In America I was taken by the hand and led around Gettysburg (an unforgettable experience) by Dan Gregor, Colonel Ken Powers and Jack McCormack (thanks for the Civil War bullet, Jack!) and got a preliminary 'briefing' from the Gettysburg National Military Park historian Bob Prosperi. A similar welcome awaited me in the wonderful Gene Autry Western Heritage Museum in Los Angeles from John Langellier and Kevin Mulroy. For his kindness in Marquette University I want to thank Professor Tom Hachey and for getting me there, Sean Keane. I am indebted to Professor James McPherson in Princeton for his time and expertise (I was delighted just to have an excuse to walk through the place). Love and best wishes are also due to Leo and Dympna Fitzsimon.

For the use of material from unpublished manuscripts I am obliged to Elizabeth Dobbs, Julie Parsons, Henry O'Kane and Paddy Devlin and for access to his South American material, Brian McGinn. Frank Harte let me use some great songs in the radio series, verses of which have found their way into this text. Frank McGuinness let me impose upon his time. In RTE Colm Connolly photocopied everything he had on Myles Keogh, Danny McDonald copied my tapes and Stephen d'Arcy and Frank Kelly did not ask half enough questions about how long certain books were missing from the RTE library. Sean Murphy in Waterford put me in contact with a lot of valuable veterans, as did Sean Fitzsimmons, while Pat Smith of Leopardstown Park Hospital gave me the opportunity to talk to two of the last surviving Irish veterans of the First World War (both now, sadly, dead).

Many of the photographs which appear in this volume were supplied by the same people who gave of their time for personal interviews. My thanks to the Gene Autry Western Heritage Museum (and John Langellier) for the Frontier War photographs. Jack McCormack supplied the bulk of the US Civil War material from his own archive. Most of the Vietnam photos came from Ed Somers, while Henry O'Kane provided me with shots taken after his capture in Korea. Mrs Rosario Mayne, widow of Herbert Mayne, responded to my request to lend me some of her husband's material. The photographs covering the Second World War chapter came from Elizabeth Dobbs, Kevin Gibney, Maurice Daly and Paddy Devlin. Many thanks also to John Cooney of RTE.

The frighteningly well-informed Kevin Myers and Jack McCormack · cast their educated eyes over parts of the text for me. My frequent collaborator Jim Lusby gave the text a professional appraisal and came back with the report: 'Must do better', as he always does. My best and most patient of friends Anne Lyster offered criticisms from the perspective of the potential consumer. My tolerant and loving wife, Iseult, read the same material for me but she also allowed family life to continue in an ever-moving stream, dividing around my island and occasionally washing up on my shores. To her I am eternally grateful, as always. Of my four children, Amber, Rory, Lara and Ross, I beg forgiveness for not taking them to the movies more often.

Introduction: For King, Emperor, President and Czar

Man, dweller in mountain huts, possessor of coloured mice,
Skilful in minor manual turns, patron of obscure subjects, of
Gaelic swordsmanship and mediaeval armoury
The technique of the public man, the masked servilities are
Not for you. Master of military trade, you give
Like Raleigh, Lawrence, Childers, your services but not yourself.

Charles Donnelly, 'Poem'

Dispossessed and disenfranchised, disciplined and dedicated; courageous, loyal, doughty and audacious – the sentimental, and not exclusively native view, of the Irish soldier fighting under a foreign flag. 'Low, vulgar men without any one qualification to recommend them – more fit to carry the hod than the epaulette' – an alternative and widely held opinion of that same 'universal' warrior. There is nothing which uniquely qualifies the Irishman to be a soldier. He is of medium height and weight for a European, is not gifted with any superior stamina or powers of endurance, is no more accurate with a rifle, is not more or less self-disciplined than the average. So why, along with the German, is the Irishman burdened with a reputation for military sagacity, craft and daring *sans pareil*? If the Germans dominate the officer class of the 'transcendent' army then the Irish must surely have provided most of the NCOs.

Is the notion of the superhuman Irish fighting man a myth or is there a certain, almost spiritual, quality about an Irishman in uniform? This is obviously a rhetorical question. Subjectivity, chauvinism and a host of maudlin irrelevancies make any definitive judgement impossible. Searching for the sort of endorsements which would enhance a positive thesis is rather like invoking the Bible to settle an argument. Contrary quotations can always be cited to prove the antithesis. No attempt, therefore, will be made to pursue that chimera except to say that the concept of the 'Fighting Irishman' carries with it an implicit element of condescension. Often unintended, the notion can be as much a patronising obeisance to undiscriminating Irish pugnacity as it is homage to Irish courage and resilience. There are hints of the nineteenth-century *Punch* view of the drunken brawling Irishman with the thickset simian appearance for whom discretion could never be the better part of valour because he was illiterate and unable to understand either concept anyway.

That the mythology even exists is curious in itself. Why should the Irish rifleman, lancer, fusilier or trooper be more aggressive or invincible than those around him? After all, the one thing which most Irish soldiers have had in common since the 1700s is that they have been fighting in someone else's army and prosecuting someone else's war. Only rarely has the Irishman fought for his homeland, seldom for anything which was native or necessarily dear to him. Periodically he might fight for (or convince himself that he was defending) his religion. But more often he risked life, limb and liver for a foreign potentate who reciprocated by putting a roof over his head and bread on his table. Certainly, on occasion, he might respond with particular truculence to an army fighting under the Union Jack, but he might, on those occasions, find himself opposed by another Irishman struggling no less enthusiastically in the British cause. It is not sufficient to dismiss such commonplace occurrences with blithe references to antagonistic political or religious traditions on this island. More often than not those two adversaries were from the same tradition.

Perhaps the real truth behind the idealised 'Fighting Irishman' lies in the very nature of war itself. It is hardly a solitary pastime. Like the various sports which could be said to have replaced it as a focus of aggressive nationalism or ethnic territoriality, it is a group activity. The British establishment, though conscious of the potential dangers, had the wit to place the Irish soldier shoulder-to-shoulder with his fellow countryman in some of the most prestigious units in its army. Other nations, often for convenience, did likewise. The result was a soldier far more motivated than one fighting for his personal survival alongside strangers.

Before pursuing the main themes of this book, it is worth introducing a brief variation. Latterly the Irish soldier, now able to wear the insignia of a native unit, has been shedding his reputation for bellicosity and reinventing himself as a mediator. For centuries Ireland did not have an army of its own except revolutionary forces which tended to be led by poets and writers rather than soldiers. Some of them were excellent poets, but a well-turned couplet is not much protection against enfilading fire or an artillery barrage – there is no substitute for military *nous*. Since gaining independence, apart from a short period of civil strife during which the new-born infant scratched herself until she bled copiously, the Irish Defence Forces have been doing what armies should do, making peace rather than war. Arguably this tiny contingent has done more good in the last four decades than all the thousands of Irish mercenaries, idealists, and journeymen soldiers of the previous four centuries. Ireland has supplied 33,000 troops for United Nations peacekeeping operations in seventeen countries. Their courage, diplomacy and restraint are in stark and refreshing contrast to those legendary fighting qualities of their compatriots in foreign armies. They have taken casualties at Niemba in the Congo, in South Lebanon and in a host of other battle zones, knowing that they must avoid, at almost all costs, inflicting casualties in return. Revenge and retaliation are not words allowed in their lexicon.

But the Irish peacekeeping role is an infant tradition and beyond the remit of this book. Before dealing with the specific conflicts which will illustrate the role of the Irishman in modern warfare it is interesting to examine briefly some of his antecedents. It is hard to think of a major American or western European military engagement of the last 300 years which has not had at least one Irishman present. They have fought for every king and queen of England, France and Spain, soldiered under George Washington, Simon Bolivar, the Duke of Wellington (himself a Dubliner), founded the navies of the USA (John Barry), Argentina (William Brown) and Austria (John Forbes), come under fire at Fort Sumter, Balaclava, Waterloo, Gettysburg, the Little Bighorn, Mafeking, Jarama and the Somme. Why? Few if any of them were forced, coerced or compelled to be in any of those dangerous, deadly, disease-ridden places. So what were they doing there? Why did other people's fights become the Irishman's fight again and again?

Often it was simple happenstance, coincidence. The Irishman had migrated and been caught up in a war. But that explanation requires further elucidation. Why did he *happen* to be there? With ever-recurring monotony the answer is that his own overpopulated, impoverished country could not support him or his family. Although the Irishman was not necessarily a conscript in the accepted sense (he could, theoretically, return to his homeland), he was constructively conscripted by virtue of economic exile. In truth, he had no alternative. Ironically, the military force which was the main beneficiary was that of the very nation which had, effectively, compelled him to migrate in the first place. Despite all the lore and lionising of 'Wild Geese', Fontenoy, Sarsfield and the 'Irish brigades' of Europe, the vast bulk of emigré Irish soldiers served in the Army of Britain.

Those who did not, those who populated the forces of continental Europe, may have had another reason for their exile. They may have had the temerity to oppose the political dominance in their country of the British establishment. After the Treaty of Limerick a huge body of Roman Catholic Irish soldiers, who had opposed the Protestant King William, left for France under Patrick Sarsfield, the Earl of Lucan. Many left with the hope of returning in the ranks of a larger French army to put King James II back on the throne. They, and their successors who followed the same route throughout the Penal Law days of the eighteenth century, were forlornly dubbed the 'Wild Geese'. Those early exiles entered the service of the King of France, the Catholic Louis XIV who was at war with most of Europe. For the next century, almost until the Revolution, there would always be an 'Irish Brigade' in the French army.

Sarsfield died in 1693 at the Battle of Landen, fighting for France in Flanders against the forces of William of Orange. During that first conflict involving the 'Wild Geese' — the War of the League of Augsburg — over 20,000 Irish soldiers died. A similar number fell in the ensuing War of the Spanish Succession. But within a relatively short period all realistic hopes of French intervention in Ireland had faded. It would be a mistake to see all the Irishmen recruited into the French forces from 1700 onwards as political exiles. The French tended to view them as mere mercenaries, which, to some degree, they were. Under the Penal Laws, applied against Roman Catholics in eighteenth-century Ireland, they were barred from serving in the British army. If they wanted to pursue a military career (often as the only alternative to poverty), they had to do so on the European continent.

The apotheosis of France's Irish Brigade came at the Battle of Fontenoy, fought in 1845 during the War of the Austrian Succession.

Four thousand Irish troops, in six infantry and one cavalry regiments, were numbered among those in the 60,000-strong French army led by Marechal Maurice de Saxe. The French were opposed by a mainly British and Dutch force. De Saxe had chosen the ground over which the battle would be fought and he had chosen well. The Irish Brigade was on the left flank of the French lines and was not involved in the early fighting during which de Saxe's main force crumbled under an intense and sustained attack led by 16,000-strong British troops under the Duke of Cumberland. Included in the ranks of this army would have been many Protestant Irish, not barred from enlistment by the Penal Laws and whose circumstances were almost as straitened as those of their Catholic fellow countrymen.

The Irish regiments, bringing with them four cannon, were sent in to dislodge Cumberland's right flank and to help save the day for the French. Amid provocative roars of 'Remember Limerick', the brigade 'sent the British reeling back', according to a contemporary account. But they suffered serious losses in doing so; at 20 per cent they were proportionately higher than any other unit of the French army. Thomas Davis, the Young Irelander, in his suitably bombastic poem 'Fontenoy', captured the inevitable racial element inherent in the ferocity of the Irish charge: 'How fierce the look these exiles wear, who're wont to be so gay/The treasured wrongs of fifty years are in their hearts today.'

There was only a theoretical element of choice involved in the enlistment of the more impoverished Irish exile to Britain, Europe or, much later, America. But over the years many Irishmen not motivated by the coercive imperative of poverty joined foreign armies. Some have been idealists, political or religious, some adventurers, some simple mercenaries.

The Boer War saw two separate Irish brigades fight on the side of the Dutch South Africans. The more significant unit, led by a future leader of the Easter 1916 rebellion, Major John McBride (working in South Africa as a mine assayer), grew out of a large Irish population in the Transvaal and a number of 1798 centenary committees in Johannesburg and Pretoria. Motivated by antipathy towards Britain and including a number of unreconstructed Fenians, the Irish battalions were opposed by an army which had an Irish Brigade of its own. The committed amateurs ran into the professionals on more than one occasion. At the Battle of Dundee the pro-Boers took a number of members of the Royal Irish Fusiliers prisoner. Some of the Irish Brigade even recognised and exchanged greetings with the defeated Fusiliers.

Irish units also took both sides in the Spanish Civil War, but while the political and religious gulf between them was clear their motivation was identical. Young idealists, like the poet Charlie Donnelly, the socialist Frank Ryan or Communist Party member Michael O'Riordan, went to Spain to join the International Brigade and to defend the Republic against fascism. But men like Dick Walsh from Carlow and Denis Reynolds from Cavan joined General Eoin O'Duffy's Irish Brigade to fight godless communism and to preserve the Roman Catholic religion in Spain.

The James Connolly Column (about 150 strong) of the International Brigade became part of the American Abraham Lincoln Battalion (which included many Irish Americans). They arrived, separately, in Spain in January 1937. Training for this group of socialists, communists and ex-IRA men was rudimentary and without weapons. Many, including the young Irishman Charles Donnelly, had not even handled a rifle before going into battle for the first time. Donnelly, who was far younger than he claimed to be (twenty-two as opposed to twenty-six) was a talented poet. The one verse he wrote in his brief and ultimately tragic period in Spain was suitably dark and brutal. While he was there on behalf of a cause he had no illusions about the deadly nature of war. Called 'Heroic Heart', its closing lines read:

Battering the roads, armoured columns
Break walls of stone or bone without receipt.
Jawbones find new ways with meat, loins
Raking and blind, new ways with women.

Donnelly had reached Spain by travelling incognito and often illegally. The 520 members of General Eoin O'Duffy's Irish Brigade had faced their own difficulties in making their way to Spain to assist the nationalist forces of the fascist leader General Franco. O'Duffy had sought volunteers for his private crusade but the enterprise had been banned by the de Valera government. Denis Reynolds from Cavan, later a Fine Gael county councillor, was one of almost 400 of O'Duffy's men who were about to be prevented from departing for Spain from Galway; only the intervention of the Roman Catholic Bishop, Dr Browne, enabled them to depart. Reynolds, a sharp featured and ascetic looking young man, was a dedicated anti-communist and saw the Spanish Republican government as communist in everything but name. Dick Walsh from Carlow saw Franco's campaign as striking a blow for the Roman Catholic church. He travelled to Spain on the same boat as Reynolds, the *Urundi.*

The Battle of Jarama, which began on 6 February 1937, drew in the Irish who sided with the republican government and those (far greater in number) who supported Franco's nationalists, but the two units did not actually meet during the course of the month-long battle. Some Irish members of the International Brigade entered the contest in its early stages. A future icon for Irish socialists, Frank Ryan – later to die in Germany after two years in a fascist prison – was wounded in the first week. The James Connolly Column was sent into action on 23 February. On 27 February the fascists went on the offensive. Charlie Donnelly was killed in an olive grove by a burst of machine-gun fire. Shortly before his death he uttered the last phrase attributed to him when he picked up a bunch of olives, squeezed them and observed: 'Even the olives are bleeding.' This epitaph is, unjustly, better known than any of his poetry.

The barb most commonly aimed at O'Duffy's battalion is that they 'never fired a shot in anger and came back with more men than they left with'. Both disparaging accusations are demonstrably untrue. The Irish 'nationalists' did suffer casualties (eleven dead) and did take part in military actions. Unfortunately, the four deaths among the battalion at Jarama were as a result of 'friendly fire' – a nationalist unit from the Canary Islands mistook them for republicans. Denis Reynolds saw Captain Tim Hyde, an old IRA man from Midleton in Cork, hit once in the arm. Then another bullet hit him; 'I saw him lifting up with the force of it, and that killed him.' Undoubtedly the Irishmen fighting with the International Brigade saw far more action than their antagonistic compatriots. Fifty-nine members of the James Connolly Column died fighting for the Republic. Carlowman Dick Walsh, who fought with O'Duffy, believes today that he was on the wrong side.

'Many Irish went out to fight on the republican side and a great number died. They were the real idealists.'

The O'Duffy brigade could be seen in a direct line of descent from another religiously motivated Irish unit, this time fighting in Mexico. The Mexican-American War (1846–48) gave rise to a major dilemma for the 2,000 Irish troops in the army of General Zachary Taylor. They were fighting against Roman Catholic Mexicans for a Protestant-dominated army in a conflict which the Mexicans were determined to dub a 'religious' war. The Irish were encouraged by the Mexicans to desert, and a large number did. These were formed into a battalion of the Mexican army known as the San Patricios. Two things must be borne in mind before we are carried away by Celtic romanticism. Most of the defectors were not seduced solely by religious zeal – promises of Mexican land and money were also a powerful attraction. In addition, the San Patricios, despite their name and their distinctive 'shamrock' flag, were not exclusively Irish. However, they were led by one John Reilly (or Riley), a sergeant in the US Fifth Infantry. His second-in-command was a Mayoman, Patrick Dalton. The San Patricios, who never numbered more than 200 and were really two companies rather than a battalion, came to grief at the Battle of Churubusco. Seventy of them were taken prisoner, fifty were hanged and twenty flogged. For some extraordinary reason Reilly was one of those who got away with a flogging. An especially agonising death awaited thirty of the San Patricios. They were placed on mule carts with ropes around their necks and made to watch the storming by the Americans of Chapultepec, the last Mexican bastion before the capital city. When the Stars and Stripes was raised over the citadel, the mules were released and the thirty men dangled.

A group of soldiers more clearly motivated by religious fervour was the 1,400 Irishmen who went to the defence of the Papal States in 1860 against the army of the northern Italian state of Piedmont. Their number included Myles Keogh from Carlow and John Joseph Coppinger from Cork, who would later distinguish themselves in the US Civil War. The Irish were treated wretchedly, not allowed to serve together in a single unit, underpaid and badly trained. Nonetheless, they are acknowledged to have fought particularly bravely for a cause unpopular in an Italy on the verge of unification.

The 1,000 Irishmen who sailed to South America to fight for the cause of independence from Spain, led by Simon Bolivar, had no particularly lofty motives in mind. They were simple mercenaries, promised wages one third higher than anything on offer in the British army. The guarantee, from an artful Wexford conman John Devereux, was spurious and most of the members of the Irish Legion reacted like the mercenaries they were when they got to Venezuela. Angered by conditions, forty officers returned to Ireland on the ships which had brought them; the rest bided their time. Their ranks were reduced by disease – dysentery, typhus and yellow fever. Their uniforms and footwear began to disintegrate. By the time the Irish Legion went into action only 450 of the original group of 1,000 were left; the rest had died, were chronically ill or had deserted.

For many their luck did not change when the fighting began; things got even worse. After an initial success as an amphibious raiding force they moved on the Venezuelan town of Maracaibo. The advance guard of the legion was wiped out by Guajira Indians and the rearguard burned to death in their huts. Only the Irish Lancers, under Colonel Francis Burdett O'Connor from Cork, fared well; that they did so was all the more astonishing – they did not boast a single horse between them. After a couple of barely mitigated disasters most of the legion demanded to be shipped back to Ireland; they mutinied and burned down the town of Riohaca. Three hundred of them were rounded up by the still loyal Lancers and dumped in Jamaica.

There was, however, a positive side to Irish aid for Bolivar. A Kerryman, Dr Thomas Foley, became inspector general of his military hospitals. Another 'Kingdom' expatriate, Arthur Sandes rose to the rank of brigadier general in Bolivar's army, while Corkman Daniel Florence O'Leary became his personal aide-de-camp. Daniel O'Connell, who saw himself as being on a par with the South American 'Liberator', sent his fifteen-year-old son Morgan to fight with Bolivar. O'Connell Junior saw little action; Bolivar made sure to keep him well out of trouble. After a year spent on the general's staff Morgan got bored and went home.

Amongst many of the forces, intermingled with feelings of idealism or the simple urge for financial gain, was the element of adventure. This often derived from a certain misplaced romanticism which evaporated with the first report of gunfire. But there were (and still are) undoubtedly many Irish soldiers who drifted from war to war largely because they liked soldiering. It is not a motivating force which most of us ordinary mortals can readily understand, but it does exist and will be encountered over and over again in the many case histories of these chapters.

1

The Irish Soldier in America

The Green, the Blue and the Grey: The US Civil War

By the hush me boys, and that's to make no noise,
And listen to poor Paddy's sad narration.
For I was by hunger pressed and in poverty distressed,
So I took a thought to leave this Irish nation.
So I sold my horse and plough, my little pig and cow,
My father's farm of land and then I parted.
With my sweetheart Bid McGee, I'm afraid I'll ne'er more see,
For I left her there in Ireland broken-hearted.

'Paddy's Lamentation'

Between 1845 and 1855 two million Irish people, mostly uneducated and of Catholic peasant stock, fled famine, disease and abject poverty not to seek their fortune but in search of an alternative to malnutrition, rampant infant mortality and an average life expectancy somewhere in the low forties. Most of them became the wage slaves of Northern American industrial expansion. Within a decade of their exile thousands would find themselves fighting on both sides in a clash of two alien cultures which would free a race even lowlier than their own, forge a new United States and bring credit and some measure of respectability to the Irish in America.

Few of those who arrived in America's great East Coast cities conformed to the stereotype of the wide-eyed Irishman drawn to this new world because of stories that the streets were paved with gold. Any

11

who did were quickly disillusioned. The first thing this archetype found out was that the streets were not paved with gold. Then he discovered that they were not even paved. Finally he realised that he was expected to pave them. The Irish were given only the most menial of jobs. Many positions to which the more educated immigrants might have hoped to aspire were in businesses which paraded 'No Irish Need Apply' signs.

The Irish survived because they were prepared to do work which the lower strata of WASP society would not undertake. Their acceptance of low wages guaranteed that there was no shortage of work in an economy which was digging the foundations of its future dominance of the world economy. Ironically, what the Irish did not appear prepared to do was to venture in large numbers into the interior of the US and become part of the agricultural economy. It was as if the land, having already failed them, was suspect.

Few who had escaped starvation in Ireland to struggle with the working-class poverty of the American Industrial Revolution had any awareness of the great debate which was tearing their adopted country apart. Many did not even speak the language of the United States of America and were unaware of just how tenuously it clung to that title. The Dred Scott case, the Lincoln-Douglas debates, the execution of John Brown, events which helped catapult the US towards a fratricidal civil war, were of little importance to a labourer whose only connection with politics was the local Democratic Party grandee of his city's embryonic political machine. As the inevitability of war grew and as the issues became clearer, perhaps the Irish labourer might have experienced the dread, probably planted in his mind by that same Democratic Party machine, that the black slaves of the South might soon be coming North to work for even lower wages than those for which he already eked out an existence.

The Union and the Confederacy did not, initially, go to war to free the slaves of the South. Granted, the motivation on the Southern side was the desire not only to retain but to expand the slave-holding constituency. But Southerners also went to war to defend their independence and to assert 'state rights' – the primacy of the individual state over the confederation. The issues were played out even in the terminology used to describe the conflict. To this day many Southerners do not refer to the Civil War, that is a Yankee phrase, but to the War between the States. Professor James McPherson of Princeton University is the author of possibly the best single-volume work on the war: *Battle Cry of Freedom*. Speaking to this writer, he simplified the issues involved as follows.

> For the Confederacy the cause of secession was slavery. The slave states felt that the election of Abraham Lincoln to the presidency as the head of an anti-slavery party (the Republicans) threatened the future existence of slavery in their society and to prevent the destruction of slavery they seceded from the Union, asserting their right to do so under the right of revolution and also their constitutional right to secede. For the Union – the Abraham Lincoln administration – the issue first was preserving the existence of the undivided United States. The Northern people, and Lincoln in particular, feared that if secession was once established as a successful precedent, as a constitutional step, the next time that a disaffected minority lost a presidential election, or felt aggrieved, they would call on that precedent and go out of the Union and this would mean the end of the United States.

But Abraham Lincoln was not an abolitionist when the Civil War began. He wanted to halt the spread of slavery and was opposed to it personally but it was not until over a year after the war began that he saw the need to accommodate the idealism of many fellow Northerners and issue an emancipation proclamation.

One by one the Southern states announced their secession from the Union. With their capital in Richmond, Virginia, they would form the Confederate States of America. Conflict was unavoidable and the first shots fired in the war which would last for four years and cause more American casualties than in all subsequent conflicts involving US forces came at the Federal base of Fort Sumter, Charleston Harbour, South Carolina. The fort had been under siege after the Federal forces refused to hand it over to the Confederate States. It was bombarded on 12 April 1861. John Thompson from Coleraine was one of the defenders of Fort Sumter and thus became the first Irishman embroiled in the War between the States.

The American preoccupation with the right to bear arms, seen to its worst effect in the permissive gun-control laws of the modern USA, was an asset to the war machines of both North and South at the outset of the Civil War. In every state of the disunited Union, militia regiments were well established. Some were hardly more than social clubs but others provided a reservoir upon which both sides would draw in the early days of the conflict. Exclusivity was as rampant among these groups as it was elsewhere in American society. Consequently the Irish tended to cluster around manifestly and identifiably Irish milita regiments, like the 69th New York State Militia, soon to acquire the nickname the 'Fighting 69th'. Its motto was in Gaelic: '*Riamh nar druid o sbairn lann*' (never retreat from the clash of spears). Units such as the 69th were regarded with some suspicion by outsiders. They reflected not just the discrimination which excluded the Irish from other units but the preference of the Irishman to seek out the company of his own. *Harpers Weekly* once referred to the Irish militiaman (who had a rather roisterous reputation) as 'not infrequently an absolute nuisance'.

The commanding officer of the 69th had made a major nuisance of himself sometime prior to the attack on Fort Sumter. Michael Corcoran was a Sligoman, born in Ballymote on 21 September 1827. Austere in appearance, with Goya-esque features and a thick drooping moustache, he traced his ancestry back to the doyen of the 'Wild Geese' – the Earl of Lucan, Patrick Sarsfield. He had joined the Royal Irish Constabulary at the age of nineteen but, drawn to the revolutionary Young Ireland movement, had resigned. He emigrated to the US in 1848 and sold oysters, became a revenue inspector and a post office clerk before taking over the management of Hibernian Hall, a popular Irish meeting place. He enlisted in the 69th as a private in 1851. He rose quickly through the ranks and by August 1859 was a colonel. The following year should have seen his last involvement with the regiment and, arguably, its disbandment as a unit. In 1860 the Prince of Wales was visiting New York and it was decided to honour his visit with a military parade of all the city militia units. All, that is, except the 69th. Corcoran absolutely refused to have anything to do with the parade. He 'could not in good conscience order out a regiment composed of Irish-born citizens to parade in honour of a sovereign under whose reign Ireland was made a desert and her sons forced into exile'. Corcoran was placed under arrest, though not held in custody, preparatory to a court martial. His stand reinforced the suspicion that many had of the Irish militia units. They were thought to be so resistant to authority that they would refuse to do battle under commanders other than their own. The attack on Fort

Sumter quickly rehabilitated Corcoran and summarily ended all thoughts of disbanding the 69th.

Lincoln called for 75,000 volunteers to defend the Union and Corcoran proceeded as if he could muster that number singlehandedly. The 69th sought 1,000 men but could have amassed closer to 5,000 had they been allowed take everyone who applied. It was a period when recruiting was relatively easy; no one had yet come home with the kind of horror stories that cause men to think about their prospects in a war.

On 23 April the 69th, with 1,000 volunteers, enlisted in the cause of the Union and marched off to fight. The 69th's first encounter with the realities of war came more than three months later at a time when its members, who had enlisted for twelve weeks, were not technically obliged to fight. They fought anyway. The First Battle of Bull Run, on 21 July 1861 (or the First Battle of Manassas — Southerners call the battles after the nearest town, Northerners after the nearest river), opened the lace curtains of adventure and romance and let in the dull light of carnage and ferocity on the Civil War. It was fought almost within earshot of Washington. Hundreds of spectators left the capital armed with picnic baskets to watch the impending battle from a safe distance. The rapid advance of the Southerners forced many to abandon their lunches as thousands of Union and Confederate troops were losing their lives.

The Union forces, numbering 40,000, were commanded by General Irvin McDowell, while the Confederates under General Pierre Beauregard numbered 35,000. The 69th was in a brigade commanded by a man yet to become a great general, William Tecumseh Sherman. The first significant Irish casualty of the war was the death of a native of Glenswilly, County Donegal — Captain James Haggerty, who was an acting lieutenant colonel of the 69th. The regiment suffered more severe casualties in an unsuccessful attempt to retake Federal guns overrun by rebels. The company led by Major Thomas Francis Meagher, 'the Irish Zouaves', fared particularly badly. Meagher had his horse shot from under him and rose to his feet screaming theatrically and futilely beneath the incredible din: 'Remember Ireland and Fontenoy'. The regimental flag, which had already cost the lives of two colour bearers, was seized by a rebel. It was regained by a third colour bearer, John

O'Keefe, who had to shoot a number of Confederate soldiers before emerging from the fight clinging to the banner.

The members of the regiment, according to independent accounts, were exceptional in that they stood and fought the advancing 'graycoats' while most around them broke and ran. When the order came to withdraw they attempted to do so in an orderly fashion, a difficult feat to accomplish given the shambles that surrounded them. In the confusion Corcoran and a number of his men were taken prisoner. Among those who went with Corcoran to the makeshift Confederate prison (thirty-seven *in toto*) in 'Liggon's Tobacco Warehouse' in Richmond, Virginia, was Donegal-born Private James McKay Rorty. Rorty managed to escape along with two other 69th members, William O'Donoghue and Peter Kelly, in September. The three headed north and got as far as the Potomac River on 27 September. Rorty and Kelly hid overnight in an abandoned house while O'Donoghue swam the Potomac. He was picked up by the *USS Seminole* and tried to persuade the captain to pick up his two comrades. The captain refused, insisting on taking O'Donoghue to the War Department for what would today be described as a 'debriefing'. O'Donoghue, however, made the *Seminole* captain swear to go back for Rorty and Kelly the following night. The two were duly picked up.

Corcoran, meanwhile, had been transferred to Castle Pinckney in Charleston Harbour, South Carolina. Conditions, he wrote, were better than in 'the ever monotonous tobacco factory' in Richmond, but 'the rank and file of the different regiments should be seen to as soon as possible. Many are suffering much from want of clothing and change of undergarments. Many are without shoes, coats or bed covering, and face a cheerless prospect with the near approach of cold weather.'

Corcoran would soon have more to concern himself with than the relatively balmy winters of South Carolina. The day after his own capture the US navy had captured a rare prize, one Walter W. Smith. Smith was a 'privateer', a glorified pirate employed by the Confederacy to prey on Union shipping. Smith was more entrepreneur than Southern patriot as he was well paid for his scavenging. The North determined to make an example of him and he was sentenced to death for piracy. By way of retaliation the South picked out, by lots, a high-ranking Union officer who was to suffer the same fate as Smith. Corcoran drew the short straw. He was moved to Charleston jail where he wrote of being 'in a common footing with the most depraved classes and locked up at night like felons'. In another of his letters he left a suitably flowery last testament, which reveals his intense Irish nationalism.

> Neither the opportunity nor the time to accomplish the object for which I held life most sacred having arrived – that of aiding to free my native land from the galling yoke of oppression under which she has been suffering for centuries – there could be no possible other cause for which I would be content to offer up my life than in the endeavour to maintain the glorious Flag which has afforded a home and protection to me and my oppressed countrymen.

Fortunately, Corcoran was not obliged to die as a hostage. Both sides backed down, he survived and was released the following year in an exchange of imprisoned officers. Just over a year later he died after a fall from a horse owned by his friend and associate, General Thomas Francis Meagher. Reports suggest he was probably drunk at the time but it may well have been a stroke rather than the fall which killed him. Had he been given the choice he might have preferred the more noble fate assigned to him by the Confederacy.

While Corcoran festered in prison, the 69th, having fulfilled its three-month obligation, returned home. The dominant Irish influence in the Civil War then became Thomas Francis Meagher. He had the manner and accent of the British upper classes, among whom he was educated, rather than of the County Waterford of his birth. Meagher was a quite extraordinary man, thirty-eight-years old when the Civil War began, handsome if somewhat fleshy; he had been one of the leaders of the Young Ireland Rising of 1848. The movement which initiated the abortive rebellion was of far greater significance than the brief and ludicrous affray at the Widow McCormack's in Ballingarry which constituted the military element of the rebellion. Meagher, along with most of the conspirators, was deported to Tasmania. He escaped from there in 1852 and made his way to America. He was practising at the Bar in New York when the war began and was already well integrated into upper middle-class New York society. One associate described him as being 'a handsome man, stately and courteous, with a wonderful flow of language'. He was not, however, universally liked – a detractor observed: 'God Almighty had just made him to step off a scaffold with a big speech in his mouth. He had a very domineering, arrogant disposition.'

Meagher, though no longer an extreme Irish nationalist by that time, was conscious of the military history of Irish emigré regiments. The Irish Brigade, which had fought for various French kings in the 1700s, provided him with a model of what he wanted to recreate, hence his invocation of that unit's success at the Battle of Fontenoy, when he was thrown from his horse at Bull Run. Meagher wanted to fashion, around the 69th New York State Militia, a brigade which would acquire a reputation equal to that of any of the multitude of Irish units which had fought for foreign powers. Inevitably, of course, Meagher also wanted to be the commander of that brigade. He was fortunate and Corcoran was not. He was dragged unconscious from the Bull Run battlefield by a trooper from the 2nd US Dragoons. While Meagher built up his fighting brigade Corcoran mouldered in a Southern prison camp.

Initially, Meagher had hoped to form an inter-state brigade, taking elements from the heavily Irish populated areas of Massachusetts and Pennsylvania. But the governors of those two states, fearing that the brigade would be associated with New York, thwarted his ambitions. The first 'Irish Brigade' consisted of three New York regiments, the 69th, the 63rd and the 88th. Many New York recruiting posters of the period were pitched at the huge native-born Irish population by equating the struggle of the Union states with that of the Irish against England. 'Young America and Old Ireland, One and Inseparable' read one; 'The Cotton Lords and Traitor Allies of England Must be Put Down! Once For All – Once For Ever' read another.

The brigade, with Meagher as its brigadier general, spent the winter of 1861 and 1862 drilling and training with the Army of the Potomac under Major General George McClellan. The Irish 'corner' of that vast army encampment (Camp California) was decorated, in Meagher's inimitable style, with some of his hunting trophies from an expedition to Central America, which included tanned jaguar skins. The winter weather was severe, the encampment muddy, wet and uncomfortable. The Roman Catholic chaplain of the 88th New York, Father Corby, recorded one occasion when he glanced out of his tent to watch a man perform the simple act of crossing a path between rows of tents. He sank so deeply into the mud that he had to be shovelled out.

The brigade was of uneven composition. It included many veterans of other armies. Some were former US regulars who had fought in the war against Mexico. Others were British army veterans, while some had fought for the Papal armies. Some were complete novices; many had been recruited 'off the boat', enlisting shortly after they left the immigrant landing point at Castle Garden in New York. Large and tempting recruiting posters, in English and German, were prominently displayed with details of potential earnings from a frequently abrupt military career. At least one recruit had seen action in Ireland itself. Lieutenant John J. Kavanagh joined the 63rd New York in January 1862. He had been one of the two rebel casualties of the skirmish at the Widow McCormack's which constituted the 1848 Rebellion. He was not so fortunate in the American Civil War, dying while leading his company in the Battle of Antietam. Another 1848 rebel, Joseph Burke of Mayo, a British army veteran, was luckier – he lived to head a brigade in the Union's Army of the Cumberland.

Meagher's choice of weapons for his brigade reveals something of his quixotic and romantic character. Unfortunately, it was a choice which was to cost many ordinary soldiers their lives. The brigadier opted for 69-millimetre calibre smoothbore muskets. He could have chosen the more modern rifled musket which was to revolutionise the slaughter of warfare. The 'rifle' was a far more effective weapon over greater distances than was the smoothbore musket. But the musket, loaded with 'buck and ball' could do horrendous damage to a wider area of human flesh when used close up. Meagher's dream was of close-quarter musket and bayonet work similar to that for which the Irish brigades on the European continent were justifiably famous. But the reality of the US Civil War was that it would be the dawn of 'modern' warfare, with the rifled musket favouring well-protected or entrenched defenders against even the most courageous massed charge.

The Civil War ultimately became a war to end slavery but there were few, if any, militant abolitionists among the Irish who fought for the North. Most were opposed to the abolition of slavery but were equally opposed to the secession of the South. The Irish of the urban ghettoes of

New York, Boston and Philadelphia were Democrats, almost to a man. Most would have voted *against* Republican Abraham Lincoln in the presidential election of 1860. The great fear of the Irish labourer was that emancipation of the slave would see thousands of blacks migrating northwards, prepared to work for even lower wages than the Irish. Indeed, in the South itself the Irish labourer was, in economic if not social terms, of a lower order than the black. Because a slave could be bought and sold he had some monetary value; an Irish navvy could not, so he had none. Being so expendable he received most of the dangerous jobs.

Many of the 20,000 Irishmen who served the Confederacy had a pressing reason to fight against emancipation. Their livelihoods were threatened in an immediate and obvious way by the abolition of slavery. Northern Democratic newspapers encouraged the anti-abolition mentality among the Irish with headlines like: 'Shall the Working Classes be Equalised with Negroes?' Archbishop John Hughes, the Roman Catholic prelate of New York who actually came to Ireland to recruit for the Union, once observed: 'We Catholics and a vast majority of our brave troops in the field have not the slightest idea of carrying on a war that costs so much blood and treasure just to gratify a clique of Abolitionists.'

So what were these thousands of native-born Irish fighting for if not for the downfall of the institution of slavery? For a plethora of different reasons. For some it was a simple and loyal answer to an urgent call from the nation which had given them shelter from the famine, disease, poverty and oppression of their native country. They felt, with considerable justification, that they had an obligation to defend the Union which had given them a refuge. James McKay Rorty, the young Donegal man, expressed these sentiments admirably in a letter to his parents explaining why he had re-enlisted in the 69th New York after his capture at Bull Run and subsequent escape. He refers to his 'attachment to and veneration for the Constitution, which urged me to defend it at all risks'.

Not everybody professed such lofty constitutional ideals. To many Irishmen soldiering was a job, just like labouring. The immigrant put his life on the line and was paid for doing so, forced by economic necessity to go to war. The story told of the two Irish soldiers on picket duty accounts for their presence and for that of many of their fellow countrymen in the ranks. The picket (lookout) lines of a Union and Confederate unit were only a few hundred yards apart. On guard, on either side of the darkened no man's land, were an Irish Federal and an Irish 'graycoat'. The rebel was anxious to find out why his fellow countryman was fighting for the Northern oppressors. The 'bluecoat's' reply was: 'I'm fighting for thirteen dollars a month. I hear you only get eleven!'

The more sought-after Irish soldier received considerably more than thirteen dollars a month. Both the Union and Confederate armies were badly in need of trained and experienced officers. Many units had been raised and were consequently led by militarily incompetent politicians. The practice of electing officers was widespread and did not always result in the selection of the most adept candidates. European forces and particularly the largely mercenary Papal Army became a prime target for Union and Confederate 'head hunters'. The likes of John Joseph Coppinger, Daniel Kiely, Joseph O'Keefe and (the most famous Irish mercenary adventurer) Myles Keogh could, quite conceivably, have fought for the South but were persuaded by the likes of Archbishop Hughes of New York to opt for the North. Carlow-born, romantic adventurer Keogh would rise to the rank of brevet (wartime) lieutenant colonel of cavalry. The more stolid Coppinger, from County Cork, would retire in the 1900s with the rank of major general.

Another attraction to the impoverished Irish immigrant was the large bounty often offered by states in the latter part of the war to attract recruits. A bounty of $200 was payable in some instances, more than a year's pay to the average labourer. Many succumbed to the inevitable temptation and became 'bounty jumpers'. They would join up in New York, accept their bounty, desert and re-enlist in Philadelphia.

A considerable number of recruits had political reasons of their own for joining. To some the pro-Confederate stance of the British government prompted their allegiance to the North. The aristocratic Southern slave owner, on whose behalf the war was seen to be fought, became identified in many Irish minds with his English counterpart. The United States and Britain also came close to war on more than one occasion over the latter's effective support for the Confederacy. To many Irishmen that was 'a consummation devoutly to be wished'.

To a substantial coterie of Irish recruits such sentiments were not simple atavism. The Fenian Brotherhood, first cousin of James

Stephens's Irish Republican Brotherhood, numbered many Federal and Confederate soldiers in its ranks. These men had joined the conflict for their own purpose, to acquire military training, expertise and weapons, all of which would subsequently be used in another Irish rebellion. Michael Corcoran, Colonel of the 69th, was a Fenian, and seen by most of his brethern as the obvious candidate to lead them against the English. (Meagher, by contrast, was not a Fenian.) The secretary of the Fenian Circle within the army was the idealistic James McKay Rorty. In his letter to his parents he had expressed 'the hope that the military knowledge or skill which I may acquire might thereafter be turned to account in the sacred cause of my native land . . . for are we not serving the "foe of Ireland's foe" ': From the Fenian perspective, however, the War between the States was a disaster on a scale which far exceeded that of the subsequent Rising of 1867. Hundreds of potential Irish rebels received invaluable military training but all too often the experience proved to be fatal. The names of many Fenians would be mentioned in the military despatches of the Union and the Confederacy but for far too many the honour was a posthumous one. In short, the Civil War totally gutted the leadership of the Fenian Brotherhood.

'I depend upon your men as I could upon no others in all the army.' So General E. V. Sumner is reputed to have said to Thomas Francis Meagher as he sent the Irish Brigade into battle at Malvern Hill on 1 July 1862. It was possibly hyperbole on the general's part, or the quote may well be apocryphal, but in the fighting up to that point the Irish Brigade had already secured a respected reputation. This was augmented at Malvern Hill where the brigade counter-attacked in the face of a Confederate advance. The manoeuvre was successful but costly, the 69th alone took 155 casualties.

Among the dead was Sergeant Haggerty, the brother of the lieutenant colonel from Donegal who had been one of the first to die at Bull Run. Private Peter Rafferty of B Company won a Congressional Medal of Honour. He was wounded once, refused to go to the rear, was wounded again and subsequently captured. His injuries disabled him for life. Lieutenant John H. Donovan of D Company was shot through the eye by a Minié ball which exited through his ear. He was left for dead on the field but survived and became a prisoner. The following day Confederate General A. P. Hill was involved in collecting the sidearms of Union officers. Spotting Donovan's wound, he remarked that the Irishman would obviously have no further use for his revolver. Donovan responded: 'I think differently. I have one good eye left and I'll risk that in the cause of the Union. If I ever lose that I'll go at it blind.' Donovan survived the war and was discharged as a captain in 1865 with his one good eye still intact.

The brigade was greatly depleted after Malvern Hill and the three-month campaign which had preceded it. The 69th alone had gone to Camp California with 750 men. Thanks to deaths, injuries, disease and desertion, by July it could only muster 295. The brigade laid up for a while and Meagher returned to New York to recruit. This time, however, it was not so easy. The romantic idealism inspired by Fort Sumter had evaporated and been replaced by a realisation of the horrors of war. It was immeasurably more difficult, even for a persuasive orator like Meagher, to cajole his fellow countrymen into a cause which they might now be far more inclined to view as someone else's. Meagher was also facing competition for recruits from his old friend Michael Corcoran, freed by the Confederates and in the process of raising an Irish brigade of his own to be known as Corcoran's Legion. Meagher managed to raise only 250 men for the three regiments of the brigade; the much depleted 69th received a mere forty of those!

On 31 May 1862 Confederate President Jefferson Davis appointed General Robert E. Lee as commander of the Army of Northern Virginia. It was the best move he made in the entire war. It was Lee's inspiring leadership and his early successes against numerically superior Union forces which convinced many rebel soldiers that their army was invincible, a belief which appeared to be shared by far too many in the Union Army. During the late summer of 1862 Lee took the war to the North, to the state of Maryland which was slave holding but had, just about, remained loyal to the Union. He ordered the army's band to strike up 'Maryland, My Maryland' as they marched towards Harrisburg, Pennsylvania, confident that his ranks would be swollen by Southern sympathisers. But, as luck would have it, he was passing through a pro-Union stronghold. He would encounter the Yankee forces at a creek called the Antietam.

Leading the Union Army was the diminutive George B. McClellan. Nicknamed the 'Young Napoleon', any resemblance to the masterly but tiny French general was purely physical. A Democrat whose heart was not really in the war, he was despised by the more radical members of Lincoln's Republican Party. He was, however, adored by most of his soldiers whose lives he was far more sparing of than some of his more illustrious successors.

Despite fortuitously coming into possession of Lee's tactical plans and having superior numbers of troops, McClellan almost contrived to lose the fight. The battle took place on 17 September 1862. It gave rise to some of the most vicious fighting seen in the war so far. Irish-American historian Jack McCormack, walking the battlefield over a century later, found two Union and Confederate musket balls merged together. Just two of thousands of bullets discharged from opposite sides of the lines, they had collided in mid flight rather than finding a human target.

The Irish Brigade was serving with the 1st Division, II Corps, in the centre of the Union line. It was ordered to attack a sunken road after an advance across an open field. Four North Carolina infantry regiments defended the road (it came to be known as 'Bloody Lane'), which was at the bottom of a rise. The first inkling they got of the Irish Brigade's advance was when they saw the tips of the green banners borne by the Irish regiments appearing on the horizon. They let fly, as did the Confederate artillery half a mile to the rear. Captain D. P. Conyngham, who served with the brigade as an officer and later became its historian, described the hail of bullets: 'The musketry firing at this point was the severest and most deadly ever witnessed before – so acknowledged by veterans in the service. Men on both sides fell in large numbers every moment and those who were eye-witnesses of the struggle did not suppose it possible for a single man to escape.'

McClellan, watching the II Corps advance, was impressed with the Irish Brigade. He commented, 'Look at the perfect line of the Irish as it moves to meet the enemy.' Almost simultaneously the brigade's standard bearers went down in the hail of fire. A member of McClellan's staff, seeing this, panicked. 'The day is lost, General,' he shouted, 'the Irish fly.' But other colour bearers picked up the banners and continued the advance. Captain James McGee of the 69th raised his regiment's distinctive colours and within seconds the staff was shattered by a musket ball. As he stooped to pick it up his hat was shot off. McClellan's account of the attack on Bloody Lane continues:

> Here the brave Irish Brigade opened upon the enemy a terrific musketry fire, and sustained its well-earned reputation. After suffering terribly in officers and men strewing the ground with their enemies as they drove them back, their ammunition nearly expended, and their commander, General Meagher, disabled by a fall from his horse shot under him, this brigade was ordered to the rear.

In fact, the withdrawal was, in purely military terms, as spectacular as anything which had preceded it. The Irish Brigade, alone of General Israel Richardson's division of II Corps, had encountered heavy opposition. Richardson was forced to watch as it was decimated. It was three hours before another brigade from the division, Caldwell's, was sent to relieve it. These two units then accomplished one of the most impressive and intricate manoeuvres ever performed in the Civil War under hostile fire. The relieving force moved up in column behind the Irish. Meagher's brigade 'broke by companies to the rear'; Caldwell's 'broke by companies to the front'. It was a parade ground drill performed in battlefield conditions. But for hundreds of Irishmen the manoeuvre was far too late, they were beyond relief. The brigade had lost over 500 officers and men wounded and killed. The 69th (here earning the nickname 'Fighting 69th'), on the extreme right flank of the division, suffered 62 per cent casualties. The 63rd New York lost 59 per cent of its force.

Conyngham described some of what he witnessed after the battle.

> The doctors were moving among the groups of the dead and wounded, staunching their wounds or easing their sufferings. The dead lay piled in all kinds of manner. Here are two men, a Federal and a rebel soldier, with their bayonets driven through each others breasts; both of them are dead and their features wear all the fierce expressions of the hate and passion of the conflict. Near them is a little drummer boy of about fourteen; a piece of shell has gone through his drum and himself together. Poor child, he has beaten

his last tatoo. Some bodies are disfigured; they have been either torn in pieces by shells or scattered about by the horses and wheels of artillery. Their clothes only keep the shattered remains together. The streams are full of bodies; the wounded dragged themselves there to drink, fell in and were drowned, while several were killed in crossing.

Antietam ended up as a Union victory but the carnage was not yet over for Meagher's brigade. Its members had another pressing engagement with the Angel of Death in the town of Fredericksburg, Virginia.

Lincoln had had his fill of McClellan and was ready to drop 'Little Napoleon' and take the controversial step of emancipating the slaves in the autumn of 1862. Neither move went down well with many of his Irish soldiers. Reacting to the sacking of McClellan, most of the officers of the Irish Brigade (Democrats, like McClellan) tendered their resignations and had to be persuaded by Meagher to withdraw them. As McClellan bade goodbye to the Army of the Potomac which he had created, organised and then misused, he was given a rapturous reception as he passed through the depleted Irish Brigade columns; soldiers broke ranks, surrounded his horse and wished him well. They were soon to have compelling reasons for regretting his dismissal.

The brigade, whose numbers were badly depleted by now, was reorganised. The 63rd, 69th and 88th New York (such as they were by then) remained as the nucleus of the unit but the 116th Pennsylvania under Colonel Denis Heenan and Major St Clair Mulholland (a future winner of the Congressional Medal of Honour) was added. Meagher also did a 'swap' with the IX Corps, getting rid of the 'Yankee' 29th Massachusetts, the only non-Irish regiment in the brigade, and getting in return the all-Irish 28th Massachusetts. McClellan's replacement was Ambrose Burnside, more to Lincoln's liking because he was prepared to take on Lee's army in a headlong advance on Richmond, Virginia (today only an hour's drive from Washington D.C.). Lee interposed his army (numbering about 80,000) between Burnside's force of 118,000 and the Confederate capital in the town of Fredericksburg. He established most of his forces in easily defended high ground outside the town. In establishing this enviable position he was assisted by Burnside's unfathomable decision to await the arrival of his main force before occupying those same heights himself.

En route to join the main force, Meagher's brigade were witnesses to a bizarre incident which had a chastening effect on a troop of superstitious Irish soldiers. As they passed the house of a dead Confederate – General Turner Ashby – his wizened and dishevelled mother ran out into their ranks calling down curses upon the men who had killed her son. As they approached the pontoon bridges which had been built across the Rappahannock River outside Fredericksburg, professional embalmers thrust pieces of paper into the soldiers' hands instructing them to pin these cards to their uniforms and their bodies would be well looked after when they were shipped home. St Clair Mulholland, second-in-command of the 116th Pennsylvania, thought the cards were 'suggestive of an early trip home, nicely boxed up and delivered to loving friends by express. The boys did not seem altogether pleased with the cold-blooded allusions to their latter end.' The brigade's distaste for the ghoulish embalmers was probably unconnected with their subsequent enthusiastic participation in the wholesale looting of the town of Fredericksburg. In this, as in battle, the Irish were well to the fore.

It was December and the Irish troops spent a cold night, unable to light fires because they were within sight of the enemy positions. It was dank and foggy and despite the presence of over 30,000 troops in Fredericksburg itself an almost eerie silence pervaded the town. One-eyed John Donovan, by now a captain and reunited with his unit after being left for dead at Malvern Hill, wrote that 'everything was quiet during the night . . . fearful calm ensued, but it was only that calm that is said generally to precede a storm.'

Burnside's tactics for defeating Lee – frontal assaults – lacked subtlety. The main focus of his attack was a hill known as Marye's Heights. Brigades were to form up in two lines, 200 yards apart. Officers were advised not to go into action on horseback as they would be easy targets for Confederate sharpshooters. As it went to meet its nemesis, the Irish Brigade was, paradoxically, a noble but sorry sight. The New York regiments were chronically understrength, the 69th, commanded by Colonel Robert Nugent, totalled 238 officers and men; the 63rd, under Major Joseph O'Neill, could muster only 162 while

Colonel Patrick Kelly's 88th had only 252. Heenan's 116th Pennsylvania had a force of only 247. The biggest element of a force of about 1,200 (an oversize regiment – less than half the size of even the smallest brigade) comprised the 416 men of the newly arrived 28th Massachusetts. The 28th was the only unit which carried its own colours into action. The green silk flags of the New York regiments were in tatters after being ripped apart by Confederate shells and bullets. For the first time they would go into action without these comforting emblems. They would be carrying only the flag of the United States of America.

Besotted by symbolism, conscious of his unit's 'place' in the Irish emigré military tradition, Meagher ensured that each man went into battle bearing a token of his Irishness. Bunches of evergreen boxwood were distributed through the ranks. Meagher placed his sprig in his cap. Mulholland, second-in-command of the 116th Pennsylvania, wrote: 'every officer and man followed his example and soon great bunches of the fragrant shrub adorned the caps of everyone. Wreaths were made and hung upon the tattered flags.' (These were the US flags.) Meagher, facilely eloquent as always, addressed his troops. Captain John Donovan of the 69th was suitably inspired: 'each man was made aware of the great and terrible work before him, and each man measured in his mind the part he had to perform'. Private William McClelland of the 88th, listening from the ranks, wrote: 'we all felt in high spirits, little dreaming, though we expected a heavy battle, that in so short a time after, so many of our poor fellows would have been sent to their final doom.'

Meagher, handicapped by an earlier injury, was unable to lead his brigade in the assault on the Heights. Ironically, the field over which the advance on the high ground took place, owned by a Confederate, Colonel Marye, had during the Great Famine grown an entire crop of corn which was shipped to Ireland for the relief of the starving Irish! The brigade readied itself for the assault behind a rise, out of sight of the Confederate riflemen. The order came for them to move forward: 'Right shoulder, shift arms, battalion forward, guide centre, march!' They walked straight into fire that John Donovan described simply as 'murderous', impeded as they went by the hundreds of bodies which had already fallen. In addition to the artillery pumping down shells from Marye's Heights, a division of the infantry, Anderson's, was sheltered behind a stone wall. Confederate's, five to six men deep, were firing in relays from behind the wall, keeping up a hail of fire not unlike that from the machine-guns of the 1914–1918 War.

Major St Clair Mulholland wrote:

> Officers and men fell in rapid succession. Lieutenant Garrett Nowlen fell with a ball through the thigh. Major Bardwell fell badly wounded and a ball whistled through Lieutenant Bob McGuire's lungs. The orderly Sergeant of Company H wheeled around, gazed upon Lieutenant Quinlan, and a great stream of blood poured from a hole in his forehead, splashing over the young officer, and the sergeant fell dead at his feet. Captain John O'Neill . . . was shot in the lungs, the ball passing completely through his body. But on the line pressed steadily, the men dropping in twos, in threes, in groups. No cheers or wild hurrahs as they moved towards the foe.

Among the troops defending Marye's Heights were a number of Confederate Irish regiments. Irish-born Colonel Robert McMillan, commanding a Georgian Irish regiment, spotted the green flag of the 28th Massachusetts as the five Federal Irish regiments advanced. 'That's Meagher's brigade', he shouted, displaying as much national sentiment as one can expect from a mercenary as he ordered his troops to 'Give it to them now, boys. Now's the time. Give it to them!' The combined Irish casualties, Union and Confederate, of that single day's fighting in a foreign civil war numbered about 20 per cent of those men estimated to have died in the Irish equivalent sixty years later.

The 28th Massachusetts lost its regimental colours on the field that day. The colour sergeant of the 116th Pennsylvania, William Tyrrell, had his leg broken by a bullet but, down on one knee, continued to keep the US flag of his regiment aloft. Five more bullets struck Tyrrell, twice that many peppered the tattered flag and both went down. Miraculously Tyrrell survived and was later promoted to lieutenant. The staff of 63rd New York's flag was shattered and the flag itself shredded, but the colour sergeant remained uninjured despite a coat full of bullet holes. The 69th's US flag was taken by a dying soldier and stuffed into his uniform so that it would not get into enemy hands. Finally, as they neared their objective, the Irish were ordered to dive for any available cover. They lay on the ground, often hidden behind the bodies of other Federal troops, and fired back at the Confederate defenders. John Donovan watched as the two lieutenants in his company were killed. Looking along the ranks of the brigade, he described 'an awful sight . . . brave fellows now stretched in their gore, who but an hour ago were the personification of life and strength and manliness'. A bullet struck him in the shoulder and was stopped from doing damage by a metallic shoulder strap. Then he was hit in the chest by shrapnel and knocked unconscious. When he recovered he was still pinned down between Confederate and Union fire. As the intensity of the battle abated he shouted a command to his company to fall back. Scarcely a dozen men, rising hesitantly and reluctantly from among the dead and dying, followed him.

Unable to advance any further the brigade pulled back. The bodies of two of its officers, Major Hogan and Captain Young, were found within twenty-five yards of the stone wall when the fighting ended. It was as close as any of the Union soldiers had got that day. As they straggled back from under the shadow of the stone wall, Meagher gathered together what was left of his brigade. Almost half had been killed or wounded (it must be remembered that far more men subsequently died of their wounds than would have been the case in twentieth-century wars). The 69th New York had lost sixteen of its nineteen officers and three quarters of its men. One of the 69th's survivors, Lieutenant Patrick Carney, had been wounded nine times. The 116th Pennsylvania had 100 per cent casualties among its officers. Altogether 545 men of the Irish Brigade had been killed or wounded. The divisional commander, General W. S. Hancock, inspected the remnant shortly after the battle ended. The brigade was drawn up, by companies, a few yards apart. He noted, with regret, one company which could muster only seven men. Then glancing to one side he spotted a single soldier, isolated from the rest. Hancock asked the soldier why he was not lining up with the rest of his company. 'This is all my company, sir', came the reply.

An unidentified Irish officer wrote a letter about the aftermath of the battle to the *New York Irish American*. 'Never since the war began have the Union forces met with such a disaster as that we have just suffered. As for the Brigade, may the Lord pity and protect the widows and orphans of nearly all those belonging to it! It will be a sad, sad Christmas by many an Irish hearthstone in New York, Pennsylvania and

Massachusetts.' Anticipating the numbers who would die of their wounds the officer added: 'The lying government papers state that all the wounded have been cared for! There are hundreds yet who have never had the blood washed off their wounds, and their gunpowdery hands and faces crusted with the clotted blood are meeting you at every turn . . . the men appear like a few ghosts among the huts. . . . As for the remnants of the Brigade, they are the most dejected set of Irishmen you ever saw or heard of.'

It may have been some source of consolation to Meagher, now leading what was effectively an understrength regiment, that the brigade's assault on Marye's Heights was to become one of the legendary sacrifices of a war which was long on martyrdom. The correspondent of the London *Times* newspaper offered this florid account of the battle:

> Never at Fontenoy, Albuera or at Waterloo was more undaunted courage displayed by the sons of Erin than during those six frantic dashes which they directed against the impregnable position of their foe. That any mortal men could have carried the position before which they were wantonly sacrificed, defended as it was, it seems to me idle for a moment to believe. But the bodies which lie in dense masses within forty yards of the muzzles of Colonel Walton's guns are the best evidence what manner of men they were who pressed on to death with the dauntlessness of a race which has gained glory on a thousand battle fields, and never more richly deserved it than at the foot of Marye's Heights on the 13th day of December, 1862.

A bizarre footnote to the butchery at Fredericksburg only served to underline the fratricidal nature of the war. The 28th Massachusetts had lost its regimental standard in the battle. Some time after Fredericksburg, Michael Sullivan, a Confederate in McMillan's Georgia Regiment, staggered, apparently wounded, into a Federal picket line. He asked to be brought to Meagher. There he handed over the 28th's flag to the astonished brigadier. He had seen the Massachusetts colour bearer shot down and had crawled out to recover the fallen flag. He had retrieved it under fire and kept it until such time as he was able to return it to the Irish Brigade. Meagher ensured that Sullivan was escorted safely back to Confederate lines.

It was inevitable, in this civil war, that Irishmen would find themselves on opposite sides. It was hardly unique in Irish military history. The conflict of ideologies is best seen in microcosm within the Gwynn family. Two brothers, both born in Ireland, served on opposite sides, Hugh becoming a major with the 23rd Tennessee Infantry, James a brevet major general in the US Volunteers. Green flags adorned with Irish mottoes and slogans (*Faugh a ballagh – Erin go bragh*) were carried into action on both sides. Irish songs could be heard sung at night in the camps of the Union and the Confederacy.

The greatest battle ever fought on the North American continent might never have taken place where it did had the Confederate army of Robert E. Lee possessed proper footwear. But many of the soldiers of Lee's army of Northern Virginia had no shoes and the town of Gettysburg, in south-central Pennsylvania, was rumoured to have a shoe factory. So it was that the rebel army numbering 65,000 took on the 85,000 men of General George Meade, recently appointed commander of the Army of the Potomac. Lee had come north, sweeping well west of Harrisburg in Pennsylvania. Warily, Meade had kept his army between the Confederates and Washington. He was waiting for Lee to turn and head south for the capital. So it was that when this pivotal battle was joined the Confederate forces advanced from the North and the Union forces from the South!

The battle began on 1 July 1863 and lasted for three days. As the tattered remnants of the Irish Brigade hurried to the field they were no longer under the leadership of Meagher. Refused permission to take his brigade out of the line while he and his officers returned to New York to recruit, Meagher had resigned his commission. Colonel Patrick Kelly led what was little more than a glorified regiment into action on the second day of Gettysburg.

In many ways, a more significant contribution to the Union cause at Gettysburg came from an individual Irishman who led a largely non-Irish unit. Patrick Henry O'Rorke, born in County Cavan on 28 March 1836, had graduated first in the West Point class of June 1861 (George Armstrong Custer graduated last in the same class). Although in his mid twenties he looked like a fresh-faced youth, his moustache and elaborate whiskers insufficient to endow him with the appearance of gravitas. He had begun his military career in the Corps of Engineers and had once, like Custer, gone aloft in a balloon to spy on Confederate positions. The Battle of Gettysburg found him as colonel in command of the 140th New York Volunteer Regiment. Twice, despite his inexperience, he had assumed command of his brigade. His unit had been ordered into the line to help defend an unsupported and unauthorised advance on the left flank of the Union force by the irrepressible III Corps Commander, Dan Sickles. O'Rorke was redirected at the last moment to a hill overlooking the Union positions called Little Round Top. Confederates were attempting to take it and this would have helped them outflank the Federals. His regiment got to the summit of Little Round Top just in time to reinforce a thin and crumbling Union defensive line. O'Rorke, having dismounted and led his men down the slope towards the Confederates, was killed by a Minié ball through the neck.

Down below Little Round Top the Confederates were attempting to break Sickle's Corps, fighting through areas that have become notorious in American history as slaughter fields – Devil's Den, the Peach Orchard and the Wheatfield. Troops from other corps were rushed in to help Sickles, among them the remaining members of what had been the five regiments of the much corroded Irish Brigade. What should have been a force of 5,000 men, now numbering less than 600, was then tossed into the meatgrinder of the Wheatfield where, after five hours of vicious hand-to-hand fighting, over 7,000 bodies lay across nine acres of fertile Pennsylvania farmland. A Massachusetts soldier wrote of the sound of the carnage witnessed by the Irish Brigade in the Wheatfield area. 'The hoarse and indistinguishable orders of commanding officers, the screaming and bursting of shells as they tore through the struggling masses of humanity, the death screams of wounded animals, the groans of their human companions . . . a perfect hell on earth. It has never been effaced from my memory, day or night, for fifty years.'

Ironically, Meagher's legacy to the brigade, the 69-millimetre smoothbore muskets with their 'scattergun' effect, proved more valuable in the close-quarter fighting of the Wheatfield than they had at Antietam or Fredericksburg. Beyond a range of 200 feet they were of little value, but the brigade had hardly entered the Wheatfield area before they were confronted with a line of Confederate infantry about forty yards distant. Colonel Patrick Kelly ordered a charge. The obsolete 'buck and ball' weapons did tremendous damage to the Confederate line and this was quickly followed up, in the classic but outmoded fashion beloved of Meagher, by a fierce bayonet charge. While the brigade regrouped, Major St Clair Mulholland of the 116th Pennsylvania spotted a larger rebel force approaching and fearing that the tiny Irish troop would be overrun, ordered a withdrawal. Mulholland may have had a premonition of incarceration in the ghastly Confederate prison of Andersonville where 25 per cent (13,000) of the Union prisoners died of disease and malnutrition. One unfortunate Irishman in Sickles Corps, Private Joseph Baker of the 57th Pennsylvania, was one of a number of Irish captured at Gettysburg; he died at Andersonville. The brigade, by now a totally spent force, contributed 107 corpses to the Wheatfield.

Lee had been unable to make any impression on the left or right flank of the Union line entrenched along Cemetery Ridge in the first two days of the battle. On the third day he opted to go for Meade's centre. The job was to be done by the relatively fresh troops led by General George E. Pickett. Thirteen thousand men were to charge, in close formation, across a mile of open ground aiming at a clump of trees in the centre of the Union line. As ill luck would have it, stationed right in front of the trees was an Irish regiment, the 69th Pennsylvania.

'Pickett's Charge' was one of those magnificently courageous and utterly wasteful failures which pervade military history. It lacks something of the pointlessness and needless destruction of the 'Charge of the Light Brigade', but was far more costly in terms of human life. The defenders of Cemetery Ridge were not armed with 69-millimetre calibre muskets. They bore modern, accurate rifled muskets which picked off the charging Confederates before they got within a hundred yards of the Federal lines – those rebels, that is, who had not already been blown apart by the Union artillery. Colour bearer for the 1st Virginia Infantry on that day, 3 July 1863, was seventeen-year-old Willie Mitchel, son of the Young Irelander John Mitchel, who had thrown in his lot with the Confederacy. Mitchel had already lost one son in the war and a second had had his arm blown away. Since colour bearers were a prime target for the best shots in the defending ranks, Willie Mitchel never made it to Cemetery Ridge. His tombstone in Charleston, South Carolina, bears the inscription: 'I could not fight for Ireland, so I chose to fight for the South.'

C Company of the 1st Virginia was an Irish unit known as the 'Montgomery Guards' after an Irish officer killed during the American Revolution. Its commander was Captain John E. Dooley whose mind, apparently unlike Mitchel's, was little concerned with the struggle for Irish independence. He was intent on simply surviving; 'when you rise to your feet as we did today,' he wrote candidly, 'I tell you the enthusiasm of ardent breasts in many cases ain't there . . . the thought is most frequently, "Oh if I could just come out of this charge safely." ' Dooley did not quite come out of the charge safely, but he survived nonetheless. He got to within about thirty yards of a Federal battery position before being downed by a shot to each thigh. Union prisons were somewhat more hospitable than Andersonville (the resources of the North were infinitely greater) and he survived the rest of the war as a POW in Johnson's Island, Ohio, and went on to become a Jesuit priest.

Among the troops awaiting the arrival of the remnants of Pickett's force under the copse of trees at the centre of the Union line was Corporal John Cassidy of the 69th Pennsylvania. A contemporary photograph reveals a tough, surly looking individual. Like the rest of his regiment, under the orders of Colonel Denis O'Kane, he waited until the advancing Confederates were within one hundred feet of his position. Then, along with the others, he unleashed his first volley. To his right he might have seen the 71st Pennsylvania falling back under the Confederate assault leaving his regiment exposed. Two companies of the 69th wheeled around to cover their flank. In his breast pocket Cassidy carried a prayer book given to him by a Roman Catholic priest, *The Manual of the Christian Soldier*. A rebel bullet hit him chest high passing through the missal and saving him from instant death. Sadly, this story does not have a miraculous ending; had Cassidy been fighting in the Second World War or thereafter he might have received the sort of medical treatment which would have saved his life, but he died of his wounds in his home town less than two weeks after the battle. His commanding officer, Colonel O'Kane, also died.

James McKay Rorty, dedicated Fenian, survivor of Bull Run and prison-camp escapee, was also in action on the final day of the Gettysburg Battle. He commanded one of the artillery batteries which was tearing huge holes in Pickett's ranks as his men charged across the mile of open ground from Seminary Ridge. He operated in an

unhurried, imperturbable manner, unphased by the incoming Confederate shells; but when the fighting was over he too was numbered
amongst the Union dead. A Union soldier wrote that Pickett's division
had advanced 'with the step of men who believed themselves
invincible'. Half of his force was killed, wounded or captured,
including three brigadier generals and eight colonels. Lee was forced to
abandon the field. The war continued for another two years but its
nature changed after Gettysburg. The Confederacy no longer posed a
threat to the Northern capital, a psychologically important factor in the
Union conduct of the war. From Gettysburg onwards Lee waged a
largely defensive campaign.

Some of the kudos which had been earned by the Irish race in the US as a
consequence of the bravery and commitment of Irish-born combatants
in the Civil War was clawed back shortly after Gettysburg when those
who had stayed at home rioted in New York at the prospect of being
drafted into the Union army. Conscription had been introduced by the
Lincoln administration and each state was expected to provide a levy of
fresh troops. But it was a curious form of conscription which allowed
those well enough off to avoid military service by paying a 'substitute'
to take their place. This led to accusations that the main supporters of
the war, the Northern middle and upper classes, were not carrying their
weight – it was a 'rich man's war, poor man's fight'. The impoverished
and overwhelmingly Democratic Irish of New York were not in a
position to hire substitutes, and rather than be forced to fight the
Confederates they fought the law instead. As Professor James
McPherson puts it, 'the Irish were ripe for revolt against this war waged
by Yankee Protestants for black freedom'. Couched in the simplistic
terms in which many Irish saw it, their situation was that they were
now to be forced to fight in a war to free slaves who would then flood
northwards and take their jobs.

They chose to protest in the ugliest possible manner, in a fashion
which took much of the gloss off the well-publicised achievements of
Irish soldiers and units in the war. The days of rioting which followed
the first attempt to impose military service on the Irish of New York led

to the lynching of a number of innocent blacks, scapegoated by the intransigent and barbaric mob. The former colonel of the 69th, Robert Nugent, was acting as provost marshal in the city at that time (effectively the head of the Military Police) and his house was burned down. The four days of rioting which followed are still the worst in American history, leaving 105 people dead. Among the targets of the mob, whose members were reckoned to be at least two thirds Irish, were such bastions of military oppression as Protestant churches and missions and a black children's orphanage.

In other exhibitions of disfavour, in a heavily Irish mining section of Dubuque, Iowa, men had their homes burned for enlisting. In Chicago a largely Irish mob of about 400 attacked a deputy US marshal and his three assistants after they had arrested two men for refusing to give their names to draft officials. In Milwaukee an Irish (and German) demonstration ended in the burning of a draft registration office. The infamous Irish secret society the Molly Maguires created an effective recruitment 'no go area' of four mining counties in Pennsylvania, on one occasion forcibly stopping a train filled with army conscripts and volunteers and ordering them off.

But overall, the Irish contribution to the Civil War was significant. In addition to the Irish Brigade there were a number of overwhelmingly Irish units, such as Corcoran's Irish Legion (155th, 164th, 170th and 182nd New York regiments), countless Irish regiments within other brigades or all-Irish companies within regiments. On an individual level there were a number of highly successful Irish-born general officers in both armies, such as William Gamble from Tyrone, (Myles Keogh's first commanding officer) and Richard Jackson from Westmeath, who commanded the X Corps Artillery. The last Union general to die in the war was Thomas Smyth from Cork. The birthplace of one of the three great Union generals of the war – Phillip Sheridan – is a matter of some dispute. He himself offered a number of different versions, but on the balance of probability, he was born in Cavan. He laid waste the 'granary' of the Confederate war effort, the Shenandoah Valley, and is acknowledged as having been the most successful Union general after Grant and Sherman.

Roughly 20,000 Irishmen fought for the Confederacy. Though there was only a handful of Irish slave owners, many of those who fought did have a vested interest in slavery. It was, after all, an institution which kept hundreds of thousands of willing blacks off the Southern labour market. Attempts were made to raise a Confederate 'Irish Brigade' to rival that of Meagher or Corcoran; however, with the Irish spread more thinly in the South than in the North, it proved impossible. The closest equivalent was the Louisiana Brigade – the 'Tigers' – which included the Irish 6th Louisiana Infantry. Because the Confederacy was so hard pressed and ultimately failed to survive it did not get around to issuing many medals for valour. The only awards made during the war were the rather makeshift medals given to the members of Company F of the 1st Texas Heavy Artillery. These were Mexican silver dollars, smoothed down and appropriately inscribed. Company F styled themselves the 'Davis Guards' (after Jefferson Davis, President of the Confederate States of America) and consisted of forty Irish gunners led by a twenty-five-year old Galway lieutenant – Richard W. (Dick) Dowling. This tiny force, occupying Fort Griffin on the Sabine River in Texas, had held off an amphibious invasion of Texas by 4,000 Union troops in four gunboats and seven transport ships. In the process they captured 400 Union prisoners who, fortunately, were unaware that the fort was so lightly defended.

The highest ranking Irishman who fought for the Confederacy was Cork pharmacist Major General Patrick Ronayne Cleburne. He was a mere private after enlisting in 1861, but was a divisional commander a year later through sheer talent and his British army experience. His loyalty to the South had nothing to do with any attachment to slave owners ('I care nothing for them'), but simply because the people of Helena, Arkansas, where he lived, 'have been my friends and have stood by me on all occasions . . . I am with the South in life or death, in victory or defeat.' He served in the Western campaign with the Southern Army of Tennessee. Cleburne, partly because of his Irish background and slowness to assimilate some of the native Southern prejudices, made the fatal error of clear-headed honesty towards the end of the war. A practical man, he submitted a radical proposal to the Confederate authorities to arm black slaves and use them against the Union forces. He could see clearly that superior Northern manpower would, inevitably, win out. Lincoln's Emancipation Proclamation had turned European nations against the Confederacy and slaves against their masters; 'slavery, from being one of our chief sources of strength at the commencement of the war, has now become, in a military point of view, one of our chief sources of weakness'. And Cleburne did not shirk the unavoidable consequence of such a move − 'if we arm and train him and make him fight for the country in her hour of distress, every consideration of principle and policy demand that we should set him, and his whole race who side with us, free'.

The proposal was endorsed by a dozen fellow officers and the document forwarded to Richmond where an appalled Jefferson Davis censored its publication. Cleburne, although he clearly merited promotion to corps command, gained no further advancement. The 'Stonewall of the West' (a reference to the qualities he shared with the great Confederate General 'Stonewall' Jackson) was, however, left in command of his division. At the Battle of Franklin the commander of the Army of Tennessee, John Bell Hood, dissatisfied with the competence of his generals, sent his forces on a futile assault against a heavily fortified Union position. Hood's vengeful and petty action cost him 6,000 men and the lives of six Confederate generals, including Cleburne. A much recounted story tells of how Cleburne, possibly harbouring the intimations of mortality which any sane man would have gleaned from Hood's demented strategy, stopped for a few moments on his way to the battlefield in an Episcopalian churchyard. Struck by the serenity and beauty of the surroundings he remarked that it would be 'almost worth dying for to be buried in such a beautiful spot'. The supremely gifted Irish-born 'Ney of the Confederacy' would be interred there within hours.

While the contribution of the Irish nation to America's private war was quantitatively and qualitatively significant, it was hardly more so than that of other immigrant races. Because of the reputation which they brought with them from Europe, allied to the casualties suffered by ethnic Irish units, it may well have been that the Irish got a better 'press' than other nationalities. Professor James McPherson of Princeton makes reference in his *Battle Cry of Freedom* to the numerical under-representation of the Irish in the Union forces. Of some two million Union soldiers and sailors, half a million were foreigners, or 25 per cent. But 30 per cent of the males of military age in the United States were immigrants. The Irish and German Catholics were the two ethnic groups who did not enlist in proportion to their share of the population.

This disparity can be readily accounted for. The Irish were under the influence of the largely anti-war and anti-abolition Democratic Party. To the impoverished and newly arrived Irish the issues involved in the war were remote. It was not their fight, and the condescension exhibited towards them by a segment of Yankee society would certainly not have encouraged them to risk their lives in the Union cause. Emancipation of the slaves posed a direct threat to their interests. Many had not applied for citizenship and so were not eligible for the draft. In addition, the practice emerged amongst big city Democratic political 'machines', like Tammany Hall in New York, of 'buying out' supporters who had been drafted. Taxpayers' money went towards the employment of substitutes for men nominated by local Democratic ward heelers; many of these were the highly politicised Irish.

However, those who did go to war, and there were many, probably bore a slightly disproportionate burden of the fighting. There was even a feeling that anti-Irish racism dictated the seemingly inevitable presence of Irish units where the fighting was most brutal and the fatalities most overwhelming. The comment of an Irish soldier at Gettysburg exposes this suspicion. On being told that his unit was being kept in reserve he observed acidly, 'In resairve? Yis! Resairved for the heavy fighting.' It is far more likely to have been simple coincidence or the result of an undoubted faith placed by American generals in Irish units that accounted for the heavy casualties taken by these troops. The Irish Brigade suffered more casualties (4,000) than were ever in its ranks at any one time. It suffered more casualties in total than all but three other Union or Confederate brigades. All five officers who commanded it were either killed or wounded.

But there was a positive side to this sacrifice. The assimilation of the Irish race into American society made a quantum leap forward. The reputation acquired by the Irish Brigade, Corcoran's Legion or the Louisiana Tigers corrected a number of misapprehensions and prejudices concerning the Irish race. They were increasingly seen as loyal Americans rather than just stereotypically ignorant, 'Ultramontanist', intemperate Papist slum dwellers. The 'No Irish Need Apply' mentality was modified as the Irish race basked in the afterglow of their contribution to the forging of a troubled but still united nation. The Irish, much discriminated against before war, acquired a new cachet. That they often used their improved status to discriminate against

Captain Myles Keogh in full dragoon uniform.
The Gene Autry Western Heritage Museum, Los Angeles.

Keogh is pictured here, with arms folded, to the right of Custer in the back row.
The Gene Autry Western Heritage Museum, Los Angeles.

Keogh's horse, Commanche, the only survivor of Custer's command at the Battle of Little Bighorn.
The Gene Autry Western Heritage Museum, Los Angeles.

Colonel Robert Nugent (standing) and Brigadier General Thomas F. Meagher.
Collection of Jack McCormack.

Colonel Michael Corcoran, 69th NY State Militia, wearing medal sent to him by San Francisco Fenians for refusing to parade his regiment in honour of the Prince of Wales.
Collection of Jack McCormack.

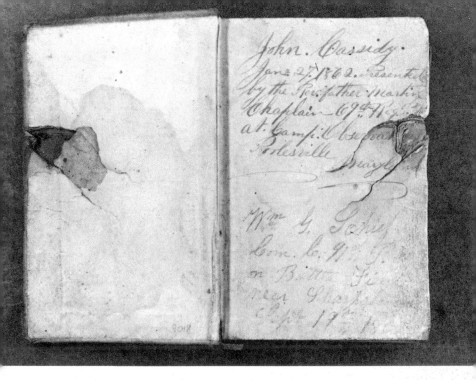

John Cassidy, mortally wounded at Gettysburg.
Joe McGinn, from Gettysburg National Military Park.

Cassidy's prayer book (above and top), showing rent made by ball.
Joe McGinn, from Gettysburg National Military Park.

Top left
Major General Patrick R. Cleburne, born in Co. Cork, killed at Franklin, Tennessee.
Collection of Jack McCormack.

Bottom left
Acting Lieutenant-Colonel James Haggerty of the 69th NY State Militia (born Glenswilly, Co. Donegal), the first high-ranking Irishman killed in the Civil War.
Collection of Jack McCormack.

Top right
Brigadier General Thomas A. Smyth, born in Fermoy, Co. Cork, the last Federal general killed in the Civil War.
Collection of Jack McCormack.

Bottom right
Colonel Patrick Henry O'Rorke, born in Co. Cavan, killed in action at Gettysburg.
Jack McCormack, Mass. MOLLUS Col., USAMHI.

'Corcoran's Irish Legion' (170th NY Infantry) near their camp in 1864.
Jack McCormack, Mass. MOLLUS Col., USAMHI.

Major General Philip H. Sheridan in the field.
Jack McCormack, Mass. MOLLUS Col., USAMHI.

Fr William Corby, the Irish Brigade chaplain (and later President of Notre Dame University), gives a benediction to his men as they go into battle at Gettysburg.
Jack McCormack, Mass. MOLLUS Col., USAMHI.

newer immigrant groups was a regrettable but perhaps inevitable consequence of that improvement.

Going West: Wars Against the Native American

During the nineteenth century, like a shadow cast by the sinking sun, the frontier line of the USA moved inexorably towards the Pacific Ocean. As it did, entire nations of native Americans, or 'Indian tribes' as they were called, were swept before it like so much dust before a broom into large tracts of land preserved for their use because they were unwanted by the white man. Those who were not brushed aside were wiped out by famine, disease or warfare.

One of those nations, the Choctaw, was a settled, agricultural people. In 1830 thousands died on a forced march from their ancestral lands in Mississippi to a reservation in Oklahoma. In the 1840s, scratching out an existence in the unpromising land to which they had been consigned, the Choctaws came to hear stories of a stricken people in a far-off land, a people who were unable to feed themselves because of the failure of their staple crop and who were dying of starvation and disease. The Choctaws knew nothing about Ireland, they lived in a remote part of the USA, far from the great Eastern port cities into which the economic refugees of the Great Famine were flocking. But still, moved by what they heard, they gathered the sum of £750 together and sent it to help the starving Irish. In the 1840s it was a large sum. To the Choctaws, who would have raised few cash crops, it was colossal.

This is one of the few recorded instances of any awareness in the 1800s on the part of Native Americans of the existence of Ireland. Many Irish, on the other hand, were to become very familiar with the Native American. The Irish 'diaspora' of the 1840s and 1850s ensured that Irishmen came into direct contact with native Indians. They saw them at close quarters and, more often than not, they killed them. The Irish who constituted 25 per cent of all immigration into the US during that period were generally impoverished, uneducated and unhealthy. The 'No Irish Need Apply' signs erected by employers were not to be found over army recruiting centres, so the Irish joined in their thousands and, incidentally, later deserted in their hundreds. In 1850 and 1851, for example, the US army (a relatively small force of between 15,000 to

25,000 men) accepted 5,000 new recruits. Of these 2,113 (42 per cent) were Irish. During the decade following the Civil War (1865–75) 183,659 men enlisted in the army. Of these 38,649 admitted to having been born in Ireland. Others, perhaps, who sought advancement in the army may not have.

John Ford and others in the US movie industry have perpetuated the stereotype of the Irish sergeant (inevitably played by Victor McLaglen or Ward Bond). Stereotypical though it is, the notion of the ubiquitous Irish NCO is not an entirely erroneous one. In Custer's 7th Cavalry in 1876, for example, there was at least one Irish-born sergeant in every single company, a total of eighteen divided among the twelve companies (although enlistment in the army did not confer any status on these lowly immigrants). The attitude of the telegraph operator in Camp Brown, Wyoming, towards servicemen was fairly typical of the time. 'None but a menial cur could stand the usage of a soldier in the army today. The majority of the officers are "dead beats" and the soldiers escaped convicts and the lowest of God's creation.'

It was to be the Indian of the Western Plains, the Lakota or Sioux, the Cheyenne, the Arapaho, who would provide the sternest and most bloody resistance to the 'bluecoats' who attempted to herd him into squalid reservations and keep him there. The discovery of gold in California in 1849 meant the first widespread exposure of the Plains Indian to the white man. He brought diseases with him from the East to which the Lakota and Cheyenne, close to the westward trails, had no resistance. He also brought blue-clad soldiers who built forts at strategic points along the trail. The Bureau of Indian Affairs appointed agents to oversee the native tribes. One of these was, almost literally, a poacher turned gamekeeper.

Thomas Fitzpatrick, born in Cavan in 1799, had emigrated to the US in 1816 and had spent the 1820s and 1830s as a 'Mountain Man', trapping beaver and avoiding Indians. He had earned the nickname 'Broken Hand' from the Blackfeet after injuring his wrist escaping from one of their war parties in Montana in 1835. He had been an army scout and his knowledge of Indian culture had helped him negotiate a treaty between an assembly of Indian tribes at Fort Laramie in 1851. Travelling among the Cheyenne, Arapaho and Sioux in 1853 he wrote: 'They were in abject want of food half the year, and their reliance from that scanty supply, in the rapid decrease of the buffalo, is fast disappearing. . . . Their women are pinched with want and their children constantly crying out with hunger.'

That hunger may have prompted a Sioux called High Forehead to kill the cow of a travelling Mormon family the following year. His people offered to pay compensation of ten dollars. But a gung-ho Irish cavalry officer, Lieutenant John Grattan, fresh out of West Point, decided to teach High Forehead a lesson. He announced his intention to arrest him. This move was in total contravention of the 1851 Fort Laramie Treaty, under the terms of which whites punished whites and Indians dealt with Indians. And the Sioux had no intention of submitting to Grattan's justice. High Forehead held Grattan in the contempt reserved by those of low caste for those perceived as being even lower. Grattan set off in search of High Forehead with a sergeant, corporal and twenty-seven troopers. He also brought a twelve-pound fieldpiece and a mountain howitzer. His intentions were clearly not passive. He issued an instruction to his troops: 'When I give the order you may fire as you damned please.' Like so many attacks by cavalry and militia soldiers on Indian settlements (Sand Creek, Washita Creek), the killing was to be indiscriminate. Ironically, it turned out to be anything but. No one knows what happened; only one of Grattan's troopers survived, Irishman John Cuddy, and he died of his wounds after being brought back to Fort Laramie. The rest of the troop was wiped out. Grattan's body was like a pin cushion by the time it was found, with twenty-four arrows piercing various parts of it. One had gone completely through his skull. His face was mashed to a pulp by the Sioux and he had to be identified by means of his pocket watch.

There were calls for blood on the frontier and in the East. An army inspector was despatched to investigate. Grattan's folly and his contemptuous attitude towards the Indians were forgotten. The inspector's conclusion was that 'the time has now fully arrived for teaching these barbarians . . . how to appreciate and respect the power, the justice, the generosity and the magnanimity of the United States.' Partly as a consequence of Grattan's killing and that of his troop the Plains tribes were to feel the power of the United States regularly over the next thirty-five years, but rarely, if ever, would they experience its justice or magnanimity. The destruction of the Native American as a military and indeed social force went hand-in-hand. It seemed to be insufficient to neutralise the threat of Indian violence; the only acceptable solution seems to have been to destroy their war-making capacity and their way of life. The architect and symbol of this ruthless suppression was General Philip Sheridan, the son of poor Cavan emigrants, who became the most prominent Irish-born military power in the land. (He never readily admitted to being Irish.) After his Civil War successes he was appointed by President Ulysses S. Grant and the army commander, William Tecumseh Sherman, to suppress Indian uprisings on the frontier.

Sheridan was a slightly Napoleonic looking figure. Short, he was five feet five inches, dark and stocky and was described by one staff officer as 'thickset and common Irish looking'. He was 'given to intense rages, mad with battle lust during an engagement, quick to censure and slow to forgive, bursting with energy, forever demanding the impossible of his men'. He liked what he saw in George Armstrong Custer, a brevet general during the Civil War, now lieutenant colonel in field command of the 7th Cavalry. Sheridan had, more or less, a free hand to do as he wished. On 15 October 1868 Sherman had written to him: 'I will say nothing and do nothing to restrain our troops from doing what they deem proper on the spot . . . I will back you with my whole authority.' There was little ambiguity about what exactly Sheridan wanted. Once, while involved in negotiations with a Commanche leader, Tosawi 'Silver Brooch', he heard the chief allude to himself as a good Indian. 'Little Phil' observed drily: 'The only good Indians I ever saw were dead.' As Henry II had asked, 'Who will rid me of this turbulent priest [Thomas Beckett]?', so Little Phil's observation was taken as a statement of intent and immediately acted upon.

In fairness to Sheridan, however, the statement, though ascribed to him and never vigorously repudiated by him, may be entirely apocryphal. Sheridan's attitude towards the people he was slaughtering was more complex. He was a both a politician and a servant of real politicians. Above all, he was a pragmatic man who believed that the Indians were an essentially Stone Age people who were hindering the progress of the most powerful nation of the Steam Age. But he probably also recognised that there was no moral justification for what was being done. Perhaps it was the vestigial Irishman in him which enabled him to empathise a little with the peoples he was obliterating. He once pointed out that if the American nation was treated the way the Indians were they would have responded in much the same way as the 'savages'.

Sheridan's 'hammer' on the frontier was the 7th Cavalry, led by the dashing, long-haired, egotistical Lieutenant Colonel George Armstrong Custer. The 7th, despite its portrayal by Hollywood as a peculiarly all-American WASP regiment (give or take an 'Oirish' drill sergeant) was, in fact, one seventh Irish and only slightly less German. The regimental marching song was 'Garryowen', a particular favourite of Custer's, as was 'The Girl I Left Behind Me'. The Irish influence can be seen in the regiment's 1876 muster roll which included over 126 Irish names out of 822 members of the regiment. There were names like Sergeant George McDermott, aged twenty-eight and from County Clare, Denis Kerr from Antrim who deserted from Company A in 1877, as did John Gilbert of Cork.

With one exception, the Irish in the 7th were enlisted men or NCOs. The exception was Captain (brevet Lieutenant Colonel) Myles Walter Keogh from Carlow, commander of Company I. Dynamic, handsome, vigorous, courageous, these were adjectives attributed as much to Keogh as to Custer. Unfortunately, he was also offensive, intemperate, drunken and violent. Keogh had been one of those fortunate enough to have been offered a commission in the post Civil War army. To achieve this had required every ounce of 'pull'. He wrote to his brother Tom in December 1865, eight months after the conclusion of the war: 'things are so uncertain here that any of us are liable to be thrown out, but one thing's certain – I have enough of powerful friends who will always see me provided for in a becoming way.' It was not until the following October that he was finally 'provided for'. Like thousands of other Irishmen in the US after the war, he had no other job to go back to. He wrote enthusiastically about his good fortune.

> I have had unequalled promotion and now when all the great volunteer army is scattered to the winds I am amongst the few to be retained in the regular army. A. S. Smith, one of our most distinguished Majors, is my Colonel. Custer, the Cavalry General, has been appointed Major. I am the fourth senior Captain. This is for one of my age almost unprecedented in the regular army, with probably the exception of General Custer and one or two others who are in higher grades.

From now on Keogh's business would be hunting the Plains Indian. His letters reveal much about his attitude towards the people against whom he was fighting. He viewed them in the way he viewed the game he liked to hunt on the prairies. 'I no longer hunt buffalo as they are so numerous and easily killed, there is no fun killing them except when fresh meat is needed. Webster antelope and particularly the large black tailed deer, this is glorious sport; a few days ago I shot a black tailed buck at 450 yards with my carbine small bore. He weighed nearly 400 pounds and his antlers are horrendous . . . I must confess that I should much rather have some nobler game, say Sioux or Pawnee. Their two tribes are combined and are now on the warpath.'

This 'game' was dangerous, however, and could fight back, as Keogh reminded his brother in a letter from Fort Harker, Kansas, on 13 August 1868.

> I am only sorry to say that the Indians have again broken out, they yesterday attacked a settlement within forty miles from here and having plundered the place, brutally ravished the women and got away — we are preparing for an Indian war during the ensuing fall. I sent you a copy of a photograph I had taken of one of my long scouts the Indians killed last year. The top of his head was cut off. This man was less brutally used than many others owing to our charging up to recapture some and pursue the Indians.

Keogh had high hopes that the army would soon begin to hit back. He had written to Tom Keogh in March of that year, applauding the fact that General Phillip Sheridan had been appointed to take charge of the campaign. 'I hope he will rush things', he told his brother.

He did. That winter Custer was sent against Chief Black Kettle's Cheyenne settlement on the Washita River, south of the Arkansas. His instructions from Sheridan were to 'kill or hang all warriors and bring back all women and children'. The orders were not only carried out efficiently, but improved upon. Not all the women and children were brought back as prisoners. Keogh, perhaps much to his disappointment, did not take part in this great victory over 'savage bands of cruel marauders' (Sheridan's description). At the time of the 'battle' he was on the staff of General Sully, commander of the district of Upper Arkansas. But the 7th had its usual quota of Irishmen involved in that action and the regimental band struck up 'Garryowen' as the troops advanced on the settlement. (Legend has it that it was so cold the bandsmen's saliva froze in their instruments and they played only a few bars.)

Keogh may not have been involved in the fight at the Washita River but he appears to have benefitted from either the 'booty' of that battle or some other skirmish. Five months afterwards he wrote again to his brother, 'we have knocked the Indians into a cocked hat, yet they are still on the warpath. We have about ninety squaws from our last fight. Some of them are very pretty. I have one that is quite intelligent. It is usual for officers to have two or three hanging around.' Sadly, this was all too common a fate among captured Indian women.

Various treaties and agreements had allocated territory in North and South Dakota to a number of Indian tribes, chiefly the Sioux, Cheyenne and Arapahoe. Included in this area were the Black Hills, sacred to the Sioux. In 1874 a military expedition, led by Custer, discovered gold in the Black Hills. Prospectors began to flood into the Dakotas in their hundreds. Initially, the army turned them away but they kept sneaking back in. Then, as the Indians began to attack the prospectors, the army went in to protect the white trespassers. More and more Sioux and Cheyenne followed irredentist leaders like Gall, Crazy Horse and Sitting Bull off the reservation and into the lands to the north and west of the Dakotas. Sheridan decided that something had to be done about this sullen retinue which was reported by Indian agents to be growing exponentially. An ultimatum was issued to all peoples to return to their reservations by 31 January 1876 or to be branded as hostile. That summer Sheridan and his generals devised a three-pronged approach for rounding up the 'renegades' thought to be gathered in an area between the Powder River and the Bighorn River in modern Montana. A force under the command of General Gibbon would advance eastwards along the Bozeman trail. A second contingent, under General Crook, would approach from the south.

On 17 May 1876, a third force of 925 men, mostly from Custer's 7th Cavalry and under the command of General Alfred Terry, left Fort Lincoln in the Dakota territory, heading westwards, with the regimental tunes 'Garryowen' and 'The Girl I Left Behind Me' ringing in their ears. Custer's immediate subordinates on the expedition were Major Marcus Reno and Captain Frederick Benteen, whose dislike of each other was exceeded only by their loathing for their commanding officer. Thomas Coleman, son of Irish immigrants, was a humble private in B Company attached to Reno's command. He recorded details of the march and subsequent battle in a colourful diary. For three weeks there were no signs of 'hostiles' but plenty of evidence of their presence: '[On 23 May] we came to a circular arbour about 200 feet in circumference, built with crotches and strong poles. There was a tree in the centre 35-feet high around which was piled a number of buffalo heads. This place was devoted to a religious ceremony called the Sun Dance, usually practised by this tribe before going on the warpath.'

The 7th Cavalry, under Custer, split off from the rest of Terry's column. By 25 June, Long Hair (his nickname amongst the Indians), with just over 600 men, had encountered his 'hostiles'. Indian agents had calculated the force at about 800 warriors. In fact it was up to five times that size! The Sioux and Cheyenne who had left the reservation and flocked to the command of Sitting Bull and Crazy Horse were camped by the Little Bighorn River in a valley surrounded by low hills and trees. Private Coleman wrote of the setting:

> It is a lovely place. The valley is one and a half miles broad and four miles long, the river winding like a snake and dotted with islands, thickly studded with timber, the water clear as crystal as it comes rushing from the mountains. Oh what a pity that such a lovely place should be the abode of such a band of bloodthirsty demons!

Custer had no idea of the size of the encampment and fearing that he had been spotted, decided to attack before the hostiles could disperse. Fatally, he then split his force into three. Benteen took three companies on a sweep to the south-east to guard Custer's flank. Reno, with three companies, was despatched to attack the village from the south. Custer took five companies (just over 200 men) to attack the other end. One company was detailed to guard the pack train.

That Reno and his three companies were not annihilated was extremely fortunate. Most of the members of his battalion managed to make their way to a hilltop where they were later joined by Benteen and his men. There they held out until dark and throughout the next day. On the morning of 27 June, after the Sioux and Cheyenne had dispersed, they were joined by the rest of General Terry's command. Unaware of Custer's exact whereabouts and with a number of seriously wounded men, Reno had opted to stay put rather than go to the aid of his commanding officer. The decision may have averted an even worse humiliation for the US army. Custer was four miles away, dying, along with his entire troop of 210 officers and men.

Only colourful and contradictory Indian accounts exist as to the fate of Custer and his troop, along with archaeological evidence, so there is little purpose in dwelling on the particulars. Among the Irish victims of the debacle was Sergeant Robert Hughes, a Dubliner in Company K who carried Custer's standard into battle. Two Irish troopers were unfortunate enough to get caught up with Custer's detachment because they were instructed to carry messages from Reno. The second message was borne by Private John Mitchell from Galway; the first had been taken to the colonel by Archibald McIlhargey from Antrim. Later McIlhargey's widow, Josie, would marry Sergeant Michael Caddle, also of Company I. Sergeant Jeremiah Finley from Tipperary was the regimental tailor and had made the buckskin jacket which Custer wore during the campaign. His body was found shot through with twelve arrows. His widow later married Private John Donahue from Galway.

It was between Last Stand Hill and Calhoun Hill that Captain Myles Walter Keogh died. At the time, it was the custom of the Indians to mutilate the bodies of their victims, thus making it more difficult for them to gain revenge in the next world. Keogh's body, however, was not mutilated by the Sioux. An explanation for this was that he wore a medal around his neck. The Sioux, who wore pendants of all kinds to ward off spirits, may have honoured this 'medicine'. The medal, indeed, may have been the one awarded to him by Pope Pius IX for service with the Papal Army and would have been large and impressive, more so than other Roman Catholic medals, scapulars, beads or crosses worn around the necks of troopers. Keogh's body was, however, looted. A year after the battle four items belonging to him were recovered from an Indian in Canada: his watch, his army gauntlets and two photographs, one of Keogh wearing his medal and a blood spattered picture of the sister of one of his fellow officers, Captain McDougall. The brave who handed over those effects also had Keogh's revolver but refused to sell it.

Dubious legends have grown up around Keogh, partly because of his swashbuckling mercenary history and also because his horse Comanche was found on the battlefield, injured but alive — the only vestige of Custer's force to have survived the battle. It was said by scouts who later spoke to Sioux involved in the battle that Keogh had been the last bluecoat to die, 'the bravest man', standing alone before the last Indian charge and killing six Sioux before he himself fell. Another account tells of a big officer with a curly moustache suddenly sitting up after the battle was over and the soldiers' bodies were being looted. He had a pistol in his hand and glared about him at the children and the squaws, who shrank back. Then a Sioux brave stood forward, took the pistol out of the wounded man's hand and shot him in the head. Cheyenne accounts of this incident say the man had two bars on his epaulettes, the insignia of a captain.

Keogh's courage in death must remain legendary, but that of two other Irishmen – Sergeant Thomas Murray from Monaghan and Private Thomas J. Callan from Louth – is verifiable. Both received Congressional Medals of Honour, Murray for a variety of acts, Callan for carrying water to the wounded on top of Reno Hill. Private Thomas O'Neill deserved a medal of some sort just for surviving. Before the retreat by Reno's battalion to the hilltop they had fled in disorder into a clump of trees. Sixteen members of the battalion, including O'Neill, a Dubliner, and Lieutenant Charles de Rudio, did not hear the retreat being sounded. They were forced to hide out in the trees for thirty-six hours while the Sioux and Cheyenne moved backwards and forwards between the village and Reno Hill. Miraculously, they managed to escape detection. Afterwards de Rudio wrote of O'Neill, 'He faithfully obeyed me and stood by me like a brother. I shall never cease to remember him and his service to me during our dangerous companionship.'

The medal won by Thomas Callan was hard earned. The lack of water on a blisteringly hot June day in Montana caused as much hardship to the Reno-Benteen group as to the Sioux who were not able to shake them from their entrenched positions. One Irishman, Sergeant Michael P. Madden, was thirsty, brave or foolhardy enough to volunteer to get water from the river. He never made it. His leg was shattered below the knee by an Indian bullet. The regimental surgeon, Dr Porter, decided that the only way he could save Madden's life was to amputate. This he did without any anaesthetic other than the soporific effects of a few slugs of whiskey. Among the typically 'green-tinged' legends which grew up were that Madden had offered no complaint as his leg was being removed and commented after the emergency hilltop surgery that if the doctor was prepared to give him more whiskey he could have the other leg as well. A more accurate account of his reaction to the amputation probably comes from his colleague Private Goldin, who records him as recalling nostalgically his service with the 7th: 'many a fine shindig we've had, too, but now I'm nothin' but a poor, damned, one-legged soldier'.

Madden may have felt his troubles were over when the relief column arrived and the Indians withdrew. The sergeant was evacuated by means of a litter dragged by mules. However, an 1877 report of the Surgeon General mentions that on approaching the boat *Far West* to be taken downriver, 'the leading mule of the litter bearing the amputated man knelt down and the patient rolled off'. Madden was, fortunately, uninjured by the obstreperous behaviour of the animal. The mule had landed him on a cactus when it performed its unexplained genuflection. Madden is reported to have cursed the animal roundly, setting everyone's mind at rest as to his condition. However, his colleague, Private Coleman of Company B, wrote: 'Although the litter he was on fell to the ground twice he never uttered a complaint.'

Thirty-two Irishmen died with Custer at the Little Bighorn; most of their names are forgotten and none, with the exception of Myles Keogh, ranked higher than sergeant. Some of those who survived were to have later appointments with violent death as the struggle of the Plains Indian continued before coming to a cold, abrupt and murderous end at Wounded Knee Creek fourteen years later. Ironically, one Irishman (and probably dozens of Indians) who had survived the Little Bighorn died at Wounded Knee. Corporal George Loyd, from Tyrone, served with G Company. He received a lung wound and died of his injuries. He was awarded a posthumous Congressional Medal of Honour.

If we are to accept Phillip Sheridan's infamous dictum about 'dead' Indians, then there were lots of 'good' Indians in evidence at Wounded Knee Creek, and many members of an Irish race which had fled poverty and subjugation had, by reason of economic necessity or the spirit of adventure, assisted in the suppression of another culture. In the one hundred years since Wounded Knee the success of the Irish race in the US has been as spectacular as the decline of the native American. As well, most of the Irish troopers who so assiduously did their duty on 29 December 1890 may not have been aware of the existence of the Choctaw Indians. They had long since ceased to be troublesome and were already sliding inexorably into the Native American pit of rank poverty, alcoholism and dependency. The troopers certainly were not aware of the supremely charitable gesture by that impoverished nation which had helped save so many lives in the country of their birth forty years before.

Black Elk of the Oglala Sioux nation lamented the dead of Wounded Knee with the words: 'A people's dream died there. It was a beautiful dream . . . the nation's hoop is broken and scattered. There is no centre any longer, and the sacred tree is dead.' The imagery could easily be that of many an Irish poet. It is ironic that the dependency of their own impoverished nation and the hostility of many of the citizens of their adopted land had forced thousands of Irishmen into the only employment which would accept them and had brought them to this place where they would seal the fate of a people far older than themselves.

2

The Great War

What Passing Bells: Unionist and Nationalist Ireland in the First World War

And wherever the fight is hottest,
And the sorest task is set,
Ulster will strike for England
And England will not forget.

from a contemporary unionist poem

Johnny Redmond has the battle won,
Says the Grand Old Dame Brittania.
He has finished what Wolf Tone begun,
Says the Grand Old Dame Brittania.
Those Shinners through the country stalk
And praise '67 and Bachelor's Walk.
Did you ever hear such foolish talk?
Said the Grand Old Dame Brittania.

from a satirical nationalist song

It is a truth, far from universally acknowledged, that nationalist Ireland shared equally the burden of Irish involvement in the First World War with the Ulster unionists. For their own distinct reasons both sides have often chosen to ignore this fact. It suited Ulster unionists to suggest that they alone were rallying to the cause while the disloyal nationalists cowered behind a legion of excuses. It suited Irish nationalists to believe that they had shunned a British-inspired imperialistic quarrel while chasing the 'golden fleece' of legislative independence. But the truth was rather different. By February 1916 almost as many of John Redmond's National Volunteers (22,000) had enlisted as had Carson and Craig's Ulster Volunteers (25,000), while a further 48,000 Irishmen of no identifiable political stripe (though mainly from the South) had also enlisted.

In Dublin, with some of the worst slum conditions in Europe, recruitment levels compared favourably with Belfast. This was despite the fact that at least half of the Dubliners who applied to join the forces were deemed medically unfit to serve in an army which had lowered its entry standards in the urgent drive to get warm bodies into the field. Hundreds of working-class Dubliners, signing up largely for economic reasons, were among the 45,000 men who joined the various battalions of the Dublin Fusiliers over the four years of the conflict. By enlisting, married men rendered their wives eligible for a 'separation allowance'. It was often the difference between mere poverty and virtual starvation for thousands of working-class families in Dublin.

The Dublin middle classes were well also represented, particularly areas such as Rathgar, Pembroke and Rathmines, which were strongly unionist. Here, where such luxuries could be afforded, the motivation for enlistment was more idealistic and patriotic. To the dependents of many of those who went because, economically, they had no alternative, the jingoistic cant of a contemporary musical-hall song must have been especially galling.

> Oh we don't want to lose you, but we think you ought to go;
> For your King and country both need you so.
> We shall want and miss you, but with all our might and main
> We will thank you, cheer you, kiss you
> When you come back again.

But thousands of sons, husbands and brothers would never come back, and thousands more would return as physical and emotional wrecks. Not even the enthusiastic send-off of the crowd which followed the departing ranks of the 2nd Battalion, the Royal Irish Regiment, to the North Wall could in the words of Anthony Brennan of Kilkenny disguise the 'painful scenes of wives and mothers bidding good-bye to husbands and sons'. Brennan himself, bound for the Western Front and the Battle of the Somme, departed with a sense of foreboding. 'The band . . . determined to get the last ounce of emotional effect out of the situation, played "Come Back to Erin". Many of us who then watched the shores of Ireland receding from view were doing so for the last time, and in my case it was to be seventeen long months before I could respond to the invitation of the band and "Come back to Erin" again.'

The first shot of the Great War from a member of the British Expeditionary Force in France was fired by an Irishman, Corporal Edward Thomas, a Tipperary man serving with the 4th Royal Irish Dragoon Guards. He fired at a German cavalry unit and missed. But one of the first of many egregious bloodlettings of an Irish unit came at Gallipoli in April 1915. It was something of a sideshow, the brainchild of Winston Churchill who wanted to divert German forces from the Western Front where fighting had already settled into the attrition of trench warfare. General Sir Ian Hamilton was charged with the task of landing a force on the Gallipoli Peninsula just across the Dardanelles from Asian Turkey. The Turks were seen as the Achilles heel of the Alliance forces. If Turkey was being overrun the Germans would have to come to the aid of their allies, thus leading to manpower shortages on the Western Front. But as the Dublin Fusiliers and the Munster Fusiliers were to discover, the Turks, fighting in defence of their own country, were a match for anything the British could throw at them.

The Gallipoli landings were to take place at a number of designated beaches on 25 April 1915. The Dublins and Munsters, part of the 29th Division, were to come ashore at 'V' beach. The story is told of a British regiment about to effect a landing in Gallipoli and passing a hospital ship crammed with Australian wounded from 'W' beach. It was an unnerving experience, but the incoming regiment managed to muster a shout of: 'Are we downhearted?' A single hoarse Australian croaked in reply, 'You bloody soon will be!' It might just as well have been a maimed Irishman; the experience of the Irish and the ANZACs had been depressingly similar.

'V' beach was surrounded, in a natural amphitheatre, by cliffs one hundred feet in height. To the right of the beach was an old fortress and beyond that the village of Sedd el Bahr. The defences on the cliffs overhead were well wired and defended by machine-guns. In a pattern which was to be repeated time and time again, right through the war, the bombardment of the Turkish positions failed to dislodge the defenders. The 1st Battalion, Dublin Fusiliers, led the attack, taken in by five 'tows' – open boats. As the boats neared the shore snipers shot the oarsmen. The tows began to drift in the strong current and as they did so they were raked by constant, accurate and deadly machine-gun fire. The lead boat contained forty men; only three ever reached shore, all wounded.

Watching this carnage, the 1st Battalion, Munster Fusiliers, along with a company of the Dublin Fusiliers, got a unique preview of their own fate as they approached the beach in an old, crudely adapted collier, the *River Clyde*. The ship beached sooner than had been anticipated, still eighty yards from the shore. A sort of ad hoc 'floating bridge' had been designed to get the infantrymen onto the beach. The Munsters poured from the deliberately gutted sides of the *River Clyde* onto this structure, which began to break up almost immediately. Men were forced to swim for the shore. Meanwhile the Turkish machine-gunners and snipers, having dealt with the Dublins, trained their sights on the foreshore.

The Munsters, slowed down by their heavy packs (200 rounds of ammunition, three days' rations, overcoats, macintosh sheets weighing about sixty pounds), were butchered as they floundered through the waves. Many never even made it as far as the Turkish bullets. They simply drowned as they sank into the deep water. The working classes of Dublin and Cork were far smaller in stature then, averaging about five feet four inches to five feet six inches in height. Two of the few Munster officers who survived the slaughter left behind their memories of those events. Captain G. W. Geddes wrote an account of his experiences which is kept in the Imperial War Museum in London. Lieutenant Guy Nightingale was also an inveterate correspondent and has left behind an invaluable collection of contemporary letters.

Among the early casualties was Brigadier General Napier. He had left the comparative safety of the *Clyde* just ahead of Nightingale. 'He was hit in the stomach,' Nightingale wrote to his mother, 'on the barge between our ship and the beach. He lay for half an hour on the barge and then tried to get some water to drink, but the moment he moved the Turks began firing at him again . . . he died very soon afterwards and when I went ashore for the second time I turned him over and he was quite dead.' Lieutenant Commander Sampson, a Royal Naval Air Service flier, was reconnoitring the area. Flying across 'V' beach he was puzzled at the colour of the water. When it became clear what had happened below him he recognised that the calm sea, from the shoreline right out to fifty yards from the beach, was 'absolutely red with blood'.

Geddes and Nightingale from the Munsters and Henry Desmond O'Hara of the Dublins were among the only functioning officers left. The Munsters had lost twenty of their twenty-six officers as casualties and 600 of 900 men. The Dublins had only four officers unhurt and had lost 550 men. Lieutenant O'Hara, who was to win a DSO the following day (the youngest officer to have done so at that time) had to assume command over the Dublin Fusiliers' battalion because all his superior officers, from the colonel down, were either dead or injured. However, the remnant over which he assumed command was scarcely larger than the platoon strength force over which he would normally have had control.

Geddes captures the horror of it all in his vivid accounts. 'Hell it has been, with a vengeance,' he wrote, 'and men who were at Mons and La Bassee say it was sheer child's play to what we've gone through here.' He himself got ashore without being hit and lay exhausted on the beach until he could drag himself up to some flimsy cover, a mere ten yards from the water's edge, which had been found by the few Dublins who had made it ashore still (relatively) intact. He estimated that he had lost about 70 per cent of his company. Geddes realised that the fort of Sedd el Bahr was undefended and that the beach to the right of his group was unoccupied. Concerned that the Turks might come down from their elevated positions to push the invading force off the beach, Geddes took a small group of volunteers to secure their right in a suicidal dash from cover. 'I had a button shot off, and got plugged through the shoulder, the bullet going clean through and coming out my back – another fraction of an inch and my career would have been ended . . . of the first four men to cross with me two were instantly killed, one wounded and one got through.'

Nightingale and Major Jarret, commander of the Munster's Y Company, joined Geddes's small force after it grew dark. Geddes crept away to get his wound treated. Soon afterwards Nightingale found himself in command. 'Jarret came up to have a look, when he was shot through the throat by my side. He died very soon and that left me the senior officer on the shore. We had an awful night soaked to the skin, bitterly cold and wet and sniped at all night.' The remnants of the two battalions were combined into one field battalion described, for convenience sake, as 'the Dubsters'. Reinforced by two companies of the 2nd Hampshires, whose landing had been aborted after the annihilation of the two Irish battalions, the Dubsters stormed the Turkish positions the following day and beat off the defenders. 'The German officers whom we have taken prisoner', Nightingale wrote to his mother (the Turks had valuable German assistance) 'say it is absolutely beyond them how we ever effected a landing at all. If there was one place in the whole world that was impregnable it was this peninsula . . . It certainly has been a tough job. The heaps of dead are awful and the beach where we landed was an extraordinary sight the morning they buried them.'

The conflict, even leaving aside the appalling casualties of the initial landing, was utterly savage. Geddes, in his account, accuses the Turks of 'killing, torturing and burning the wounded – this is reported on every side'. Statements like this may be dismissed as hyperbole but Nightingale rather blithely accepts responsibility for atrocities on the British side. 'We took 300 prisoners', he claims, 'and could have taken 3,000 but we preferred shooting them. All the streams were simply running blood and the heaps of dead were a grand sight.' The casual brutality and callousness of such a claim is indicative of the effect the fighting was having on the participants. It is important to bear in mind that Nightingale was relating such events to his own mother. In another letter, also written to his mother, on 9 June he records the death of a newly arrived officer. The contempt and lack of sensitivity of the veteran for the 'green' recruit spills from the page. 'One was hit last night during dinner and fell into the soup, upsetting the whole table, and bled into the tea pot making an awful mess of everything, and we finally didn't get dinner till after dark.'

Nightingale could clearly see the physical and indeed the psychological effect the bitter fighting was having on his peers. Geddes returned to his company some days after having his wound treated. Nightingale was clearly fond of him; theirs was a friendship forged *in extremis*. He could not avoid the evidence of overwhelming stress experienced by his friend, nor indeed by Henry Desmond O'Hara. 'Geddes is a ripping commanding officer to work with', he wrote, in true 'boy's own' style, 'but he is frightfully worried and his hair is nearly white! I've never seen fellows get so old so quickly. This morning I saw a fellow called O'Hara in the Dublins whom I hadn't seen for about a fortnight and I hardly recognised him.'

Ironically, given the purpose of the entire exercise, the next months of fighting degenerated into trench warfare. The experience of the Western Front was replicated. Snipers took a heavy toll of the unwary. Victims of raids and patrols lay in no man's land, decomposing. The stench of death was everywhere. Not even large quantities of chloride, lime and creosote could disguise the smell. Soldiers were kept constantly busy digging and reinforcing trenches, but the work was not therapeutic. O'Hara wrote to his fiancée that the men were all bordering on lunacy, the conditions were so terrible. The Turks were defending their homeland against invaders and they were doing so with exceeding bravery. Nightingale concurred. 'Simply tons of fellows are going off their heads from strain and worry – mostly fellows who have been wounded and come back, but there are very few now who have gone through from the beginning and are not the worse for it.'

O'Hara's fragile psyche was assailed by fatalism. He told his fiancée in one letter that he didn't think he was going to live long, and indeed he did not. He died of his wounds some weeks later. Guy Nightingale, however, did not die in Gallipoli. He also survived subsequent service (this time with the 16th [Irish] Division) on the Western Front. His often frenzied letters with their mixture of callousness, bluster and naivety were obviously not sufficiently cathartic. He lived until 1935, an alcoholic recluse for most of that time, and on the twentieth anniversary of the Gallipoli landing he commemorated the event by committing suicide.

News of the calamity at 'V' Beach was released in dribs and drabs. Nightingale, for example, perceptively noticed, when newspapers covering the landings were sent to him, that although the bulk of the casualties incurred by the Munsters and Dublins had come on the first day of the campaign, the casualty lists were spread over a number of days in order to lessen the impact. This meant that the men of the 10th (Irish) Division did not necessarily appreciate the enormity of the disaster that faced them when they landed at Suvla Bay in the northern part of the Gallipoli Peninsula in August.

It was part of a plan by Sir Ian Hamilton to drive a wedge across the peninsula, thus cutting off the Turks between the new invading force and the existing force in the south. The actual landings at Suvla Bay were tame affairs in comparison with the carnage at 'V' beach. It was only afterwards that administrative incompetence was to blight the entire operation. James Cahill, aged ninety-six, speaking to the author just a fortnight before his death in December 1990, recalled assembling on the beach and heading towards the first objective. 'It was a muddle up to get there, because you're under shellfire and men were lying around dying and roaring and the order was: "Form up in three lines." The commanding officer comes out and he says, "Any man showing signs of cowardice, you shoot him."'

It was in the Suvla Campaign that D Company of the 7th Battalion, Dublin Fusiliers, met its nemesis. The company was a largely middle-class group consisting of rugby, soccer and Gaelic footballers who had assembled at Landsdowne Road in order to enlist. Edgar Poulter was amongst them: 'We all turned up and, incidentally, paid half a crown for the privilege of joining up', he recalled. He was discouraged by his first impressions of Suvla Bay where the Turks had laid numerous mines. 'They said look out for land mines. I saw the odd fellow coming back with his leg blown off or wounded with stick bombs or land mines . . . we all began to feel a little funny in the pit of the stomach. We saw the first wounded we'd ever seen coming back.' The troops, once they had disembarked, waited around the beach for further orders. Nobody seemed to know what to do next. The logistics of the operation went haywire. Men stood, sat or lounged in the heat of an August day without supplies of water, provision for which appeared to have been forgotten. Edgar Poulter's experience was typical. 'At seven o'clock that night we were told to occupy Chocolate Hill. From the time we landed to the time we got to Chocolate Hill we'd had nothing to drink. It was a long time. We landed without filling the water bottles. I don't know whose mistake that was. But we didn't remedy that till late that night. And you couldn't use the artesian wells because there were bodies in the wells. The Turks had dropped bodies in the wells and polluted the water.'

Later that same night Captain Paddy Tobin of D Company began what might have been the first of a fascinating series of letters to his father. It was also the last. The correspondence was to end abruptly on the arid slopes of Kiretch Tepe Sirt a week later. Tobin was a much loved and respected Catholic officer in a company which largely consisted of Protestant Southern unionists. His letter captures the atmosphere of the Suvla landings well, conveying a sense of the heat, thirst, noise, danger and fear which prevailed. 'Well, at one spot it was hell', he told his father. 'We had to cross a spit of sand not twenty yards wide, with water on both sides. This the Turks had ranged to a yard and here we lost many poor fellows. . . . We had been running along hard, for about a quarter of a mile in heavy sand before this and we had not much energy left. With a final effort we dashed across it and reached a little sheltered bank like the Alps at Dollymount, only not so high, where we rested. Well across that neck I expected every minute to fall . . . I found myself under the bank in a paroxysm of fear and chattering my prayers between my teeth.'

While organisational chaos reigned on the beaches, inertia seemed to grip the command structure, allowing the Turks to consolidate and to reinforce the three battalions which had been stationed in the Suvla area. Finally, the commander of the 10th Division, General Sir Bryan Mahon, was ordered by the corps commander, General Stopford, to attack a ridge held by the Turks. Kiretch Tepe Sirt ran north-east to south-west, finishing at Suvla Point, which overlooked the bay. The attack began on 15 August; the Irish advanced along the northern edge of the ridge, the seaward side, gaining a foothold by means of a ferocious and costly bayonet charge. But on the far side of the hill things had gone badly for the 5th and 6th Inniskillings. Within an hour they had suffered 350 casualties and to no purpose – they had been unable to take the southern heights of Kiretch Tepe Sirt. This left the Irish defenders on the far side of the hill woefully exposed to the Turkish landward entrenchments. The rocky upper slopes, covered with boulders, provided perfect cover for the defenders who could not be dislodged by rifle or machine-gun fire. All that night the Turks lobbed down grenades, causing multiple casualties among the defending 6th Irish Fusiliers, 6th Munsters and 7th Dublins. They had no hand grenades of their own with which to respond.

Private Albert Wilkin of the elite D Company, 7th Dublins, caught five grenades and threw them back at the Turks. The sixth killed him. In other circumstances he might have been awarded a Victoria Cross but his heroism, alongside dozens of similar acts of bravery, merited only a posthumous 'mention in despatches'. Repeated efforts to take the ridge with bayonet charges were beaten back. In one instance Major M. C. Harrison (who had assumed command of the 7th Dublins after Colonel Downing was shot in the foot by a sniper) sent part of D Company (the 'Footballers' Company) to put a stop to the incessant grenade attacks. Four members of the raiding patrol came back alive! The Irish defenders were reduced to throwing rocks at the Turks and attempting to roll boulders down onto their trenches. Repeated requests by brigade command for reinforcements to complete the job begun by the 31st Brigade were ignored.

After the deaths of Major Harrison and Captain Poole Hickman, an eminent barrister in civilian life – Captain Paddy Tobin – briefly assumed command of D Company. Lieutenant Ernest Hamilton, a Trinity College medical student, described Tobin's death in a letter of condolence to his parents.

> He controlled the fire and steadied the men. Such gallantry and coolness I have never witnessed. We fought like demons against three times our numbers and held on too. Our knoll came in for at least six attacks. During one of these your son was killed, shot through the head. He caught me by the shoulder, and when I turned round he had passed away . . . His death affected the men so much that I thought all was finished, but spurred [on] by his example they fought for another hour as they never fought before.

Finally the decision was taken to abandon the gains made on the northern slopes by the 30th Brigade. The order came to withdraw. Hamilton led the remnants of the 7th Dublins from the slopes of Kiretch Tepe Sirt; he was the only surviving officer. He left behind him at Suvla Bay dead comrades of the calibre of Tobin, Hickman and Lieutenant Ernest Lawrence Julian, Reid Professor of Law at Trinity College. The annihilation of the 7th Dublins and the virtual obliteration of D Company in the course of the Suvla operation would deprive the country of a number of capable intellectuals it could ill afford to lose.

The needless waste of the lives of those first Irish volunteers was made more poignant when it became known why the 10th Division had not been reinforced or otherwise assisted. Because of a row at corps level, Mahon, the 10th's commander, having issued instructions for the attack, proceeded to resign. Stopford, the corps commander, had been sacked by Hamilton shortly after the assault on Kiretch Tepe Sirt began. His replacement, Major General de Lisle, was insufficiently familiar with what was actually going on to appreciate the urgency of the appeals from the 30th Brigade for reinforcements. When he finally agreed to send them, the positions on the northern ridge of Kiretch Tepe Sirt had already been abandoned.

Five days later the 29th Division, with the now separated and reinforced 1st Munsters and 1st Dublins, were at the sharp end of Winston Churchill's floundering initiative yet again. They arrived at Suvla Bay and their subsequent experiences were, if anything, even more horrific than at 'V' beach. An attack from the vicinity of Chocolate Hill ended in a rout. The Munsters set out with a force of 700 and lost nine officers and 400 men. Heavy shelling caused the gorse which covered the battleground to catch fire and break up the attack. Machine-gun fire mowed down most of the advancing troops and many of the seriously wounded, unable to crawl to safety, were burned alive by the flames. When the survivors were numbered, two companies, who would have had over 300 between them, could only muster twenty-four and thirteen men respectively. Guy Nightingale, who along with his men had not slept for three days, wrote to his mother that he was so exhausted, 'I'd have welcomed a bullet through any part of my anatomy.' At one point he had to lie in the bottom of a trench while a gorse fire passed overhead. 'Barrett, my old servant,' he wrote to his mother, 'is still out there; dead, I hope, for his sake, for those who are still alive and wounded must be suffering agonies from thirst and exposure.'

Between 19 and 20 December 1915, Suvla was evacuated. The rest of the peninsula was abandoned between 8 and 9 January 1916. Winston Churchill had, by then, already resigned as First Lord of the Admiralty. Captain Geddes of the 1st Munsters regarded the whole enterprise as 'a desperate venture'. 'I felt we were for it', he wrote. After 'V' beach, Guy Nightingale was concerned that 'they'll try and make out it's been nothing at all out here . . . whereas it's been hell and frightfully mismanaged'. After the first days of the Suvla relief operation he concluded, 'we've played all our cards on this new landing and failed'. His final evaluation of the entire exercise would have found an echo right around the 10th and 29th divisions, in whose ranks hundreds of Irish soldiers, regulars and new volunteers had died needlessly. 'I am sure everybody's opinion out here is live and let live and Turkey for the Turks!'

Not very long after Corporal Edward Thomas from Tipperary fired the first shot of the Great War, the conflict degenerated into a static grinding war of attrition. From Flanders and Picardy (the French-Belgian border region) to Germany, trench warfare replaced any semblance of mobility. The so-called 'sausage machine' began to pulp the flesh and bones of millions of young European men. In certain areas German and British or French lines were within easy grenade-tossing range of each other.

The Dublin-born writer Monk Gibbon, who was with the Army Service Corps, describes lines near Sailly which were only a few yards apart in his book *Inglorious Soldier*. Along other parts of the front the opposing forces might be facing each other across half a mile or more of no man's land. It also did not pay to be unusually tall in these trenches. Sergeant de Margry, who served with the 2nd Battalion, Royal Irish Regiment, 'couldn't help remembering the many dire warnings I had been given about my height [six feet] being a great handicap in trench warfare as the parapets were sized for men of average height, so that I'd be one of the first the Germans, and especially their snipers, would spot as a likely target!'

The regime was one of seemingly interminable boredom, interspersed with periods of back-breaking work and moments of sheer terror. The former nationalist MP and poet, Tom Kettle, who was a lieutenant in the 16th (Irish) Division, sums it up well:

> In the trenches it is the day-to-dayness that tells and tries. It is always the same tone of duty: certain days in billets, certain days in reserve, certain days in the front line. . . . A few casualties every turn, another grating of the saw teeth of death and disease, and before very long a strong unit is weak. . . . Everybody going up to the trenches from the CO down to the last arrival in the last draft knows it to be a moral certainty that there are two or three that will not march back. Everybody knows that it may be anybody. In the

trenches death is random, illogical, devoid of principle. One is shot not on sight, but on blindness, out of sight.

The prospect of sudden arbitrary death from a snap German raid, a stray mortar, a grenade or random shelling was ever present. Something in the make-up of the soldier, even the raw recruit, helped him rationalise and accept the possibility of death while undertaking one of the many raids on enemy lines upon which British army units would habitually embark. But random death, of the kind described by Wilfred Owen in his poem 'The Sentry' ('There we herded from the blast/Of whizz bangs, but one found our door at last'), was harder to come to terms with. As Charles Miller, an officer with the 2nd Inniskillings, put it: 'All that kind of thing was exciting. It is less exciting to be torn to pieces by a screaming piece of metal fired from several miles away.'

At different points along the front policies varied when it came to 'counting coup' on the enemy. In some sectors it was relatively peaceful. In others, where a more 'live and let die' spirit prevailed, raids and patrols, mainly under cover of darkness, were more frequent across no man's land. The object was often to return with prisoners for interrogation by command intelligence. Tommy Ervine of the 8th Royal Irish Rifles was bayonet man on a permanent patrol. On one typical raid he was accompanied by, among others, an ex-boxer named Jack McVicar and a man called Skates. Skates tossed a hand grenade into a group of unsuspecting Germans.

> We came around and found them – aw, it was a pitiful sight to look at them! Then there was a dugout with sixty or seventy steps down into it. Someone threw a couple of mills bombs [grenades] down before they could get out and they were cut to pieces down there. Well, three or four were alive and could walk and we got them to bring back. We didn't like to shoot them. We couldn't just go and murder a man. But we had to get away quick because the noise of Sammy's bombs alerted them. They sent up flares after us but we got back.

Survival in the trenches was a lottery. A soldier could follow all the rules, take all reasonable precautions and still become the victim of whatever random force dictated that he, and not the man beside him, was to die. You were lucky or you were a casualty! Incidents like the one recorded by de Margry of the Royal Irish Regiment were typical. He was nabbed for fatigue duty after he had settled into a dugout hoping to sleep off the exhaustion of a tiring day. Reluctantly he left the relative comfort of the dugout for a few more hours of digging and shovelling. 'Some few seconds later there was a blinding flash and a terrific explosion and as we automatically turned round to see what had happened we were horrified to find that some heavy shell had completely obliterated the dugout I'd only just left, and that all that could be seen of it was a huge crater about which some of the smoke and dust from the explosion could still be seen; but of the poor chaps I'd left sleeping there, no sign of them could be seen anywhere.' De Margry's previously hostile attitude towards the NCO who had disturbed his rest underwent an instant transformation!

Adding to the natural discomfort of the trenches was the hard physical work the ordinary soldier was expected to perform – officers had a more comfortable time of it. Most of this was done at night because it was safer and did not attract the attention of the enemy, which meant you could not expect much sleep during your stint in the forward trenches. Even in reserve, however, the work regime was constant. Anthony Brennan from Kilkenny spent three weeks working eight hours a day on a tunnel underneath the German lines. Later he was responsible for building dugouts capable of accommodating up to thirty soldiers. Sandbags were constantly being added to the trench defences. Such physical labour was frequently rendered useless (or more onerous) by the weather. The winter of 1915 was appalling; conditions in the trenches became worse when the rains came. Brennan would watch as 'our beautiful brick-fashioned structure of sandbags, so nice to look upon during the dry summer days, collapsed ignominiously after a few days of heavy rain. All along the front traverses fell in, usually at about 2.00 am, and tired men just settling down to a couple of hours' sleep after a wearisome ration party, or a spell of sentry duty, were hauled out to dig a way clear from "fire-bay" to "fire-bay" until daylight made the task impossible.'

The ubiquitous rats compounded the misery. Brennan spent one of his first nights in France keeping them at bay with an entrenching tool. Jack Campbell, a Dubliner and a member of the original British Expeditionary Force, still remembered the rats at the age of ninety-six.

They brought death as well as discomfort: 'We were in an old loft, my company. It had been used for a long time by troops coming up for rest. There was a young lad alongside me and in the night-time he shouted, "Ow, I've been bit." Well, we got a bit of candle and right enough a rat had taken a bite out of his cheek. We put a first-aid dressing on and he saw the medical officer in the morning but apparently it was too late because two or three days later he died. His face and his neck were black and swollen from the poison of the rat.'

The only creatures Campbell remembers as being more inexhaustible in supply than rats were body lice. Jim Maultsaid was with the 14th Royal Irish Rifles in the 36th (Ulster) Division. A talented artist, he left behind an extraordinary war journal liberally peppered with drawings and cartoon-strip commentaries. One of his sketches, entitled 'Wiping out the Pests', describes a bizarre but functional game which soldiers used to play. 'For a bet of a franc or so we often sat around a candle . . . took off our shirts and commenced to hunt for little pests. A time limit of ten minutes was laid down and the winner was the man that caught the most. Not a nice or pleasant subject to talk about but true to life and often played by number 14 platoon with grim and determined earnestness.'

Cold, particularly in winter, and wet at any time of the year, the front-line soldier also had another more surprising enemy: hunger. Jack Campbell often went hungry as German and British artillery deliberately targeted each other's supply transport. 'Around 9.00 or 10.00 at night the word would be passed along: "Sorry lads, no rations tonight, the transport couldn't get through." I think it was by mutual agreement that that finished because the Germans couldn't get the rations up and we couldn't either, so what was going to happen to the men in the trenches?'

In April 1916, details of the Easter Rising took a while to filter through to the members of the largely nationalist 16th Division. The reaction of most to news of their erstwhile comrades in the Irish Volunteers (before the split brought the larger National Volunteers into existence) was one of indifference. There were none of the demonstrations or even desertions anticipated by Army Command. In some cases soldiers exhibited outright hostility to the Rising. Nationalist Party MP

Stephen Gwynn said of his unit: 'I shall never forget the men's indignation. They felt they had been stabbed in the back.' Anthony Brennan of the 2nd Battalion, Royal Irish Regiment, recalls the Munster men in his unit as being 'all mildly interested, nobody took the thing very seriously'. But Southern Irish battalions became suspect. 'The army authorities were of a different mind. Our sojourn in the country was prolonged for a few more weeks to guard against any possible sympathetic reactions to affairs in Dublin.'

The front-line soldiers, whether or not they had strong nationalist sympathies (and most in the 16th [Irish] Division had) were more concerned with their own survival; more Irishmen died on the Western Front that week in the Hulluch gas attack than in Dublin. But some may have had the prescience to realise that the leaders and participants in the 1916 Rising would become icons while they would become virtual outcasts. Tom Kettle certainly did. He was in Dublin on leave during the Easter 1916 period, but unlike other army officers was not called upon to suppress the Rising. He wrote shortly afterwards: 'These men will go down in history as heroes and martyrs; and I will go down – if I go down at all – as a bloody British officer.'

The Battle of the Somme

There was no especially sound reason for undertaking a massive offensive on the Somme, except that by the early summer of 1916 British generals needed to launch a massive offensive somewhere. The French army was being pummelled by the Germans at Verdun and was desperate to have the pressure relieved.

Like so many other essentially meaningless battles during the Great War, the Battle of the Somme was as mismanaged as it was futile. It cost 150,000 lives on both sides with 300,000 wounded. Twenty thousand British army troops died on the first day of the offensive. A high percentage of those were from the 36th (Ulster) Division. The date 1 July 1916 is almost as significant to unionist Ulster as is 12 July 1690. In fact, the first day of the Somme was actually the 226th anniversary of the Battle of the Boyne. (This was due to the change to the Gregorian calendar in 1752.) Few of the Ulstermen, however, were aware of the significance or the symbolism of the date.

The 36th Division was recruited on similar lines to those of the North of England service units, the so-called 'Pals Brigades'. The idea seemed sound enough. The inhabitants of urban streets and rural towns and villages would fight more vigorously if they were placed alongside their friends and peers. So, the men of East Belfast became the 8th Battalion, Royal Irish Rifles. The Tyrone Volunteers formed the 9th Battalion of the Inniskilling Fusiliers and so on. The division was overwhelmingly unionist, Carson's Ulster Volunteer Force transplanted to the mud of Picardy. 'They were a covenanting army', writes Phillp Orr in *The Road to the Somme*, 'oath-bound and committed as much to the collective survival of Protestant Ulster as to the survival of the Britain they fought for and were part of.' But when they died, in their thousands, as they did on 1 July 1916, entire urban streets and rural towns and villages would lose their sons in frightening numbers.

The 36th was in the line near the village of Thiepval, close to the Ancre River, a tributary of the Somme. Stretching across no man's land was the formidable Schwaben Redoubt, a system of well-established German defences which included concrete fortifications and strategically positioned machine-gun emplacements. The 36th's objective, on the first day of the battle, was to overrun three German trench lines across a sunken road, the first of which was about 500 yards away. Beyond the third German line were two further entrenched defences, the second of which lay just over a mile from the 36th's own front line. On the face of it the goal seemed modest enough. An entire division, squeezed into an area measuring less than two miles across, was being asked to advance one mile in a day. But battles are not fought across maps. Some of the Ulstermen had a clear presentiment of what was to happen to them. One soldier, a former teacher, wrote to the secretary of his local Orange lodge: 'There is no doubt that when you receive this note I shall be dead. There are all the signs that something bigger than has ever taken place before in this war is about to be launched. The more I brood on what may happen the surer I am I shall not survive it. All of us say, "It'll be the other fellow who'll be killed." I feel that I am one of those other fellows.'

For five days prior to the 'off' the British bombardment of the German lines was merciless. It intensified on the morning of 1 July. The object of the bombardment was to keep the Germans in their deep, well-protected dugouts while at the same time ripping apart the barbed wire which guarded their front lines. Unfortunately, however, the bombardment had to be lifted to permit the 36th Division to advance on the German trenches. This allowed the German machine-gunners the vital seconds they needed to get back up to their positions. It was a story which was to be repeated right along the entire battle front.

In an order which aroused much controversy (and which was, in two instances, ignored), battalion commanders and their immediate subordinates were instructed not to go 'over the top' with their men. The attrition rate among officers was already too high. Colonel Ambrose Ricardo, commanding officer of the 9th Inniskillings, obeyed the order and watched as his men ventured into no man's land. 'They got going without delay – no fuss, no shouting, no running; everything orderly, solid and thorough, just like the men themselves. Here and there a boy would wave his hand to me as I shouted good luck to them through my megaphone, and all had a happy face.' The division, almost uniquely, would manage to achieve most of its objectives that day, but at a Pyrrhic cost.

Once 'over the top', Tommy Ervine, of the Royal Irish Rifles, did not get far before being hit. He spotted the German soldier responsible. He was picking off quite a few of Tommy's East Belfast comrades. They were ploughing through a waterlogged shell hole and 'as they were coming through that water the German had his sights trained on them and he was shooting them all. And he spotted me and he fired at me and that's when he hit me. Well, then I fired back at him later on and I hit him in the face.'

Lieutenant Henry Gallaugher, a Donegal man and a member of the Manorcunningham UVF, serving with the Inniskilling Fusiliers, shot more than twenty Germans on 1 July and took many more prisoner. Along with Major Gaffikin (9th Royal Irish Rifles) and Major Peacocke (11th Inniskilling Rifles) he attempted to consolidate the early morning gains which the 36th had managed to make against the odds. They clung desperately to their positions in the third German trench line of the Schwaben Redoubt. Because neither division on either side had been able to advance (the 29th – back from the horrors of Gallipoli – and the 32nd), the Germans had been able to outflank the bubble-like Ulster salient which pushed out from the British lines. The Inniskillings and Rifles were simply not going to be able to hold their ground.

The fates of those three men form an interesting microcosm of the tragic side of Irish participation in the First World War. Gaffikin, hit by grenade shrapnel, died that day while he was being evacuated. Gallaugher was killed the following year in the battle of Messines Ridge when the 36th (Ulster) Division and the 16th (Irish) Division, fought side by side. Peacocke survived the war only to be murdered by the IRA at his home near Cork in 1921.

Most of the Ulster casualties on 1 July were inflicted by the German machine-gunners. The 36th had attacked uphill towards a well-defended and fortified position. Its losses were horrendous, its achievements unrivalled. Jim Maultsaid's account of the carnage and confusion is both graphic and poetic:

> The slopes of Thiepval run red with the blood of Ulstermen, dead in heaps, dying in hundreds. God above us, this is glorious war! Huddled together, surrounded, the end is near. Rifle flashes stab the half darkness. Friend and foe are now almost unrecognisable. All is utter confusion, every man for himself. We are fighting back to back, a last hope. Bullets nip and zip around us. The gunflashes of the Germans are not thirty yards away. We yield ground as little parties are simply wiped away, clean away. Survivors crawl back, turn around, fight, then retreat again, but still facing their front, dying in their tracks.

Maultsaid himself was hit and subsequently rescued from no man's land by two unknown riflemen.

The failure (due to unsustainable losses of their own) of the 29th and 32nd divisions, flanking the 36th, to advance meant that the sacrifice of the Ulstermen was useless. Most of their gains were negated by German counter-attacks against the bulge in the line created by their own courageous advance. Casualties were of nightmarish proportions. By the time they were pulled out of the Somme offensive on 11 July, the 36th had suffered 5,000 casualties, most on that first day. William Montgomery of the 9th Royal Irish Rifles, drawn from West Belfast, wrote about the aftermath of 1 July to his father: 'Mother would have cried and quite possibly you also when I called the remnant of my company to attention. . . . Not a few of the men cried and I cried. A hell of an hysterical exhibition it was. It is a very small company now. I took 115 other ranks and four officers (incl. myself) into action. I am the only officer and only thirty-four other ranks are with me now out of the 115.'

Because of the composition of the battalions, organised in 'Pals' companies, whole streets and neighbourhoods in Ulster lost dozens or hundreds of their young men. Mourning would begin with the arrival of a small buff-coloured envelope. It took a couple of days for the sheer enormity of the loss to sink in. Instead of the customary Orange parades on 12 July that year, a five-minute silence was observed all across the province. The people of Ulster, according to playwright Frank McGuiness, author of *Observe the Sons of Ulster Marching Towards the Somme*, could have reacted in either of two ways to their tragedy. 'They could either turn in hatred against the forces who had led these young men to the slaughter or they could, if you like, celebrate the men's lives and the bravery of their deaths and their courage. And they took the second course, not surprisingly, I think, because that possibly made the scale of the tragedy endurable.'

Contrary to popular myth, the men of the 36th were not the only Irishmen to waste their lives that day. The 1st Battalion of the Royal Dublin Fusiliers, very different in composition from the unit which had been decimated at 'V' beach, was detailed to take the village of Beaumont Hamel on 1 July. They were, however, cut to ribbons by mortar and long-range machine-gun fire before they could even get to their forward trenches. Beaumont Hamel was not taken until the last day of the Somme offensive in November. Ironically, it was to fall to the 10th Dublin Fusiliers.

On the other side of the Ulstermen was the 32nd Division, which included the 2nd Inniskillings. Its target was the village of Thiepval. Charles Miller was one of the more fortunate officers on that day. He was attached to Brigade HQ and was not required to go over the top. His job was to establish contact with his battalion after the attack had begun and to keep track of their progress.

> It might have been a pretty hazardous job but actually it was a complete sinecure. There was no need to tell the brigade where the 2nd Inniskilling Fusiliers were that day. Three companies of them were lying like swathes of corn within twenty yards of our line.

Mortal man cannot get through a sort of tier of machine-gun bullets knee high, breast high, and head high so they could only go as far as possible and then die because the Higher Command had underestimated the skill of the Germans in building concealed concrete machine-gun emplacements. The Brigadier stopped the fourth company from attacking, and was very nearly Stellenbosched for so doing by the Divisional General.

Anthony Brennan, whose 2nd Royal Irish Regiment was in reserve on 1 July, became aware of the scale of the casualties when his unit relieved the Gordon Highlanders. 'The Gordons began collecting their dead comrades. I remember walking along a line of corpses, most of them, alas, in their early twenties.' In the German trenches he passed and repassed a German soldier, seriously wounded, who kept calling out for water. 'Few of us would refuse such a request if left to our own initiative. We had strict orders not to fall out, even for one of our own comrades. In the course of the night I had occasion to pass him several times and finally on the return journey, when we found that the poor fellow had died.'

The 1st Battalion, Royal Irish Rifles, was with the 8th Division, attacking the Ovillers Spur. Lieutenant W. Lake gives a graphic and typical account of the first moments of the assault. He watched as another company went over the top and was mown down. 'The men simply got up and fell back into the trench, either killed outright or badly wounded. Those who did get further were never seen or heard of again, as far as I know.' Understandably, witnesses and victims of such a calamity cracked. Lake saw his company commander 'crawling along the trench quite oblivious of the groaning bodies that were under him. There was a glazed look on his face which was streaming with blood and in his mouth was a cigarette that would never light because of the blood on it.' Lake never saw the captain again. A few moments later he had to deal with another victim of 'shell shock'. He became conscious of 'a man who was making horrid noises like a trapped animal and with his mouth wide open'. Lake instructed a beefy sergeant to punch the man to avoid panic spreading. It was a vicious blow but it had no apparent effect, 'so stepping over to the man, I pointed down the trench and shouted in his face: "Go". He turned and fled and we never saw him again. He was paralysed by fright. The instinct of self-preservation said "run" and his military training said "stand fast". It was a clear case of conflict between desire and duty and I was to come across it again.'

The onset of war had drawn a response from the nationalist as well as the unionist community. Political leaders such as John Redmond promoted enlistment. In a speech at Woodenbridge, County Wicklow, which was ultimately to spell disaster for his party, he urged Irish nationalists to go 'wherever the firing line extends, in defence of right, of freedom and of religion in this war'. Redmond's call to arms encompassed an idealistic plea on behalf of German-invaded Belgium, a nation which was small, independent and Catholic. But the message was also clearly conveyed that on this occasion, although nominally part of a British force, Irish soldiers would be fighting as representatives of a newly independent nation state. Home rule was now officially on the statute books, its operation suspended for the duration of the war. The notion was, of course, anathema to the unionists of the 36th (Ulster) Division but Redmond actually harboured a rather fanciful hope that should 'Irishmen come together in the trenches and spill their blood together . . . there is no power on earth, when they come home, can induce them to turn as enemies one upon the other.'

Just as the 36th (Ulster) Division was based largely on the UVF, so the 16th (Irish) Division was mainly composed of members of their Southern equivalent, the National Volunteers. The difference was that while the UVF was assimilated almost directly, unit by unit, into Kitchener's New Army and its members were allowed to choose their own officers, the National Volunteers were not trusted to the same degree. They were recruited in a ham-fisted manner and frequently had outside officers imposed upon them. In fairness, however, many of the Volunteers' officers had insufficient training or experience for the management of military units.

Reinforcing Redmond's message, several nationalist party MPs joined up. Stephen Gwynn and Willie Redmond, John Redmond's brother, were the two outstanding examples. Both were far too old to fight and, had they been English, could not have been conscripted for that reason. But it was important to both not to ask others to do what they were not prepared to do themselves. Both were given commissions in the 16th (Irish) Division. Gwynn survived the war but Redmond died at the battle of Messines Ridge in 1917. His body was carried across no man's land by men of the 36th (Ulster) Division. General Gough, commander of 1 Corps to which the 16th was attached, was an Irish unionist, but he commented on Gwynn and Redmond in the following terms: 'Among many whom I knew there were Captains Willie Redmond and Stephen Gwynn. Brought up, as I had been, in an atmosphere of hostility to home rule and all who supported it, I found in these two – and in many other Irishmen in this division, home rulers though they may have been – a loyalty, a devoted sense of duty, and a gallant spirit, which won my esteem and affection.'

The Great War is notable for the poetry which emanated from its trenches and charnel houses. Men like Rupert Brook, Wilfred Owen and Siegfried Sassoon are the most celebrated internationally but two Irish poets encapsulated much of the pathos and ambiguity of the personal struggle of many Irish nationalists. Thomas Kettle was a former nationalist MP while Francis Ledwidge was both a trade unionist and an enthusiastic Gaelic revivalist.

Emmet Dalton, subsequently an IRA leader in the War of Independence, served with Tom Kettle in the 9th Dublin Fusiliers. Dalton remembers him as 'a very charming and delightful man and I spent a little time with him, such little time as was available because within two days we were in the forefront and within three days he was dead.' Kettle read Dalton a poem which he had just written to his daughter. A poignant and evocative sonnet, it compares favourably with the best work to emerge from the war. Kettle titled it 'To My Daughter Betty, the Gift of God':

> In wiser days, my darlin' rosebud, blown
> To beauty proud as was your mother's prime,
> In that desired, delayed, incredible time,
> You'll ask why I abandoned you, my own,
> And the dear heart that was your baby throne,
> To dice with death. And, oh! they'll give you rhyme
> And reason; some will call the thing sublime,
> And some decry it in a knowing tone.
> So here, while the mad guns curse overhead,

And tired men sigh, with mud for couch and floor,
Know that we fools, now with the foolish dead,
Died not for flag, nor King, nor emperor,
But for a dream, born in a herdsman's shed,
And for the secret Scripture of the poor.

Kettle's disenchantment and fatalism are palpable. He had seen the 1916 Rising put down viciously and must have spent much of the next five months contrasting the more meaningful sacrifice of those members of the Irish Volunteers with the meaningless slaughter of his own men. Yet he felt it his duty to return to his battalion and to his death. 'I suppose he felt sad', Dalton commented, 'to think that he was fighting on the Somme when his own fellow countrymen, the men he loved, were suffering persecution, as it was, in his homeland.'

Ledwidge, a Meathman who spent his life near the banks of the River Boyne, was a mass of contradictions. He opposed Redmond on the issue of enlistment and spoke against it in any available forum. He was accused of being pro-German yet he joined up, in October 1914, severely embarrassing those who had questioned his sympathies. He saw action at Gallipoli and was killed when a shell, quite literally, blew him to bits at the Battle of Ypres in 1917. The announcement of his death in the local *Drogheda Independent* was almost curt. 'The poet Francis Ledwidge was killed in Flanders on 31 July, aged twenty-six.' His moving tribute to the executed poet and 1916 Rising leader Thomas McDonagh is yet another graphic example of the ambiguity of many Irish nationalists towards their part in the war, post 1916.

He shall not hear the bittern cry
In the wild sky where he is lain,
Nor voices of the sweeter birds
Above the wailing of the rain.

Nor shall he know when loud March blows
Thro' slanting snows her fanfare shrill,
Blowing to flame the golden cup
Of many an upset daffodil.

But when the Dark Cow leaves the moor
And pastures poor with greedy weeds,

Perhaps he'll hear her low at morn
Lifting her horn in pleasant meads.

He may have suspected, when he wrote those verses, that he could well have been writing an appropriate epitaph for himself.

Another associate of Emmet Dalton's on the Western Front was Jack Hunt. He outranked Dalton in France but the roles were later to be reversed. Hunt, from a poor Catholic family, had been a career army man. He had left the forces and earned a paltry income drilling students at St Andrew's College in Dublin. When war was declared in 1914 he re-enlisted. He went into action with Dalton and Tom Kettle at Ginchy in September 1916. Hunt received a Distinguished Service Order, Dalton a Military Cross. In 1922 Hunt, under instructions from Dalton, founded the training school for the new Free State Army. An important thread does, therefore, exist linking the Irish army through the Dublin Fusiliers to the trenches of the Western Front.

Guillemont and Ginchy

What the first days of the Somme assaults were to the 36th (Ulster) Division, the small towns of Guillemont and Ginchy, targetted midway through that campaign, were to the 16th (Irish). Both objectives had proven to be impregnable and by September 1916 the floundering Somme offensive had already lasted for ten weeks. The 6th Connaught Rangers was one of the units of the 47th Brigade, 16th Division, ordered to attack the village of Guillemont on 3 September. By then, such had been the ferocity of previous attacks none of the village was left standing; however, the Germans were holding onto a series of underground tunnels, galleries and dugouts.

Lieutenant J. F. B. O'Sullivan described the overture to the attack as his battalion approached their jump off positions. 'The stench from bloated carcases overwhelmed one to the point of vomiting. . . . We waded slowly through the cold sludge, tripping and tangling in the wire, and stumbled over a dead man lying on his back with arms and legs stretched out like an X. He was actually half afloat in the mud and nodded his head solemnly as each of us sloshed by.' The 47th took Guillemont with a charge which was described in a newspaper account as 'one of the most astonishing feats of the war – almost too fast in its impetuosity.' Casualties were enormous; almost half of the 2,400 soldiers in the 47th Brigade were either killed or wounded.

One of the Connaughts, Private Thomas Hughes from Coravoo near Castleblaney, County Monaghan, won a Victoria Cross. He was wounded early in the attack but, according to his citation, 'he returned at once to the firing line after having his wound dressed. Later, seeing a hostile machine-gun, he dashed out in front of his company, shot the gunner and single-handedly captured the gun. Though again wounded, he brought back three or four prisoners.' He received his VC, still on crutches, from the King of England. He lived with the pain of his wounds for the rest of his life and, like a significant number of VCs, died an alcoholic.

On 9 September the 16th Division was sent into action at the village of Ginchy. The night before the battle, Tom Kettle wrote to his brother:

> We are moving up tonight into the battle of the Somme. The bombardment, destruction and bloodshed are beyond all imagination, nor did I ever think the valour of simple men could be quite as beautiful as that of my Dublin Fusiliers. I have had two chances of leaving them – one on sick leave and one to take a staff job. I have chosen to stay with my comrades. I am calm and happy but desperately anxious to live. . . . The big guns are coughing and smacking their shells . . . the men are grubbing and an odd one is hitting home. Somewhere the Choosers of the Slain are touching, as in our Norse story . . . with invisible wands those who are to die.'

They had already touched Kettle. He died leading his men into the assault on Ginchy the following day.

The 2nd Battalion of the Royal Irish Regiment was not part of the 16th Divison but was involved in the Ginchy attack. Private Anthony Brennan fell in for roll call and then had one of the luckiest breaks in his brief career as a soldier. He was told to fall out and instead of having to face possible death was sent on a Lewis gun course. One of Sergeant de Margry's friends in 2 RIR turned to him before roll call and calmly remarked, 'I'll say goodbye to you now, as I know I shan't come out of this alive.' De Margry saw his company CO, Captain O'Reilly (holder of

a DSO and an MC), hit. He offered to help but was told to press
forward. A close inspection of the captain's injuries revealed that he had
been shot through the chest from side to side. He did not even make it
back to the field dressing station. The sergeant, having dealt with a
German machine-gun emplacement, was subsequently concussed by an
exploding shell. He became separated from his unit and got caught,
along with a nineteen-year-old Lewis gunner, in a German 'creeping'
barrage. As dusk began to fall another shell exploded beside both men,
burying them. He was rescued after eight hours but by then his
companion had suffocated to death.

Casualties, once again, were excessive. Nearly 11,000 men of the
16th Division had taken part in the attack (435 officers and 10,410
other ranks). The division suffered 4,500 casualties. Over 1,000 men
were killed, but for what? Another few square miles of Picardy? The
strategic advantage gained was slight, the losses numbing. By the
middle of September 1916 many of those who had originally joined up,
at Redmond's behest, in the defence of home rule were dead. The 16th,
from now on, would regularly be reinforced with drafts of non-Irish
soldiers. Redmond's volunteer force was broken, while back in Ireland
the philosophy which underpinned its existence was being overtaken by
events.

As Terence Denman points out in his excellent history of the 16th
Division *Ireland's Unknown Soldiers*, there are few Irish names to be
found in the visitor's books of the cemeteries around Guillemont and
Ginchy, where hundreds of Irish soldiers are buried. Perhaps
symbolically interred there was the spirit of old-style Redmondite
constitutional nationalism. As Denman points out, 'The year 1916
conjures up for most of the Catholic Irish the fighting on the streets of
Dublin, not the shell holes of the Somme battlefield.'

The entry of the USA into the conflict in 1917 brought more Irishmen
to France, mostly by way of New York City. The 165th Infantry
Regiment was overwhelmingly Irish-American with a fair sprinkling of
Irish-born emigrants. The designation 165th was, however, not very
popular with the members of the regiment. They still thought of
themselves as the 69th New York State Militia Regiment, the so-called
'Fighting 69th' of Civil War fame. Such feelings were shared by the

celebrated American poet Joyce Kilmer ('I think that I shall never see a poem as lovely as a tree') who remained in the 69th as a sergeant although offered a place in Officer Candidate School. He was still serving with the 69th when he was killed by a sniper's bullet in 1918.

Despite misgivings among the Irish-American community about sending troops to fight alongside the British army, American patriotism, stirred up by President Wilson, encouraged enlistment among Irish societies and Catholic parish athletic clubs. One of the most dynamic officers in the unit was Major (later Lieutenant Colonel) William 'Wild Bill' Donovan. He began the war in command of the 1st Battalion. Donovan won the Croix de Guerre and the Congressional Medal of Honor. In the Second World War he commanded the OSS, the predecessor of the CIA.

There is one revealing footnote to the 69th's service in France. The regiment was stationed in Longeau, in the Vosges Mountains. It had reached its base after enduring an uncomfortable three-day march through snow. The uniforms brought from the US were not standing up to the rigours of the war, and suggestions were made to replace them with the only available alternative, British army khaki. Regimental chaplain Father Francis P. Duffy's diary entry for 25 January 1918 focuses on his efforts to mediate in the blazing row which erupted. One Irish-born member of the regiment complained: 'What the blazes do they mane by insultin' min fighting for thim like this? I'd stand hangin' rather than put wan of thim rags on me back.' The 69th almost mutinied, refusing to 'wear the rags of the oppressors of Ireland'. Many of the uniforms which were issued were simply slashed to ribbons. Father Duffy pointed out to the regimental CO, Colonel Barker, 'there are soldiers with us who left Ireland to avoid service in the British army. But as soon as we got into the war, these men, though not yet citizens, volunteered to fight under the Stars and Stripes.' The idea was dropped.

Nevertheless, there was probably another sort of politics at play here: politics of the military variety. A proposal existed to 'brigade' American troops in British and French divisions rather than in formations of their own. General Pershing, commander of the American Expeditionary Force, was strongly opposed to the idea. It is possible that the offending uniforms were issued to the regiment most likely to rebel against them in order to use this display of hostility as an example of the futility of any such plan. The 69th was probably 'set up'.

One of the features of the Great War which has, happily, been seldom repeated since was the extensive use of gas. It was the one thing which troops on both sides seemed to fear most, to an almost pathological extent. Irish units did not manage to escape this barbaric instrument of death. On the day the 1st Dublin Fusiliers were being butchered at 'V' beach, the 2nd Battalion was being virtually wiped out at Ypres by a German chemical weapons attack. Two hundred and fifty men were gassed to death. Every single officer from lieutenant colonel down to second lieutenant was either killed or wounded by the gas or the subsequent assault. Nonetheless, the 2nd Dublins held their position.

The second major gas attack came the following month, May 1915, in the Ypres battle. Once again hundreds perished, but two particularly poignant stories concern the youngest and one of the oldest troops to die that day. Private John Condon from Waterford, serving with the Royal Irish Regiment, could not even legitimately be described as a man. He was a boy of fourteen. His family was aware that he had enlisted but did not know that he was in France. His body lies beside that of Thomas Carthy from Clonmel. Carthy was forty-seven-years old, one of thirteen children from a Church of Ireland family.

The very week of the Easter Rising the 16th Division lost 700 men near Hulluch in the space of a few minutes after a chlorine gas attack. Clouds of the gas, released from 3,800 cylinders, drifted towards the Irish-held trenches. The 'sack' gas helmets, still worn in 1916 (later replaced by the full gas mask) were inadequate. The subsequent German attack, however, was repulsed. Later, Lieutenant Lyon of the 7th Leinsters had the unenviable task of burying the dead. 'They were in all sorts of tragic attitudes, some of them holding hands like children in the dark.'

A similar attack two days later illustrates why gas was not used even more extensively. On this occasion 3,600 cylinders were used by the Germans, the gas hovering over the 16th's trenches and causing the deaths of one hundred men of the 48th Brigade and a further 180 casualties. However, the wind changed and the gas was blown back across no man's land; as a result the Germans suffered a total of 1,500 casualties. Many of those who survived gas attacks would have occasion to wish that they had succumbed along with their comrades. When interviewed, Jack Campbell, a survivor of a gas attack on the Somme in 1918, had suffered from its after-effects for seventy-two years.

At the time Campbell had been involved in a working party. His gas mask had been slung over his shoulder, stretching down by his side. A sudden barrage of shells knocked him over and he felt the impact of shrapnel on his hip. But there was no mark where he thought he had been hit. Later that evening, at about 8.00 pm, he was sent out with a stretcher party and was caught in another barrage, this time of gas shells. He immediately put on his gas mask. 'I hadn't it on two minutes when I began to feel groggy; I began to get sick into the gas mask. Well I had to pull it off or I would have suffocated, I couldn't breathe or anything. Anyway I staggered around for a while and I went down.' He was carried to safety but the gas had already done its damage. His mask had, in fact, been pierced by the shell fragment which should have hit him in the hip.

The 16th (Irish) Division and the 36th (Ulster) Division finally fought side by side at the Battle of Messines in June 1917. When the two units had trained in England, close to each other, there had been occasional incidents involving a 'clash of traditions'. But at Messines the bigotry of war replaced religious and political differences and all antagonism was focused across no man's land, although not many of the Irish troops actually felt much antagonism towards the men they were setting out to kill. The signal for the assault was to be the detonation of a huge 'mine' which had been placed in a tunnel underneath the German trenches. Aware of what was about to happen, members of the 2nd Battalion of the Dublin Fusiliers (now serving with the 16th Division) got down on their knees before 'zero hour' and said a decade of the rosary for the Germans who would die in the blast.

It was at Messines that Henry Gallaugher from Manorcunningham in Donegal, who had distinguished himself with the 36th on 1 July at the Somme, was killed. The most emotional loss for the 16th was that of Willie Redmond. His body was brought in by Dublin soldiers of the Ulster Division. Adding poignancy to his death was his own knowledge that the political philosophy for which he was avowedly fighting — constitutional home rule — had had its day. 'Don't imagine', he had told Stephen Gwynn, 'that what you and I have done will make us popular with our people. On the contrary, we will both be sent to the right about at the first general election.' Like his dead brother, John Redmond did not last to see the Sinn Fein landslide in the 1918 General Election. He died in March 1918, his policies moribund.

The 16th and 36th divisions were also side by side, but in less propitious circumstances, at the Third Battle of Ypres, usually known by the more evocative name of Passchendaele. The Third Battle of Ypres is justifiably viewed as one of the more obscene encounters of a virtueless war. Both Irish divisions had been part of the Second Army of General Plumer, one of the few outstanding British generals of the conflict. They had been transferred to the Fifth Army of the Irish-born General Gough, a far less capable soldier. The offensive in the Ypres salient was due to begin on 31 July, with the two Irish divisions in support. The objectives not seized on the first day of battle were to be captured the following day, but the rain began to fall and the operation was postponed. Rain then fell incessantly for a month, turning the battlefield into an ugly, lethal swamp.

During the first fortnight of this continuous downpour the 16th and 36th remained in their trenches waiting for orders to renew the offensive. Most of the Irish battalions remained in forward areas for that period, acting as reinforcements or working on fatigue duty. They endured unspeakable hardships from the weather and from two weeks of constant German bombardment. The 16th was responsible for the Frezenberg sector of the line where conditions underfoot were so awful that it was almost impossible to resupply the troops. When the battle was finally renewed on 16 August the Irish troops had been bombarded, starved, soaked mercilessly, gassed, machine-gunned and exposed to trench fever. Hundreds had been killed or wounded. Soldiers were then expected to throw themselves into a battle which would be fought over stamina-sapping terrain composed largely of mud and water-filled shell holes.

The Germans were as well entrenched as they had been at the Somme, their concrete pill boxes resisting almost any artillery the British could throw at them. Father Willie Doyle, the 16th's most famous chaplain who would die during the Passchendaele battle, commented: 'I have been through some hot stuff at Loos, and the Somme was warm enough for most of us, but neither of them could compare to the fierceness of the German fire here.' The Third Battle of Ypres was pressed forward until early November in unimaginable conditions by an uninspired and inhumane general staff which substituted doggedness and obstinacy for common sense, good organisation and basic humanity. That August, in just over two weeks of misery followed by two days of butchery, the 16th Division lost over 4,000 men (dead, wounded and missing) while the 36th lost more than 3,500. In his book *Orange, Green and Khaki* Tom Johnstone contrasts the approach of the English officer General Plumer to his Irish troops at Messines and that of Irishman Hubert Gough to the same two divisions at the Third Battle of Ypres. Gough, the man who precipitated the 1914 'Curragh Mutiny', 'ended the hope that between Orange and Green factions, the friendship and esteem engendered by successful collaboration in France would endure after the war. That, for Ireland, was the real tragedy of Third Ypres.'

The violent endgame for the 16th (Irish) Division came on 21 March 1918 during a massive German offensive. The growing political crisis in Ireland meant that forward Southern Irish units were not entirely trusted. The winter of 1917 and 1918 had been unusually harsh and manpower was so depleted that defences were overstretched. To deal with this problem the British had gone over to the German system of 'defence in depth', seen to good effect at the Third Battle of Ypres and based on the building of 'strong points' in the line where soldiers would base themselves during bombardments. The theory was excellent, but in practice the 'strong points' in the 16th's forward trenches were little more than glorified observation posts.

The German assault on 21 March followed a relentless five-hour bombardment. A thick fog shrouded no man's land and favoured the attackers. Visibility was down to ten yards in some places, making visual communication between observation posts impossible and increasing each unit's sense of isolation. The 16th Division cracked under the weight of the German attack and was criticised for retreating. The commander-in-chief, Field Marshal Haig, whose military genius was never equal to the task of avoiding unnecessary loss of life amongst his troops, watched his lines collapse before the German onslaught. Badly in need of someone else to blame, he fastened onto the 16th Division. 'Certain Irish units did very badly and gave way immediately the enemy showed', he commented. The Irish had cut and run, was the accusation. The Irish had also been in the front line, in some cases for up to two months, and only retreated (so they claimed) when other units withdrew and left them exposed. The fact that nearly 600 men were killed in action would suggest that, if they did 'run', they did not do so fast enough. The casualty figures reduced the 16th to a point where it was no longer, in effect, a division at all. Their numbers hovered around 5,000. The debacle of the Twenty-First March reinforced the patronising stereotype of the Irish soldier as being offensively aggressive but lacking the discipline for determined defence.

After the overwhelming rejection of British rule in 1918, to have been an Irishman from the twenty-six counties and to have fought in the Great War was to be part of a twilight world. Service with the British army between 1914 and 1918 was, more often than not, a fact one suppressed rather than boasted about. It was something the fictional sisters in Brian Friel's *Dancing at Lughnasa* never openly acknowledged about their brother, the cleric Father Jack. Their fellow countrymen, engrossed in the struggle for and the exercise of independence, grew dubious of Great War veterans. Just as the High Command of the British army had often doubted whether these Irishmen could be fully trusted, so did the 'new' Irish. This suspicion cost some 200 ex-servicemen their lives at the hands of the IRA during the highly charged War of Independence between 1919 and 1921. Some 'rehabilitated' themselves quickly and no stigma was attached to them. Emmet Dalton and Tom Barry became active in the IRA, putting their experiences on the Western Front and in the Middle East, respectively, to good use against the army which had trained them.

According to journalist and historian Kevin Myers, 'It just became convenient and preferable to consider that Irish nationalism could find only one expression and that was in the path taken by Pearse and the others who took over the GPO. It became exceedingly unfashionable to say, "Yes, you can be Irish and have served in the British army" and be not one whit less Irish because of that.' A mealy-mouthed approach to the veterans and the fallen of the Great War was reflected in the crumbling decay of the War Memorial Park designed by Lutyens in Islandbridge. First there was a row over its construction and then it was allowed to slowly disintegrate. It has only recently been restored to its original splendour by the efforts of the Office of Public Works. Just as petty was the refusal to allow the War Graves Commission to place headstones over the graves of those First World War soldiers who had died of their wounds while back in Dublin and who were buried in

Glasnevin cemetery. The commission was told that the headstones were 'too small'. To this day these graves remain completely unmarked.

Perhaps, in retrospect, the Great War can be seen as a defence of the British Empire and of British interests rather than of 'Little Catholic Belgium'. This may be the *ex post facto* perception or reality, but it was not the understanding of the Southern Irishmen who fought. They were asserting their Irishness by fighting along with other Irishmen in defence of a small, predominantly Catholic country. Many were also struggling to retain the gains made by their political leaders. This, of course, applied equally to the unionists. Tom Kettle's poem 'Cancel the Past' is almost an appeal to the republicanism unleashed by Easter 1916 to have some understanding for men who fought a similar fight but in a different manner. The poem concludes:

> Soldier with equal soldier must we sit,
> Closing a battle, not forgetting it.
> With not a name to hide,
> This mate and mother of valiant 'rebels' dead
> Must come with all her history on her head.
> We keep the past for pride;
> No deepest peace shall strike our poets dumb;
> No rawest squad of all Death's volunteers,
> No rudest men who died
> To tear your flag down in the bitter years,
> But shall have praise, and three times thrice again,
> When at the table men shall drink with men.

But exactly how many Irishmen did enlist? Was the contribution from Ireland lukewarm in comparison with that of England, Scotland and Wales? Did Ulster send a higher proportion of its young men to serve than the rest of the country? Professor Joseph Lee in his seminal *Ireland 1912–1985: Politics and Society* says 'it would seem that enthusiasm for the war was never as widespread in nationalist Ireland as the media, dominated by pro-war elements, suggested.' He bases this claim on recruitment figures which show that 26.9 per cent of all men of military age in Scotland joined up, as did 24.2 per cent in England and Wales, while only 10.7 per cent of the relevant figure in Ireland enlisted.

Whatever the level of enthusiasm among those nationalists who enlisted (and both the enthusiasm and political philosophy of troops is impossible to gauge), the figure of 10.7 per cent is not an accurate reflection of the numbers of Irishmen who fought in the Great War. Many of those men in the relevant age group (about 40,000 of them) were working in English factories, replacing those who had enlisted. As has already been pointed out, recruitment, largely on the basis of economic necessity, was very much an urban phenomenon. Such were the conditions in the working-class slums of Dublin – the main urban centre – that up to half of those who sought to enlist were rejected on medical grounds.

Furthermore, the British percentage would be artificially inflated due to the eventual introduction of compulsory military service. Many of those Scots, English and Welsh who fought did so because they had no choice. Conscription was never introduced in Ireland; all the Irish who enlisted (except some conscripted in Britain) were volunteers. Neither does the figure of 10.7 per cent take into account the number of Irishmen working in Britain who enlisted from there. Many became members of 'Irish' units based in Britain, like the 'Tyneside Irish' or the 'London Irish'. The fact that they enlisted in Britain means they do not figure in the Irish percentage and they further inflate (though only marginally) the British ones.

How many Irishmen fought? It is impossible to tell accurately because of the numbers who enlisted in Britain. However, we do know that 135,000 joined up between August 1914 and November 1918. In addition, we have a figure of 20,000 already serving with regular army units and 30,000 reservists who were immediately called up. That makes a total of 185,000. There is also a fairly reliable method of arriving at a reasonably accurate figure from studying the *Irish Memorial Records – 1914–1918* at the War Memorial in Islandbridge in Dublin. This is a series of books containing (sixteen to a page) the names of nearly 50,000 men who died with Irish regiments and the names of Irishmen who died fighting with British regiments. The important statistic to bear in mind is that 10 per cent of all who fought in the Great War died. Therefore, by extrapolating from the figure of 50,000 dead we come up with a total 'force' of 500,000. However, there is a snag. The *Memorial Records* contain the names of many men who are not Irish. These were English, Scottish and Welsh soldiers who had fought in Irish battalions. A random sample of a number of pages indicates that between 20 to 25 per cent of those named are non-Irish. If we assume the higher figure to be true, this would indicate that roughly 13,000 of those commemorated in the books are not, in fact, Irish born, leaving us with a figure of about 370,000 men. This may be a slight overestimation, however, as the statistics of the 16th Division would indicate a non-Irish death-rate figure of closer to 30 per cent, putting the total at around 350,000.

With a figure of up to 35,000 Irish dead, few Irish families could have remained untouched. The author himself had two grand-uncles (one maternal, one paternal) who died in the conflict. John Patrick O'Reilly was an eighteen-year-old bank official from Baileborough, County Cavan, who enlisted after hearing a Roman Catholic priest sermonising about 'little Catholic Belgium'. When his father discovered he had enlisted he attempted, unsuccessfully, to have him discharged. Attached to the 2nd Battalion of the Royal Irish Rifles, he died on the Somme on 29 September 1916. He was a machine-gunner and was killed by a stray shell during a lull in hostilities.

Thomas Coonan from Ogenolloe, Killaloe, County Clare, was twenty-three when he died. He was the son of William and Margaret Coonan. He, too, was a machine-gunner with the 4th Guards Machine-Gun Regiment (formerly the Grenadier Guards) and died on 7 May 1918, the holder of a Military Medal. The interval between the deaths of these two men was more than nineteen months. Yet they are buried barely ten kilometres apart on the Somme battlefield, testimony to the immobility and stasis of the Great War. Thomas Coonan and John Patrick O'Reilly, however, at least have relatives who remember them (in most cases without ever having known them). Families like the Stackpoles, friends of Kilkenny man Anthony Brennan, were wiped out by the war. Brennan, in his memoirs, writes about his friend Jimmy Stackpole who was killed at Passchendaele in 1917. His older brother Reggie had died in 1914 and their father, Sergeant Stackpole, followed them in 1918.

So why is this story omitted from most school history books in the Republic of Ireland? Why is it left almost entirely to Northern unionists to honour the dead of the Great War, and have members of that community blown to pieces by the IRA in Enniskillen when they attempt to do so? Professor R. F. 'Roy' Foster, in possibly the best one-volume survey of Irish history ever written – *Modern Ireland – 1600–1972* – characterises the neglect of this aspect of Irish history as independent Ireland's 'policy of intentional amnesia about the extent of Irish commitment to the war effort before 1916'. Terence Denman says:

> History is usually written by the winners, and Irish history is no exception. The fate of tens of thousands of patriotic Irishmen who, in response to the granting of home rule, chose to follow a different path to Irish nationhood by volunteering to serve with the British armed forces rarely attracts more than a passing reference, and that often pejorative. At best they are regarded as the misguided dupes of an ever 'perfidious Albion', at worst as lickspittles and traitors. Indifference, embarrassment or suspicion all too often confront those who show an interest in their story.

Frank McGuinness, a Donegal man, has tried to rectify this one-sided approach to Irish history in *Observe the Sons of Ulster*. He reflects the educational experience of tens of thousands of Irish people. 'We were simply not told about the First World War. I did not know so many Irish people had fought in the First World War. Their lives and their courage were written out of history. We were taught only that in 1916 there was a great battle which occurred at Easter and that this was the foundation of our country, the Free State. But we were simply not given information about another crucial day in our history which was 1 July 1916, at the battle of the Somme, where I think the destiny of the country was written as well.'

Kevin Myers agrees. 'There was the deliberate falsification of history which took place which suggests that only a few thousand traitors and renegades, people of no account, served in the British Army in the First World War, and that was said repeatedly. It belonged to a very primitive Christian Brother version of Irish History which actually describes two sorts of Irishman. There were "Men of Ireland", the sort who might join the British Army, and "Irishmen". And being an "Irishman" conferred a kind of moral superiority which meant it was impossible for you to have served in the British Army.'

It is unfair to second-guess the motives of those who fought in the Great War. Many did so for idealistic reasons; they did not take the 'shilling'. Those forced to take the 'shilling' to feed impoverished families deserve sympathy, not lofty Hibernian censure. These men had to fight to survive. It is a melancholy and ironic fact that many of them did not. Many of those who survived did so in name only. The story of Guy Nightingale has already been told. He saw the worst that man could do and succumbed to the experience of that savagery twenty years later, after a broken life. Ernest Hamilton had been a bright, highly promising medical student at Trinity College before he joined up. He survived Kiretch Tepe Sirt but was later court-martialled and 'dismissed in service' for persistent drunkenness. He never returned to his medical studies and spent the rest of a thoroughly miserable life as a chronic alcoholic. Not even the heroes were immune from the psychological consequences of their actions. A high percentage of the many Irish Victoria Cross winners went the way of Ernest Hamilton.

Three quarters of a century on the Great War still engendered bitterness in the heart of ninety-four-year-old Jack Campbell. His attitude towards Germans was understandably jaundiced by a lungful of chlorine gas. But his comments on his former enemies are well nigh unprintable. Like Guy Nightingale and Ernest Hamilton he had been unable to shake off the physical or psychological legacy of a wasteful conflict which scarred the lives of those who offered their service. 'I've gone through the pain and the misery and the hardship of that on down through the years and the longer I live the longer I'll suffer.' Aged ninety-six, he died in Leopardstown Park Hospital in Dublin on 18 November 1992, ironically, the morning on which this chapter was completed.

3

Ireland and the Second World War

The Political Background

While the rest of Europe was embroiled in the Second World War between 1939 and 1945, the Irish Free State remained steadfastly neutral. While Europe and the Far East were experiencing something approaching the apocalypse, Ireland was going through the Emergency. Such a designation could be seen as a typically euphemistic Irish response which underscored the country's cavalier attitude to a struggle between the forces of good and evil. This was, more or less, how Winston Churchill saw Eamon de Valera's policy of remaining aloof from the struggle against Nazism.

Ireland's neutrality, however, was both an expression of its sovereignty, a function of its government's republican background and a non-combative status which was of a very partial nature. An independent foreign policy was seen as a vital ingredient of Irish independence. The authorities were predisposed, therefore, towards non alignment. In addition, there was a tendency in government quarters, from de Valera downwards, not to distinguish between the imperialism of the First World War and the more idealistic nature of the 1939 to 1945 conflict. For those who wished to put such a construction on the Second World War, it was simply 'unfinished business', a carry over from the Great War.

And, of course, the Free State government had its own unresolved issue with Britain: the continuing 'Ulster Question'. The 1937 Constitution, drafted by de Valera, with Articles 2 and 3 laying claim to sovereignty over Northern Ireland, militated against any Free State involvement in an alliance with the keepers of the 'fourth Green field'. This, and a sound regard for self-preservation on the part of a nation remote from the conflict, kept the Irish out of hostilities. But Ireland operated a distinctly pro-Allied neutrality, particularly after the entry of the US into the war. When Allied air crews were downed in the Free State they were escorted to the border and handed back. German crews became 'guests of the nation'. Despite the 'microphone diplomacy' indulged in by de Valera and Churchill during the war, in which the British prime minister effectively accused the Irish leader of stabbing Britain in the back, citizens of the Irish Free State did make a significant contribution to the defeat of fascism in Europe. Although never officially encouraged to do so, thousands of 'Free Staters' travelled north to Belfast to join the British forces. Many deserted the Irish army to do so. The contribution of the people of Northern Ireland was, proportionately, far greater and easier to evaluate.

No definitive figures exist to indicate the numbers of Irishmen who served in the British Armed Forces in the Second World War. Hundreds, it must not be forgotten, fought with the US, Canadian and ANZAC forces. Lord Killanin, an Irish veteran, has made repeated unsuccessful attempts to get the British War Office to divulge such a figure. It may be, quite simply, that the information is not readily available. Free Staters had to travel to Belfast's Clifton Street or to Britain if they wished to join up. There they would simply merge with the Ulster or British recruits. John P. Duggan points out in his book on Irish neutrality that there were 165,000 Irish next-of-kin addresses on record in the British army. There is an assumption (and it is just that, a mere assumption) that half of the Irish who served in the Second World War were Southerners. Therefore, as many as 80,000 Free State soldiers could have fought in the British forces between 1939 and 1945. (Roy Foster puts the figure at about half this total.) This figure does not include the many Irish exiles living in Britain who would have enlisted or been called up.

Licking Hitler: The War in Africa and Europe

The overwhelming proportion of Irishmen involved in the Second World War served with the British army, and most would have enlisted in Belfast. Clifton Street was the home of the main recruiting centre. When William Shorten from Dundrum took the train from Dublin to Belfast he was far from unique. 'There were hundreds on the train from Dublin, both deserters [from the Irish army] and ordinary civilians joining up. They distributed you amongst the regiments . . . two of us went to the West Yorks. A mate of mine who went up to Belfast was sent to the South Staffords.' Paddy Devlin from Galway City was seventeen when he joined up. His father had fought in the Great War but his parents did not know that he and a friend of his, Jimmy Jordan, had gone to Belfast to enlist. Without his parents' written consent he was told he needed to be twenty-years old to join up, so he aged rapidly. He was offered a choice of units and opted for the Royal Sussex Regiment on the flimsy basis that he liked the county's cricket team. He ended up, however, in the Queen's Royal West Surrey Regiment, known simply as 'the Queens'.

For many of these raw recruits the first weeks and months of army life involved a heavy exposure to the joys of 'square bashing' and a rigorous physical fitness regime. Devlin, a handy footballer, found himself on the regimental soccer team, along with ex-Shamrock Rovers and Ireland player Tommy Brennan. Centre-half on the team was a figure familiar to most of the Gardai in Dublin: 'Aberdeen' Norman. He was the leader of the infamous 'Animal Gang'. 'They had fled Dublin after a fracas at Baldoyle Race Course where a member of a rival gang had been killed. The dispute was over who should supply the bookmakers with chalk and water for their blackboard, it was a racket the bookmakers had to pay to avoid trouble. This group had crossed the border and lost themselves in the British army to avoid the Irish police.' Later Devlin would transfer from the Queen's after volunteering for airborne duty with the Royal Ulster Rifles. The Animal Gang stayed put. Devlin, in his unpublished memoirs, assumes that they would have been sent to North Africa. They were. Another Dubliner, James Gannon, who fought with the Hampshire Regiment, saw a number of them beating a hasty retreat during a skirmish in the desert.

It was in North Africa that most Irish soldiers were 'blooded', but many had served with the Expeditionary Force which travelled to France shortly after Chamberlain was finally forced to accept that Herr Hitler's intentions were anything but honourable. Captain Andy Parsons from Athlone was a medical officer with the 13th Infantry Brigade who had joined up at the start of the war after a period in the Merchant Navy as a ship's doctor. He went to France with the British Expeditionary Force in 1940 and his first experiences of the British army were of headlong retreat as the Belgian army surrendered and the Germans made rapid progress towards northern France. Parsons kept a comprehensive and often gripping diary of his war experiences, which captures something of the confusion of the army as it abandoned all pretence at offering serious resistance and made for the dubious sanctuary of Dunkirk.

In the course of that retreat Parsons, more or less by default, became the medical officer (MO) of the 2nd Inniskilling Fusiliers. His first experience under fire, on 29 May 1940, was an unexpected and unnerving one. He had just set up a Regimental Aid Post in a Belgian farmhouse near Hoogestadt when it came under shell fire. Inside the house itself he came across 'two fusiliers too frightened to speak coherently. One had his foot half blown off, and there was an ever-increasing pool of scarlet blood spreading over the white tiled floor.' The courtyard outside had taken the worst of the blast. 'Seven or eight men were lying on the cobbles, one of them blown to pieces with his intestines hanging out on the ground, another with both legs blown off and a third with one leg amputated at the groin. I had a horrible impression of khaki and crimson against the grey background of the cobble stones, and all around were dead white faces and groans and helpless struggles. Over all was a foul stench of burned flesh and powder.' Parsons, who had a single bandage and a bottle of Dettol to deal with the crisis piled the wounded onto a truck and drove at sixty miles an hour, under a heavy bombardment, for Hoogestadt. Predictably, many of the wounded died on the way.

The Inniskillings reached Dunkirk on the night of 31 May. As he approached the beach in darkness, Parsons could hear shells screaming over their heads and landing on the shore. 'Every few minutes there was a roar as a low-flying aircraft tore along the beach and a shattering noise as it machine-gunned the troops, who they knew were crouching there.' Parsons's unit finally got as far as the mole (a sort of pier or causeway) on which soldiers were gathering for embarkation. It was about a mile long and was packed with troops. But there was no movement or any sign of the Royal Navy. 'My thoughts were far from cheerful. I thought that as soon as it got light a couple of fighters would just fly along the pier with their machine-guns blazing and would kill off most of the thousands of men who were on the mole and who had not a scrap of cover of any kind.'

As they waited small groups would find excuses to push their way to the front of the queue. Stretcher cases became uncommonly popular. 'At least six men would be carrying each stretcher and seven or eight more men with the wounded man's kit – two to each haversack and two more carrying his rifle between them.' In the course of a five-hour wait only two shells hit the mole. 'All we could do was to lie down on the concrete and listen to the bombs whistling down till they lit up the sky with a lurid red flash. After one of these bombings we saw the Methodist padré attached to the brigade being carried past on a stretcher. From the glimpse I got of his face as he passed I decided that he was dying, as afterwards I heard was the case.' Parsons was finally evacuated from Dunkirk on board a cross-channel steamer, *The Maid of Orleans*.

The Desert War

Many of the 200,000 British army evacuees from Dunkirk next saw action in North Africa. But for most of the men who would belong to the Eighth Army, the desert was their first experience of war. Just getting there could be as hazardous as anything they would encounter in actual desert fighting. Sapper Don Mooney of the Royal Engineers, fresh from Trinity College, was far more concerned about torpedoes than tanks until he arrived in Egypt. The convoy in which he sailed zigzagged right across the Atlantic to avoid well-known submarine waters; this meant that the journey to South Africa would take nine and a half weeks. Mooney's abiding memory of a short rest in Durban was of the 'White Lady'. 'She used to stand on the point docks in Durban as the troop ships came in and she'd sing us in. She was always dressed in white with a big white hat and a dirty great megaphone. She sang all sorts of songs, a sort of South African Vera Lynn, I think she was.'

The blazing sun was the next serious threat. Private William Shorten from Dundrum in Dublin had deserted the Irish army in April 1940, attracted not by the money (the wages were the same, two shillings a day) nor by the cause, but by a desire for adventure that was not about to be satisfied in the army of neutral Ireland. He enlisted in Belfast and served in the West Yorkshire Regiment. He learned his first lesson in desert warfare the hard way. 'A thing we were never to do was take off our shirts and it was something I did while we were digging air-raid shelters. I suffered something terrible. I got a complete sunburn; it wasn't stroke but I suffered for weeks with my back. And you couldn't report sick because it was a charge. You weren't supposed to take off your shirt.' His back bled for weeks whenever he had to wear a pack.

Had Shorten been in the right place he might have received a sympathetic hearing from a fellow Dubliner, Dr Niall Hogan of the Royal Army Medical Corps. Hogan had been working in a hospital in Blackpool and had joined up because he thought 'it would be fun'. Even today he retains a mocking and impious approach to the British army and to his own war service which would certainly have infuriated many of his stiff-spined superiors. His journey to North Africa was enlivened by the consumption of all the medicinal brandy on board an otherwise 'dry' ship, *The Viceroy of India*. His major contribution to the war in the desert, by his own account, came after landing in Algiers. Thousands of troops were coming ashore every day and many were billeted in tents in the Jardins d'Essay, an area about half the size of Phoenix Park. Here, an altogether unexpected aspect of warfare revealed itself to the future surgeon!

Within the space of a few days the area had become, quite literally in Hogan's own words, 'a shithouse'. The Dubliner, along with a dentist named Humpherson, was given the salubrious task of turning this execrable hell into a sanitary heaven. He devised a system of 'shallow-trench latrines'. 'Lines were policed by soldiers at each end, and shovels laid along, so that every time anybody crapped they had to cover it up . . . and we used to shift these once every twenty-four hours.' The assistant director of Medical Services for the area was so impressed with this innovative procedure for disposing of tons of human detritus that he sent a message to Hogan's CO suggesting that the Irish doctor be mentioned in despatches. The CO, who was not greatly enamoured of the irreverent Hogan (the feeling was mutual) decided against putting the necessary paperwork through. Such are the quirks and petty jealousies which can deny decent men the Victoria Cross!

Hogan's wicked sense of humour would have been tickled by the predicament of a fellow Dubliner, Private Desmond Fenning of the Royal Horse Artillery. His first stint in the desert was on the Suez Canal with a Glasgow ack-ack regiment. Their job was to protect their stretch of vital waterway from German or Italian aerial attack. The only problem was that they were an artillery regiment in name only. They had no artillery with which to stave off enemy planes for the first six months of their tour. That they managed to keep the Luftwaffe at bay was due to an imaginative ploy surpassing even that of Hogan's shallow-trench latrines. 'That end of the war was a bluff, sheer bluff. We set about making wooden guns which we put all down along the canal. Right enough it kept the Germans away, and the Italians.'

For many thousands of recruits and volunteers the Desert War was their first experience of action. Whole days of boredom and drudgery would be interrupted by hours or minutes of terror. Everyone's reaction to death, the possibility of their own or the fact of someone else's, was different. Brian Clarke, a career soldier, would reach the rank of colonel before his retirement to a home in Wicklow overshadowed by the Sugar Loaf Mountain. He was second-in-command of a rifle company in the Royal Irish Fusiliers. His response to his first critical situation was to get on with the job he had been ordered to do, despite an unnerving prologue. 'I was brought into contact with the realities of war when I saw a young captain lying dead; somebody had put a veil over his face and the flies were beginning to buzz round it. I continued on with my company and we went into action.' He came under fire almost immediately and had to assume command of over one hundred riflemen when his company commander, Frank Rothery, was killed.

Desmond Fenning soon discovered that war was not all about wooden guns and keeping the enemy guessing. 'I found the dead body of an Italian soldier, poor unfortunate, and he must have been there a long time because there were only his bones and uniform left. His hand, separated from the arm, was still clutching his rifle. I was ashamed afterwards because I had done nothing to bury him.' Captain Andy Parsons, the MO from Athlone, was serving with the 1 Buffs, attached to the Staffordshire Yeomanry Armoured Regimental Group, when the second battle of El Alamein began. He knew on 23 October 1942 that 'this was the day'. The Eighth Army aimed to push Rommel's vaunted Afrika Corps right across the North African desert. This veteran of the 1940 British Expeditionary Force reckoned that what the next twenty-four hours held for him would make Dunkirk 'appear as of no more significance than a nightmare of childhood'.

He had become inured to the horrors of war after months of tending to some of the worst wounds which the military hardware of the time was capable of inflicting. But some of the things he saw on the first day of Alamein were almost too much for him. His abiding memory is of hundreds of burned-out vehicles, tanks, jeeps and trucks of all types. 'The mass of burned-out vehicles at close quarters presented a disgusting mixture of sights and smells; twisted, blackened metal and burned bodies with their characteristic yellowish look lying in grotesque attitudes among the wreckage or on the grey sand. Everywhere was the smell of burning rubber and over-cooked flesh.' One of his self-imposed tasks was to search for identity discs among the dead, a job which physically sickened him at times because of the effects of fire on the human body. Another hazard commonly faced by medical officers, the booby-trapping of bodies, was exacerbated at Alamein as the Afrika Corps retreated. Parsons remembers that ten days into the battle they discovered 'a dead Highlander, cordoned off by the sappers with white tape to indicate that he was dangerous.' The Irish MO knew that Montgomery's Eighth Army was winning the battle when the Germans started to abandon their own dead on the battlefield. 'Unless the Germans have to leave in a hurry, they get their dead buried first and it was a cheering sight to see the grey-clothed bodies just lying there on the white sand.'

After ejecting the Germans from North Africa, the task of doing the same thing all over again in Italy fell to the Eighth and Fifth armies. Sicily was the stepping stone from North Africa but by September 1943 Montgomery was ready to send his troops across the Straits of Messina to land for the first time since the ignominy of Dunkirk on mainland Europe. The Italian dictator, Mussolini, had been deposed in July of that year and as the amphibious assault force was on its way to effect a landing on the beaches at Salerno in southern Italy the new Italian government surrendered. This probably did not help the subsequent assault on the town. The German Wehrmacht troops based in southern Italy, aware that an invasion force was coming, simply moved in and took over the Italian defences. The Fifth Army, whose members were told of the Italian surrender while in convoy to Salerno, did not expect much resistance.

William Gannon, a small, slight man from Dolphin's Barn in Dublin, by now an accomplished sniper, came ashore after the first wave. 'We were walking over bodies. There were more killed in that landing than they ever told you about. They didn't tell the truth.'

Gannon watched as three LCs in turn hit a sandbank and mistakenly discharge their troops. 'The ramp goes down and you run. But they were running into about ninety feet of water. They didn't know they were on a sandbank. That was it, they were all drowned.'

Desmond Fenning with the Royal Horse Artillery had a dry landing and was astonished to see hundreds of infantrymen sitting around under armed guard, for all the world like prisoners of war. They had mutinied! Fenning could not find it in his heart to blame them. These were men who had been through the Desert War. They had had enough. Even Montgomery, never greatly sympathetic towards human frailty, had acknowledged to Alanbrooke, Chief of the Imperial General Staff, that 'there is no doubt some of my chaps are getting tired. Continuous and hard fighting is a great strain.' Fenning could see that the Germans had 'knocked hell out of the first units that went in there. All the officers, I believe, were killed or wounded and had to be evacuated. Finally, the men themselves reckoned they couldn't take it any longer and they withdrew.'

Four short months after the Salerno landings came the assault at Anzio. This was a landing of 50,000 troops intended by General Alexander to speed up the capture of Rome. It was sixty miles behind the German front lines and only thirty-five miles from the capital. The landings were initially successful, but the Germans moved quickly enough to ensure that the Allies did not manage to break out towards Rome as they had hoped. Anzio was where Captain Alfred Denis – 'Andy' – Parsons had his interest in the Second World War ended by a German 105-millimetre shell which probably should have killed him. As a doctor, he was not spared the immediate knowledge of how serious his injuries were. 'My right thigh had been split open, it seemed, from end to end, and the hole in it was rapidly filling up with steaming, bubbling, scarlet blood.' Straightaway he knew that his sciatic nerve had been damaged.

As he lay in a field hospital awaiting evacuation, Parsons had plenty of time to do what many in his situation had done before and would continue to do, wonder whether it would have been better to have died. 'All the things that have made your life worth living are finished forever,' he confided to his diary, 'the only thing left for you is to drink yourself to death as quickly and quietly as possible, like many a better man before you.' But Andy Parsons did not drink himself to death. He was awarded the Military Cross for consistent gallantry during the desert and Italian campaigns, married Lizzie Dobbs, whose story appears elsewhere in this book, and settled in the South Pacific. His life ended in tragedy and mystery when he disappeared along with the rest of the passengers and crew aboard the *Joyita* in October 1955. Parsons was a doctor in Samoa and was travelling on a routine trip to the island of Tokelau. In an episode which bears a chilling resemblance to the story of the infamous *Marie Celeste*, the *Joyita* was later found abandoned.

Elsewhere in Italy another Irish doctor, Niall Hogan, was fighting a losing battle of his own against the invisible antagonist of all armies, sexually transmitted diseases. His problems were multiplied by the fact that he was based in Naples, long (but perhaps unfairly) celebrated as the birthplace of various venereal diseases. 'One of the things we used to give the troops was a little packet with ointment, condoms, which were issued free, and various instructions.' Racy little nostrums were devised to persuade soldiers to take precautions. 'They put up on some of the buildings, on the Opera House, for example, "If you get it she's got it, if she's got it you've had it." That was one sign.' The British forces also jealously (the appropriate phrase) guarded the virtue of their female members. There was a special sign to discourage fraternisation with Americans. '"Look before you jeep or you'll be Yanked into eternity" — that referred to going out with American soldiers in motor cars.'

The invasion of France in 1944 is dealt with elsewhere but one of the last major operations of the Second World War was the crossing of the Rhine towards the end of March 1945. For Paddy Devlin of 1 Battalion, Royal Ulster Rifles, it was the second and last time he would go into action on board a glider. As part of the 6th Airlanding Brigade, his was one of only eighty-eight gliders (from a total of about 400) which landed unscathed. Devlin's unit came down near the village of Hamminkeln, and Devlin himself was in charge of a Bren gun which he used to deadly effect on a truck full of enemy soldiers; later, however, he became a target for a German machine-gun crew at the edge of a small copse of trees. He was hit just twenty yards short of safety in a ditch but fortunately had opted to try and avoid the bullets by running in zigzag fashion. 'I didn't get a chance to zigzag, but I must have turned to "zig" because instead of getting a burst in my stomach I had turned slightly out of the line of fire and I got a bullet through my forearm, one along the side and across the small of my back.' Devlin could not move, a fact he now believes saved his life. Had he attempted to crawl forward the machine-gunners probably would have finished him off. His luck had held out in another respect; on his back, inside his pack, was a landmine which had not been hit. His war ended when he was brought to a regimental aid post.

Lord Killanin served to the end of the war without 'killing anyone personally', but a visit to the concentration camp in Belsen affected him profoundly. Almost fifty years later he still finds his personally recorded mental images of that horror as 'terrifying'. 'I have great difficulty in putting it out of my mind.' The Crocodile flame-throwing tanks, which had been instrumental in persuading thousands of Germans that discretion was the better part of valour, were now put to an altogether more macabre purpose, cremating the piles of emaciated bodies of those inmates who had not managed to cling to life long enough to be liberated.

Occupied Germany, after the death of Hitler, had more than a hint of hell about it. Breughel might have captured it well on canvas. The film *The Third Man*, though set in Vienna, conveys something of the turpitude and amorality which pervaded the immediate post-war period. The population of Germany was sullen but cowed. There were many on the Allied side, ruthless and self-serving, who were determined to take advantage of this. Into this Dantesque environment Louthman George Berrill was plunged after his service in the Pacific came to an end. He describes his job as being akin to that of the notorious Black and Tans in Ireland between 1919 and 1921. He was part, he claims, of a highly secretive unit which waged war against black marketeering. However, in a crumbling society where respect for human life had been obliterated by five years of war, his unit acted as executioners for others who had assumed the roles of judge and jury in cases of 'antisocial activity'. 'We went out at night-time . . . to try and find them. Shoot them, that's what we did mostly. But they were mostly ex-service blokes, British, Polish, Russian, German, the lot. They were in gangs and they used to run big businesses. You could get anything from them.' The excuse for this unofficial 'hit squad', Berrill alleges, came when the mayor of a German town and his entire family were murdered by black-market gangsters. After that the gloves were off. 'We got orders to get rid of them, so that's what we did. Just set up

a Bren gun outside houses and when they came out, shot them. That
saved a lot of trouble, I suppose.'

This narrative, so far, has concentrated, with good reason, on the lives
of the ordinary Irish soldiers who fought in the most destructive and
intense conflict in history. But there were, in the British army, a
number of extraordinary Irish soldiers, mostly veterans of the Great
War, who guided the fortunes of thousands, and sometimes hundreds of
thousands, of soldiers. Most belonged to an extremely able Northern
Irish 'warrior class'. Strictly speaking Field Marshal Alan Brooke
(Viscount Alanbrooke) could not be classified as Irish were it not that he
so often described himself as such. Brooke actually spent most of his
early life in France. He was a member of the famous Northern Irish
house of Brookeborough and served during the war as chief of the
Imperial General Staff. In many respects he was Churchill's military
right hand, though his modest claim was simply that he had 'turned
Churchill's inspirations into military sense'. His war diaries were the
basis of two books by Arthur Bryant; in *Triumph in the West* he tells an
amusing story about himself. Alanbrooke was in Rome and had severely
injured his foot prior to a private audience with Pope Pius XII. To
lessen the pain his batman gave him a huge brandy, and 'when I entered
the room swaying on two sticks and breathing brandy I am certain the
Pope wrote me off as one of those drunken Orangemen from the North
of Ireland that are beyond praying for.'

   Field Marshal Harold Alexander (first Earl Alexander of Tunis), on
the other hand, was very definitely Irish. Born in Tyrone into the same
stock as Alanbrooke, he had served with distinction (DSO and MC) in
the Irish Guards during the First World War. Commanding 1 Corps,
he was the last officer evacuated from the Dunkirk beaches in May
1940. He later led the Allied forces in North Africa and succeeded
(where most failed) in having a smooth relationship with Montgomery.
He then assumed command of the British and American armies
invading Italy. His physical courage was legendary, as were his
diplomatic skills and his unflagging confidence. Alexander's attitude,
however, towards a maverick Irish general under his command was
ambiguous. In this respect he was far more charitable in his dealings
with Brigadier General Eric 'Chink' Dorman-Smith than most of his

colleagues, including fellow Ulsterman Alanbrooke. Dorman-Smith, friend of Hemingway, enemy of Montgomery, scion of a land-owning Monaghan family and unrepentant Irish nationalist, was a staff officer of undoubted ability and imagination. However, he was not one to suffer fools gladly and he saw as foolish many whose opinions of themselves were as inflated as their rank. This was part arrogance and part intellectual impatience. He gives us an excellent précis of his philosophy in a letter to his wife which begins, 'I'm damned if I'm going to be a yes man or a toady, or pretend to like men whom I think are crooks just because they might give me promotion.'

Dorman-Smith's greatest achievement in the Second World War was at the shoulder of General Auchinleck before and during the first Battle of El Alamein, the battle which stopped dead the forward progress of Rommel's Afrika Corps. Dorman-Smith was undoubtedly influential in the choice of El Alamein as a pivotal and defensible position and his involvement in the disposition of the Eighth Army and conduct of the battle were also crucial. But this contribution went unrecognised while his testiness and unsuitability as a 'team player' told against him. He was sacked, along with Auchinleck, by Churchill. His subsequent history placed him well beyond the pale. He returned to his Monaghan estate and 'went native'. He Gaelicised his name to Dorman-O'Gowon, refought the Desert War when the memoirs of Alanbrooke and Montgomery disparaged Auchinleck, and became involved in the 1950s border campaign as an IRA sympathiser.

At the opposite end of the Irish political spectrum was inveterate unionist Sir Hubert Gough, former commander of Fifth Army (which included the 16th and 36th divisions) in the First World War. Scapegoated and sacked in 1918, one of his functions in the Second World War was what the Americans might call 'a booster'. He wanted to recruit an Irish division similar to the 10th, 16th and 36th divisions in the Great War. Paddy Devlin remembers him recruiting volunteers from other units for the 6th Airborne Division. 'He had only one arm, the sleeve of his uniform was pinned up. He had a black patch over one eye as a result of his wounds. He said he was pleased to see us, all from Southern Ireland, like himself, and he was going around all the battalions of the army asking Irishmen to volunteer for the Airborne Forces.' He got eight volunteers from among the Irish in the Queen's Regiment.

Gough's hopes of an Irish division (normally three brigades) did not materialise, although an Irish brigade (the 38th) fought in Italy. Churchill, despite his lack of enthusiasm for a neutral Ireland, did approve of the formation of an Irish brigade (normally three battalions). He wrote to the War Office in October 1941: 'I think now the time is ripe to form an Irish Brigade, also an Irish Wing or Squadron of the RAF. If these were taken in hand they would have to be made a great success of.'

Fliers: The RAF and the Fleet Air Arm

Limited horizons and limited options kept most Irish recruits of the British forces in the army. Most of those, in turn, went into the infantry. But many Irishmen did find a home in the RAF. Sam McAughtry, the Belfast writer, was a tough, gregarious young Protestant from Cosgrave Street in Belfast with visions of joining the Royal Navy. But he was an impatient lad and the navy kept him waiting for up to month before accepting him! The RAF took him on the spot. A month is a long time when you are eighteen-years old.

Eric Dunlop, a Dubliner, was working in Belfast when war broke out. During the early days of the 'Phoney War' the conflict did not impinge that often. But after Dunkirk he realised that 'the German menace was no longer a remote, impersonal thing cushioned from us by a huge effective French army . . . I quickly realised that the old world of 1939 had vanished and I should now have to listen to my conscience and try and decide what, if anything, I should do.' Despite being a neutral Southerner he joined up, opting for the RAF partly because he felt 'it was better to be in a service where you either survived intact or were written off. I didn't feel the army was my cup of tea.'

Sam McAughtry's horizons were limited by comic-book images. His ambition stretched no further than being a rigger in the RAF; he had a hazy idea that riggers were devoted servants who patched up the aircraft of their pilots and occupied the role of staunch, stout, working-class supports and props to their aristocratic masters – hard-nosed Jeeves to an airborne Wooster. 'I could see myself doing this and tightening up the equipment and patting the pilot on the head, he would nearly always be a double-barrelled-named guy . . . It turned out to be a

Wellington Barracks, London, 12 August 1914. Soldiers of the Irish Guards prepare to leave for France to join the British Expeditionary Force.

Imperial War Museum.

The Somme: the Battle for Ginchy, where Tom Kettle died on 9 September 1916.
Imperial War Museum.

Sgt de Margry of 2nd Battalion, Royal Irish Regiment, 'couldn't help remembering the many dire warnings I had been given about my height [six feet] being a great handicap in trench warfare, as the parapets were sized for men of average height.' This officer (centre) of 12th Royal Irish Rifles looks similarly disadvantaged.

Imperial War Museum.

Lizzie Dobbs, pictured here in her WRNS uniform.

Dr Andy Parson, a medical officer with the 'Buffs', whose war ended with a near fatal injury at Anzio.

Kevin Gibney of the Fleet Air Arm pictured here in Scotland in 1943, just prior to becoming Commander of 827 Squadron.

Dunkirk in flames. Captain Andy Parson was one of the lucky ones: he was evacuated on the steamer *The Maid of Orleans.*
Imperial War Museum.

Photograph taken by Maurice Daly on one of the many Pacific islands which saw horrendous Japanese casualties.

Maurice Daly (left) from Castlemaine, Co. Kerry, among the graves of casualties of the war in the Pacific.

terrible job. It's a flight mechanic, really. What I didn't know was that all these unpleasant jobs had to be done as a rigger. For example, if the pilot was sick you had to clean everything up. You had to lie on your back in puddles of iced water and stitch these canvas aircraft. It was most unpleasant.'

McAughtry received his basic training at Padgate in Lancashire. Denis Murnane, who joined the RAF to escape a career in law, did some of his earliest training in London, marching up and down outside a temporary arsenal in Regent's Park with an empty Lee Enfield rifle. Later he transferred to Torquay. One day while engaged in every soldier's pet hate, drilling, he heard planes overhead. He ignored them until 'the next thing we knew three German fighters were shooting up the promenade. So we all dived off and took cover. There was a detachment of British troops on a headland near the Grand Hotel and a cook rushed out and grabbed a Lewis gun. And I suppose more by luck than judgement he managed to shoot one of them down.' Did he get a medal for his courage and presence of mind? No! 'He was court-martialled the next day for firing the gun without permission.'

It was this sort of pettiness which irked Sam McAughtry. Apt to be undisciplined at the best of times, the Belfastman constantly kicked against the traces. He particularly hated taking the insults of the NCOs, which were an inescapable part of basic training. Within thirty-six hours of his introduction to the RAF he was on a charge for striking a Cockney corporal. It was a misunderstanding over bed sheets. McAughtry, who had never had more than one sheet in his entire life, was offered two and handed the second one back. 'Everybody burst out laughing, including people I suppose who were just as innocent as I was. But this corporal kept this up with me and I hauled off and belted him one.'

Sean Drumm from Tipperary was one of a class of fifty who graduated from RAF Bishops Court, County Down, in 1943 (only seven survived the war) as an air gunner. He was posted to Bomber Command at Silverstone, North Hants. His tour would end after either thirty missions or 200 hours of operational flying. He was looking forward to seeing action but was given pause by two veteran gunners he met by chance on a train journey one day. They had flown twenty missions and were displaying all of the telltale signs of being 'flak happy'. They were not optimistic about their chances of completing thirty missions and advised Drumm not to be too eager to get into a front-line squadron. Neither of them managed to survive, he later discovered – both had been killed on their thirtieth mission. It was a galling experience for the enthusiastic young gunner.

An occupational hazard for Irishmen in the Second World War (except those in largely Irish units) was that, irrespective of their names, they were almost invariably dubbed 'Paddy'. Most shrugged their shoulders and accepted their new persona. Certain things appear to have been expected of the lovable, feckless Paddy which, while they sat comfortably with some, were alien to the characters of many dour Northerners and middle-class Southerners. Sam McAughtry rather played up to the role assigned to him, that of a typically robust, hard-drinking, hard-fighting, hot-tempered extrovert. He enjoyed being Irish and felt that it conferred a certain status. His first St Patrick's Day in the RAF was spent in Padgate and he accompanied a Falls Road Roman Catholic, Paddy Johnston, into the town, wearing a sprig of shamrock tucked into his cap. 'This was spotted right away by the locals and the people we were serving with. They treated us differently. A light came into their eyes when they saw the shamrock . . . of course, I wasn't long in picking all this up. I loved it.

'It's no wonder the Irish won so many Victoria Crosses because the English expected you to be like this. I was inclined to play up to the Irishness a lot and do daring things and be cheeky with sergeants. Now, your typical archetypal North of Ireland man, from Ballymena or wherever, was not naturally this way. Yet I saw them come out of their shells whenever they were referred to as "Paddy". I used to sit on the bed in the barrack room and watch some guy who was Scotch-Irish by nature, reserved and cautious, and I used to watch them to some degree come out of their shell and become "Irish".'

Not everybody was enchanted by this mystical Irishness. Warrant Officer Denis Murnane was going home on leave to Ireland via London, dressed in civvies, when he was accosted by two burly soldiers in a pub who inquired about his accent. On being told that he was Irish one of the heavies responded, 'You're one of those bastards who won't give us the ports.' Looking at their combined size and weight, Murnane would have been happy to hand over the Treaty ports on the spot. Attempting to reason with them he pointed out that he, personally, was in the RAF and was going home on leave. This elicited the rational response,

'You're still one of those bastards who won't give us the ports.' Murnane was looking anxiously for the nearest exit when he felt two large presences on either flank. 'I thought, my God, I'm really going to be clobbered here. Then one of them said, "Are you having trouble?" I knew immediately he was from Northern Ireland. The other two looked at him and said, "But he's from the South." The Northerner replied, "It doesn't matter a damn, he's Irish."' The English withdrew from the field of battle. Murnane adjourned to the bar with his deliverers and discovered that one was a Catholic from the Falls Road and the other was Shankill Road Protestant.

Second World War planes came in all shapes and sizes, from the Lancaster Bombers on which Sean Drumm was a gunner to the Swordfish on which Kevin Gibney, from Howth in Dublin, served as a navigator. Gibney had joined the Royal Naval Air Service in 1938. By the time he was demobbed in 1946 he would have been awarded a DSC and bar. (Uniquely, he almost won a DFC as well but this was denied him as it was awarded only to RAF fliers.) His early experience in Coastal Command, based in Detling Aerodrome near Maidstone in Kent, was of the rather flimsy Swordfish open-cockpit plane. There were nine in his squadron. 'It wasn't a terrific advance on what was flying in 1918.' But it had a very low landing speed, was extremely manoeuvrable and could set down in a very small area.

Sam McAughtry, after his flirtation with the romance of being a rigger, was promoted by design, but almost in spite of himself, to the back seat of a Beaufighter. This was a twin-engined long-range fighter, 'a brute of an aircraft . . . they could take enormous punishment but they were anything but aerodynamic. It was like flying a table.' The two-men crews of the Beaufighters in the Mediterranean preyed on enemy shipping. 'I had lost a brother at sea so it seemed to me singularly fitting that I should blow ships to pieces.' He had plenty of opportunity, picking off German craft in the Aegean Sea from bases in the Western Desert. 'I found myself in this little backwater of a war in North Africa after Montgomery and all his wonderful Eighth Army had gone. We were left in a silent desert.' German convoys did not have much 'top cover' (defensive fighters) left by the time McAughtry arrived there in 1944, though his job was still dangerous. The chances were fair to middling that if the German flak did not get you the booze would. After a mission, 'you would come back to this dreary desert'. Mc-

Aughtry's 'golden parachute' from the RAF on demobilisation was a drink problem as boundless and menacing as the desert which had helped bring it on. It was as tough to win that battle as it was to come out alive from the countless skirmishes with Mediterranean convoys.

Eric Dunlop was destined for the Far East, a posting in India with number 60 Bomber Squadron and an enduring relationship with the Blenheim. This slow and rather ponderous twin-engined beast had a crew of three: the pilot, a navigator-gunner who sat in the nose, and a wireless operator-gunner who sat aft in a turret. In a country where the elephant has particular pride of place, the lumbering Blenheim must have seemed an oddly appropriate aircraft. Dunlop writes about an early brush with death on board one. It was during a night-time flying exercise; the pilot was 'Spud' Murphy. As they were about to take off, travelling at ninety miles an hour, the starboard engine cut out. 'My heart chilled instantaneously with fright. The pitch darkness ahead rushed at us.' The plane belly-flopped back to earth. 'There was an all-pervading smell of dust and hot, tortured metal. I was petrified. Then we hit something solid with our port wing and swung right around.' As soon as they came to a stop Dunlop, Murphy and the rear gunner, Sergeant Allen, jumped out and ran to get as far away from the potentially explosive plane as possible. It did not go up. Apart from Allen, who twisted his ankle, they emerged unscathed.

Sam McAughtry was not as fortunate with his pilot as Dunlop was. He was partnered in the Beaufighter by a northern England flier whom he called 'William Price'. He was incompetent, precious and a prodigious whiner who was upset by McAughtry's apparently cavalier attitude to pre-flight briefings and RAF rules. The Belfastman was not then as attached to the written word as he subsequently became. He relied on his memory to retain the gist of a briefing and never bothered keeping a flight log. He was as fond of Price as the Englishman was of him. One of Price's eccentricities was to adopt an erratic flight pattern at the first sign of flak. He would duck and weave like a boxer with a glass jaw.

> This could be highly dangerous . . . when you're going in to attack a target the thing was to get straight in and straight out again and not mess about. If you started weaving and doing things to save yourself you'd had it, and he tended to do this kind of thing. He

was poor at take offs and he was even worse at landings. He tended to land about twenty or thirty feet up, he pulled everything back and you just hit the deck like an elevator out of control. Once he broke an airplane in two like that. My future was tied up with this guy; I did about ten or twelve operations with him. But luckily he was 'taken ill' and moved away – being an officer I think he got away with it.

What Price would see which would cause him to weave were small, innocuous looking puffs of black smoke, every airman's enemy – 'flak'. Eric Dunlop flew nearly seventy missions over Burma as a navigator-bomb aimer before winning the Distinguished Flying Cross in 1943. His most uncomfortable encounter with flak was when bombing a Japanese airbase on the Irrawaddy River. 'I saw these black puffs start to appear, above me and behind and through the glass where I was trying to aim the bombs. I just felt on edge but not unduly disturbed. I had an unhappy feeling that I was very exposed and that wasn't very pleasant. But if you're concentrating on the job there's nothing much you can do about it.'

Flying for Bomber Command across Europe, Denis Murnane grew accustomed to it. 'You feel the bumps as the air shocks rock the plane. The worst moment is coming up on the target where you have to go in as straight and level as possible and literally everything is coming up at you. You see the tracer, you see the bursts. I would say anyone who said they weren't frightened were either madmen or great liars.' Sean Drumm, with number 630 Squadron, served under Wing Commander Guy Gibson, the 'Dambuster' hero, in number 5 Group, Bomber Command. His squadron was assigned in November 1944 to attack German supply barges at Cravenhurst on the Dortmund-Ems Canal. It was a low-level attack and it failed; the targets were missed. Gibson was not satisfied so the squadron was sent in again and was promised that it would be sent back day after day until the job was done properly. Drumm's Lancaster flew in 'line astern' (one plane after another). 'As we dropped the 1,000-pound bombs from such a low height, we were flung up in the air with the force of the explosions. A flight engineer was awarded the VC for climbing out on the wing of his aircraft to extinguish a fire.' This time the operation was a success. 'We didn't have to go again to the Dortmund-Ems.'

Sam McAughtry went in 'line astern' in one memorable operation against a small ship which was lodged in a cove on an Aegean island. The squadron could not go in on a broad front, firing their rockets together 'which usually kept the gunners' heads down'. McAughtry's plane went in third, having watched the preceding Beaufighter overfly the ship and hit the rocks. As they flew in he could see their starboard tailplane disintegrate under fire. He was glad of the resilience of his Beaufighter.

After dozens of night missions, one final daylight raid would be the last for Denis Murnane. Hit by flak over Germany, his wing caught fire and the crew was forced to evacuate. It was a time to test a man's faith, or lack of it. 'We had this Scot who always professed himself to be an atheist. When we opened the hatch to jump the last thing I saw him do before he went out was bless himself.' Murnane, reluctantly but of necessity, jumped with him, counted to ten and pulled his parachute cord. 'After a few seconds I realised that the parachute wasn't opening. I discovered that the cord, which was a sort of a steel wire, had been cut. My first thought was "Some bastard's sabotaged this."' The parachute finally functioned when he took off his gauntlets and removed a split pin, but on opening 'it looked like a lace curtain'. Murnane realised there was a lump of shrapnel in the chest pack. He hadn't felt it hit as he descended, but had the pack not blocked it he would have been dead before he hit the ground.

Kevin Gibney came to grief after an operation over Calais. The expedition had gone smoothly enough but nearing the English coast on their return his plane was shot at by nervous British gunners and ditched in the Channel. 'I got out with the gunner, swam underwater for a while, held the gunner with me but regretfully the pilot didn't make it.' Gibney managed to swim ashore where he was picked up by the King's Own Scottish Borderers. Then Gibney, or rather his family, suffered one of those periodic mistakes which the military lovingly refer to as 'snafus'. Gibney's parents were informed by telegram that he was 'missing and presumed dead'. It took forty-eight hours to correct the mistake.

One of the best-known Irish fliers of the war, Wing Commander 'Paddy' Finucane, was all of twenty-one when he died in July 1942 in an operation over France. Winston Churchill wrote of him in his memoirs: 'It was always said that the Luftwaffe would never get him and it was actually a ground shot from an unusual single machine-gun post which hit his Spitfire. He flew slowly out to sea, talking calmly to his comrades. Finally, when ten miles from the French coast, he sent his last message, spoken probably as his engine stopped: "This is it chaps." He crashed from about ten feet above the sea, and his machine sank at once. Finucane had always vowed not to be taken prisoner, and it was probably this that made him fly out to sea rather than inland, where he would have had a good chance of survival.'

Rather than have Finucane conform to Sam McAughtry's Irish stereotype, Churchill almost squeezes him into the mould of the 'stiff upper lip RAF type' so beloved of fiction and film. Churchill allows Finucane a heroic end but, sadly, most deaths were much more commonplace and mundane, and therefore real. Sam McAughtry's squadron members (commanded by Squadron Leader Foxley-Norris, later Air Chief Marshal) were given specific instructions not to fire their guns at night so as not to reveal their positions. On a random night, in a random raid, one airman forgot his first principles and did just that. He was picked out from the ground and shot down. Unlike that of Paddy Finucane's, his death was not textbook Biggles. He left his radio on transmit as he burned to death. McAughtry and the rest of the squadron shuddered as they heard rather than listened. 'He began to scream and he began to pray. It was ghastly. It was a chilling thing. There was no wise cracking coming back that night.'

Eric Dunlop managed to avoid being shot down in the Far East; however, he always saw weather conditions as a far greater threat than gunfire. 'If you could survive the weather you were 30 to 40 per cent sure of surviving the war in the Far East. From April to May the monsoon built up, the clouds built up into huge cumulus edifices up to 20,000, 30,000 feet with terrific electric currents and terrific upcurrents and downcurrents . . . get into one of those and you'd be pulled apart.'

Soldiers, understandably, can take no responsibility for wars made by politicians. This is one of the reasons why some men are able to emerge from wars unscarred, savouring positive memories and capable of suppressing negative ones. Sam McAughtry reckons he got at least as much out of the war as he put in. 'I was given the opportunity, and hundreds like me, for such an education that money couldn't buy.' He lived with millionaires (the Westinghouse brothers), drank and argued with men who were to become MPs and writers, learned about English literature from a teacher who had been conscripted. 'I couldn't get enough of it.' Nevertheless, he does not and could not ignore the negative side: death, misery, alcoholism, brutishness – however, he chooses to recall 'people who had left school at fourteen and who came out as majors, flight lieutenants, squadron leaders. Now they weren't going to dig up the streets anymore. They became doctors, solicitors, civil servants; it made an awful lot of difference to those people.'

Minimal recognition would have made a difference to Denis Murnane. He shares something with many American Vietnam War veterans, a feeling that he is partly to blame for the horrors of Dresden and other German cities which fell victim to Sir Arthur 'Bomber' Harris's area-bombing philosophy. This amounted to little more or less than the carpet or blanket bombing of German centres of civilian population. Most of those who condoned it at the time as fair retribution for the Blitz blended into the background when it was subjected to post-war criticism. Harris, rightly or wrongly, carried the can. So, by extension, did his bomber crews.

> This was rather caused by the Labour government at the end of the war. The horrors of Leipzig and Dresden came out. But we never heard those cities had been declared open cities by the Germans. They may have said they were but we never heard. And of course they were filled with refugees streaming in, trying to get away from the advancing Russians. But a lot of us felt bitter that of all the campaigns Bomber Command never got a ribbon. All power to the Battle of Britain, boys. They kept the Germans at bay for the early years of the war. But their total loss was 169 pilots killed. [The casualty rate in Bomber Command was around 60 per cent.] They got a Battle of Britain medal. I think we deserved some form of recognition. But there wasn't any.

On the Ocean Wave: The Naval Services

The romantic image of the woman in war is that of the gentle mopper of fevered brows, the ministering angel with a cheery smile, a good word for everyone and a neat, trim pair of ankles. Florence Nightingale and Vera Lynn, meet Marlene Dietrich. The imagery is, of course, from a male perspective and while it is not a complete fantasy, it is only a portion of the story.

Dublinwoman Lizzie Dobbs spent some of the war mopping brows and emptying bedpans, but she also trained as an officer and a signals decoder. She spent a year as a nurse before joining the Women's Royal Naval Service on 23 December 1942. Shortly after completing her training she was posted to *HMS Blackcap* near Warrington in Lancashire. There she met her first husband, who was serving on *HMS Illustrious*. Like many wartime marriages it ended in tragedy. He died while retraining in a Barracuda airplane in Scotland. 'He just came out of a cloud and went straight into the sea. . . . I found, of course, afterwards that I really had known very little about him when I got all his books and things sent back to me, but then that was the war.' Lizzie Dobbs was subsequently earmarked for officer training and began a career in codes and ciphers, working in Plymouth. 'We worked in the side of a cliff, it was called the Moat. It was underground. It had been built to hold about thirty people but there were about 200 there, it was terrible. The air was so bad in it that every now and then you had to climb up a ladder and get out at the top, take a breath of air and go down again.' This was in the period just prior to D-Day. But she missed the invasion itself. An old flame, Dr Denis 'Andy' Parsons, whose name has already been mentioned elsewhere in these pages, had been seriously wounded at Anzio and was invalided home; Lizzie managed to get compassionate leave to see him. Presumably the trip was worth it, because they decided to get married.

Lizzie Dobbs's last year in the WRNS was spent in Italy. 'We had a very good social life. I feel ashamed at having to say it but I really enjoyed myself in Italy. I met an awful lot of people.' Naturally, being friendly with an admiral helped. Admiral Cunningham lived in the villa once occupied by Lady Emma Hamilton. Dinner parties there led to meetings with more admirals until she had cultivated the acquaintance of quite a few of them. Lofty and magisterial lips were seen to tremble when she departed Italy to return to England and marriage.

In terms of the risks they faced at the height of German U-boat activity in the Atlantic and elsewhere, sailors in the Royal Navy and the Merchant Navy faced equal hazards. One difference, however, was that merchantmen did not take and were not equipped to take aggressive action. But they were targetted as consistently and effectively as the destroyers and battleships of the Royal Navy. Dubliner Dermot Clarke rode his luck for four years as a radio officer in the Merchant Navy. His first ship was sunk sixteen days after he signed off. He had wanted to get involved in the war to satisfy a craving for adventure and his appetite was well satiated by the time the war was over. His second ship was destined for West Africa. Their zigzag route took them through the Sargasso Sea, 'where it was almost impossible to be torpedoed', and towards the Equator. There they picked up survivors of a torpedo attack – twelve men who had been adrift for twenty-three days. Their ship had been attacked at night and most were virtually naked. 'One of them in particular I remember was a redhead. He had holes from the sun burned into him. You could put your thumb or your fist into them. Can you imagine a tropical sun coming down on your body in the morning and throughout the entire day. The next morning the sun comes up on top of the sunburn. That, for twenty-three days.'

Clarke's third trip was on board the *Dalcroy* out of Glasgow. His ship was on the extreme port side of a North Atlantic convoy which was attacked by submarines. The *Dalcroy* was hit, and swiftly lowered two lifeboats into the water. These barely managed to avoid the ship's huge propellors which the engineers had left running in their haste to evacuate. Clarke, as radio officer, carried a torch which he used to signal to the nearby *Stockport*. They were picked up and the *Stockport* then spent the next seven days rescuing survivors from thirty-nine torpedoed wrecks in the convoy.

There were soon so many on board that only the deck had space left. Some who had been plucked out of the water were too far gone and died of hypothermia; their bodies were put back overboard. Clarke himself tried to hoist one survivor over the ship's side with a rope. But the man's arms were frozen and he was unable to hold the rope tightly enough to allow himself to be lifted aboard. The ship's propellor drew closer and the sailor started to scream: 'Stop the engines, stop the engines!' Clarke could only stand and watch as he was ripped apart. The *Stockport* delivered the survivors of the convoy to safety in Iceland and headed back out into the Atlantic to pick up survivors from yet another convoy which was being attacked. In the course of the operation it was torpedoed itself, going down with all hands. 'Those men should have been given the George Cross. They saved hundreds, thousands of people. Not one of them survived and I never heard of any recognition for them.'

The Second World War added a number of evocative names to the list of those already associated with victory, defeat, triumph, disaster, atrocity, evil or heroism. The very name Belsen is enough to provoke an angry shiver. Omaha Beach inspires sadness and a feeling of waste. Dresden conjures up the biblical images of the 'Slaughter of the Innocents'. But the name Bari will mean little to anyone. In the final volume of his personal history of the Second World War, *Closing the Ring*, Winston Churchill makes a passing reference to Bari as an exception to the dominance by the Allies of the Italian skies. He talks of a 'very damaging surprise attack on our crowded harbour of Bari on December 2 [which] blew up an ammunition ship with a chance hit and caused the sinking of sixteen other ships and the loss of 30,000 tons of cargo.' What he does not mention, and what was successfully concealed by the British authorities for many years, was that part of that cargo of 30,000 tons was a store of chemical weapons ready for possible use against the enemy. One of the ships in Bari Harbour (which closely resembled the harbour of Dun Laoghaire) on that Sunday morning in December 1943 was called *The Director*. It was delivering hundreds of jerry cans full of petrol. On board was Radio Officer Dermot Clarke.

The prelude to that disastrous day was inauspicious. Clarke sat on his boat deck and watched as a minesweeper hit a mine and began to sink. Lifeboats were sent out and brought back the survivors. They passed under Clarke's vantage point. 'There were men with no legs . . . one man had the top of his head gone.' It was a profoundly upsetting experience for Clarke and his comrades but it was only a sickly *hors d'oeuvre* from the unpalatable main course which was to follow. *The Director* was moved from its berth to the Bari equivalent of the Dun Laoghaire coal harbour. The ship had just been tied up when the German air-raid started. Sticks of bombs were dropped across the line of ships, many of which had been carrying munitions cargoes. The actual explosion sparked off by those first bombs was so massive that it blew most of the water out of the harbour area and one ship, almost a mile out to sea, touched bottom. The protection of a high wall meant that *The Director* avoided the worst of the blast. Then a Stuka dive-bomber dropped four bombs towards Clarke's petrol-laden ship. Had there been a direct hit, a massive secondary explosion would almost inevitably have killed everyone on board. All four bombs hit the water close to the ship but none went off. 'Another bomb hit the pier just beside us and stuck there like a tilting tombstone. It was still there all next day. It didn't explode.' Clarke believes he owes his life to a number of 'unknown heroes', imported labourers forced to work for the Germans in munitions factories but who sabotaged bombs in order to render them harmless.

Casualties littered the harbour. Many of the people in the old town of Bari had run for the shoreline because they thought the town was being attacked. They had assembled on a small beach adjoining the harbour. 'When the ships blew up, that mass of people became just one mass of pulp and the old town was virtually obliterated.' Moreover, in addition to the original casualties military and civilian personnel continued to die for days afterwards. This was from the effects of the mustard gas which the British had stored on one of their ships. Nevertheless, this was not admitted even to the Americans, who only discovered the truth when their own experts found out the cause of the deaths. Nobody told the local population, who innocently proceeded to eat the thousands of contaminated fish thrown up by the massive explosion. Untold numbers of deaths resulted from this poisoning. *The Director* was ordered to leave the blazing port and sail for Taranto, a risky operation given its cargo of petrol.

Three weeks later the ship returned to discharge its cargo at last. Clarke remembers the sickly smell of decay pervading the harbour. The clean-up operation had not been well organised and had been obviously exacerbated by the mustard gas fears. There were still dozens of bodies in the water. Walking by the pier Clarke spotted something peculiar in the sea. On closer examination it turned out to be a female head. 'Eventually they got rowing boats with nets between them and they just brought them in.' The bodies were unceremoniously dumped in common graves. Shortly after, Clarke signed off *The Director* and returned home on leave. He met two friends of his, the Treacy brothers. Billy Treacy was, by coincidence, to replace Clarke as radio officer on *The Director*. Sailing near Port Elizabeth in South Africa a few weeks later, the ship was torpedoed and Billy Treacy was killed. It was the third successive ship Clarke had left which went down on its very next trip!

Timothy Ronan did not experience anything like Clarke's luck. The radio officer from Rosscarberry in County Cork was on board a British merchantman torpedoed in the South Atlantic on 20 January 1941. The ship, eight days out of Capetown, fell victim to the German pocket battleship *Admiral von Scheer*. 'Meeting that battleship was a terrifying experience; I was on watch at the time. I sent out the distress signal but we were in the doldrums there and the wireless signal didn't go very far.' The crew, none of whom were actually killed, got away in lifeboats and were taken prisoner on the *Admiral von Scheer*. 'Then we were put on a German prison ship called the *Nordmark*, it was an old banana boat. We were kept in the hold of the ship and never saw daylight except on the odd occasion when they allowed us on deck.' Toilet facilities were whatever use you could make of a tar barrel. 'When the ship rolled, the contents spilled all over the floor.' Ronan spent four months on board the prison ship before being transferred to Europe via the port of Bordeaux.

Dubliner David McCaughey was nineteen-years old and learning the hotel business in Cardiff when war broke out. He was put in charge of an ARP post during the bombing of the city. The experience made him want to 'hit back somehow'. So he opted to join the navy and within months had sailed on two of the most notorious convoys of the war, codenamed *PQ 17* and *Pedestal*. *Pedestal* comprised twenty-four destroyers, eight cruisers, three aircraft carriers and two battleships all attempting to convoy fourteen merchant ships into Malta. They managed to save only four!

PQ 17, by contrast, travelled through the freezing waters of the North Atlantic to carry relief supplies, on board twenty-four merchant ships, to the Soviet Union. The order was given to scatter the convoy because of fears that the *Tirpitz* was about to attack. This was not, in fact, the case and played directly into German hands. The ships were picked off one by one. McCaughey pulled countless frozen bodies from the sea; survivors, he reckoned, could live for about two to three minutes in the Arctic waters before they froze to death. Despite their attempts to kill him he developed an admiration for the German pilots who strafed the convoys. If they were hit they would almost certainly die in the freezing water. The ships could not stop to pick them up because of the presence of submarines. 'You had nothing but admiration for these people. You'd hear over the ship's radio these fellows calling for help but they'd had it, I'm afraid.'

Later in the war as the Allies succeeded in rolling back Hitler's early successes, McCaughey began to work on landing crafts transported from the US. His first experience of an amphibious assault was the invasion of Sicily. 'We hit the beach harder than we should have and we couldn't get off again.' They were being shelled, so they left the landing crafts and McCaughey took a shot in the leg. He was evacuated to Malta where accommodation had been provided in caves for hundreds of potential wounded. McCaughey had the place almost to himself. He recovered in time to rejoin his craft for the invasion of Italy, at Reggio. Being Irish in the Royal Navy was slightly different from the experiences of Irishmen in the other services. It was, after all, neutral Ireland which had denied the use of three vital ports to the navy. 'That meant lives,' says McCaughey, 'these ports would have been very useful to the navy. But other than that there really was no antagonism.'

Operation Overlord: The Irish at D-Day

It was to be the biggest seaborne invasion in military history. Nothing before or since has equalled it. For most of the Americans and Canadians it would provide their first experience of war. This was equally true of the British forces but for some of them it would mark a return to mainland Europe from where they had so ignominiously departed in hundreds of motley craft at Dunkirk four years previously. They would be funnelled, in their tens of thousands, from the south coast of England through five Normandy beaches, codenamed Utah, Omaha, Gold, Juno and Sword, and begin the storming of Hitler's 'Fortress Europe'.

Paradoxically, the invasion plans were a well-kept 'open' secret, so much so that the Germans never really knew exactly where to expect an invasion. An imaginative system of subterfuge helped. A 'ghost' army was created in East Anglia by means of detailed signals traffic which was designed to convince the Germans that the invasion of Europe would come via Calais or even further north. The corpse of a man who had died of pneumonia was dumped at sea and washed up in Spain carrying documents which suggested that the landings would be from the south. 'Overlord', as the Normandy invasion was codenamed, was also a logistical and technical nightmare which worked more like a dream. Ready-made harbours were constructed, towed across the Channel and set up for use in the days after 6 June. An oil pipeline (PLUTO – Pipe Line under the Ocean) was laid across the sea to Normandy from England. It was, relatively speaking, a triumph of meticulous planning.

Thousands of Irishmen contributed to the invasion of Normandy, many of those taking part in the struggle on D-Day itself. Many more got in on the act early, dropping into France by parachute or glider on the night of 5 June to seize vital objectives. The planning for D-Day began in 1941. Units were trained and prepared to perform specific tasks in Normandy eighteen months before the invasion. The Royal Ulster Rifles (up to 30 per cent of whose members were from the Irish Free State) appear to have been singled out. They would become the only British regiment with two battalions involved in D-Day. The 1st Battalion had been turned into gliderborne troops and would serve with the 6th Airlanding Brigade, overflying the beaches on the evening of 6 June, which the 2nd Battalion had fought across that day.

Those who were involved in the planning of Operation Overlord were known as 'bigots' (a palindrome of 'To Gib' – 'Gib' referring to Gibraltar, a haunt of the intelligence officers involved in the early planning). It was like being part of a dubious sect or Masonic organisation. When military people met, they might ask the other if was he 'bigotted'; if the response was a baffled or hurt silence then the conversation would quickly be turned to cricket or the weather. Lord Killanin was on the staff of the 30th Armoured Brigade, which was attached to the 79th Armoured Division. 'How there was no breach of security I'll never know because I came back on leave to Dublin a fortnight before D-Day. I knew everything, I was "bigotted". No one tried to stop me. If I'd been disloyal or alcoholic I could easily have spilled the beans. I knew absolutely everything except that there was going to be a postponement of D-Day by twenty-four hours because of the storm.' He could be forgiven for his lack of foresight; not even General Eisenhower himself was privy to this information.

Lady Killanin (at the time, Sheila Dunlop from Galway), who worked at Bletchley Park where German signals traffic was decoded, knew that an invasion was planned. However, her boss in Hut 6 was far better informed and was concerned with the weather in June 1944, the worst for twenty years. 'I seem to remember this huge gangling man with an enormous pipe gazing out of the window for several days beforehand. We learned afterwards that a dance which was due to be held the night before the original date of the invasion was a bit of a problem because they didn't know whether to cancel it or not. They decided in the end that if they cancelled it, [this] would show they knew something was going to happen. So on we went with our dance.'

Part of the planning process entailed considering the defences which the seaborne troops would encounter upon landing. The British army was haunted by the horrors of Gallipoli and planners were not disposed to take a sanguine attitude towards the defences which Field Marshal Rommel had installed to repulse an invading force. Preparation was thorough and innovative. The decision was taken to land at low tide when German mines fixed to metal stakes would be exposed above the water level. Special 'flail' tanks were designed to carve a way through the minefields laid across the Normandy beaches. Lord Killanin remembers these 'funnies', as they were called, with some affection. The infantrymen who followed the safe paths they created across the sand recall them with even greater enthusiasm.

However, the Allied leaders expected to meet more sinister weapons than landmines. They had grave fears of a renewal of chemical warfare on a scale not seen since the Great War. David McCaughey, a Dubliner with the Royal Navy, operated a landing craft (LCT) on Omaha beach. 'Certainly the Allies were expecting gas at Normandy because I was equipped with special socks and a tube of something or other, to cover all my shoes with . . . the holes where the laces go and a cape, and of course you had your gas mask.' Paddy Devlin, from Galway, was with the 1st Battalion, Royal Ulster Rifles, the gliderborne troops. 'Just before D-Day we were issued with new suits of battle dress that were as stiff as planks and had a white residue on them. We were informed that they had been soaked in a solution to prevent lice. . . . I read after the war that they expected the Germans to use a liquid gas. . . . Our battledress was soaked in a solution to counteract this gas. I must admit I believed the story about the lice.'

Testimony to the superb organisation of D-Day (which probably saved thousands of lives) was that the whole operation was aborted on 5 June and the entire fleet was turned around and brought back to port without the ensuing effects of crippling pandemonium. The invasion had a three-day 'window' in June when the tides and moon were right.

But the weather on 5 June, the date originally selected by Eisenhower, was so appalling that paratroops could not be dropped over their targets with any degree of accuracy and the seas were so heavy that troops could not be transferred from ships to LCTs without the risk of chaos and even carnage. The decision was taken to postpone the operation.

David McCaughey's 'mother' ship set off at about midnight on 5 June, sailing along the south coast of England. 'Of course we were all blacked out. Suddenly we got a signal to do a 180 degree turn which we couldn't understand at all. How we didn't all hit one another I don't know.' Eisenhower trusted in the reports of his weather experts that he could expect some remission from the stormy conditions on 6 June. At the same time that McCaughey and the huge flotilla of ships were re-embarking twenty-four hours later, 24,000 airborne troops were boarding planes or gliders to be dropped into occupied France. Their job was to seize specific targets: towns, bridges, German gun batteries, and delay any German attempt to relieve their beleaguered forces defending the beaches.

The British component of this force was the 1st and 6th Airborne divisions. The Royal Ulster Rifles, gliderborne troops, formed part of the 6th Airlanding Brigade, attached to the 6th Division. Galwayman Paddy Devlin (who had added two years to his age to get into the army) had joined this force eighteen months before. The Rifles landed on the evening of 6 June. Devlin has written a detailed personal account of both his experiences in Normandy and later during the crossing of the Rhine, where he was wounded. His story parallels that of the other Irishmen in the 1st Battalion, Royal Ulster Rifles. Their target, on 6 June, was the small town of Ste Honorine, about ten kilometres inland of Ouistreham. The operation began inauspiciously for Devlin and his section. An inexperienced pilot, unused to towing gliders, pulled up his undercarriage too soon after take off and the glider flopped back to earth. A reserve plane got them off the ground later, after everyone else had gone. 'I remember thinking, if we are last to land the Germans will concentrate their fire on us but then I thought maybe they will have run out of ammunition so I relaxed and enjoyed the flight.' Some of the men sang. 'I remember humming in my head a popular song of the time, "It Makes No Difference Now". It didn't!'

Gliderborne troops are at their most vulnerable when landing. If not exactly sitting ducks, they are large and ungainly, presenting a relatively easy target to ground fire. Tension mounts in the moments after the towing aeroplane slips its rope. 'After we cast off it was very quiet, no battle noises apart from what sounded like the sharp rattle of hailstones hitting our wing. I did not associate it with bullets at the time . . . we quickly emerged and instead of taking up all round defensive positions around the glider until we unloaded our spares and handcart, we just stood about having a pee and wondering at the spectacle as hundreds of gliders swooped in to join those already down.'

The 6th Airlanding Brigade had come down at Ranville a few kilometres from their target; poles with Teller mines attached to them on the original landing zone had not been fully cleared by paratroopers. The landings were unexpectedly smooth and successful 'though the Germans gave us quite a reception. I know that when we were leaving the landing zone afterwards and making our way to our objective . . . there was a paratrooper lying against this bank who'd been helping to defend the area for us to come in and he said to us: "Were you lot in those gliders that just came in?" and we said, "Yes". "Well," he said, "I don't know how you're not all dead, you should have seen the shit the Germans threw at you."'

Some weeks later Devlin was to face the stark reality of what his own fate might have been. Near Bonneville villagers told his 'section' about a crashed Dakota with thirty paratroopers and two pilots on board. The bodies had not been touched by the Germans or the French. 'The macabre bit was that they were only skeletons, still wearing helmets and with their burned weapons beside each man. No attempt had been made to get out, so a flash fire must have killed them as they sat in their seats.' Devlin might have shared the fate of another Irishman in the 6th Airlanding Brigade, Quartermaster Sergeant Dunphy of the Devonshire Regiment. He had served in the 1914 to 1918 War with the Connaught Rangers and rejoined when called up as a reservist in 1939. His glider's tow rope broke about a mile off shore and the glider was swallowed up by water. All aboard were drowned. Dunphy's body was never recovered and he has no grave. His name is included on the memorial to the missing at Bayeux.

The airborne troops encountered telling resistance on the nights of 5 and 6 June from the German defenders of Normandy. But they also shared that period with many ordinary French people (as well as resistance fighters). Despite the obvious danger, many French men and women were anxious to express their gratitude to their liberators. Some, however, if they could not entice the airborne troops to celebrate their freedom from the 'Boche', went ahead and did so on their own. Paddy Devlin met one such reveller on the road to Ranville: 'a very drunk elderly Frenchman waving a bottle of wine about and shouting, "De Valera, Irlande". Somebody must have told him we were Irish but he didn't appear to realise that de Valera was neutral.'

One of the most tragic engagements of those pre-invasion hours was the attack on the German Battery at Merville on the night of 5 and 6 June. Reconnaissance had shown four huge guns, inland and well protected, capable of doing untold damage to the troops on Juno, Gold and Sword beaches. The defences were deemed to be far too solid to be sure of destruction from the air, so it was decided to send in an airborne force to deal with the guns. The 9th Battalion of the Parachute Regiment was chosen for this task. It was led by Lieutenant Colonel Terence Otway from Tipperary; one of his junior officers was Lieutenant Mike Dowling whose family came from Port Laoise. Among Otway's troops were a number of Irishmen, some of whom had transferred from the Ulster Rifles. Both units had trained side by side.

The plan was for the paratroopers to drop and group. Just before the assault was to begin, three gliders would land inside the battery's perimeter defences. This would be a signal for the paratroops to emerge from cover. The battalion, which consisted of 635 men, had been well schooled. Otway had led them repeatedly for a week over a specially landscaped field in Newbury which mimicked the Merville battery. There had also been hours of briefings. Each unit knew exactly what its responsibilities were. But it all went spectacularly wrong. An RAF bombing mission which was supposed to soften up the Merville defences was an unmitigated disaster. One of the lead bombers was shot down near the objective. It crashed into a village and the planes coming behind, assuming this was the battery, unloaded their bombs. The actual target remained untouched.

After this came the transport planes carrying the paratroopers. Most of the troops were given their jump commands too early by the jumpmasters. They landed in swamps or areas which had been deliberately flooded by the Germans. Most were never seen again, many, no doubt, drowning before they had a chance to disengage from their parachutes. One of the three gliders never made it to the target.

The two that did were waiting for a signal before crash-landing; clearly they were not going to drop into the lion's den unless the operation was due to proceed. But what was left of Otway's force had no equipment with which to signal. The two remaining gliders aborted the mission, overshot the target (one just barely managing to do so) and crash-landed elsewhere.

The terse report of the lieutenant colonel from Tipperary tells us what had happened on the ground. 'By 0250 hrs the Battalion had grown to 150 strong, with 20 lengths of Bangalore torpedo. Each company was approximately 30 strong. Enough Signals to carry on. No 3″ mortars; one machine gun; one half of one sniping party; no 6pdr. guns; no jeeps or trailers, or any glider stores; no sappers; no field ambulances but six medical orderlies; no mine detectors, one company commander missing.' The last line of the report reads like the punch line to a black joke. 'The commanding officer decided to advance immediately.' His actual words, as recorded by survivors, were: 'Everybody in, we're going to take this bloody battery.'

This tiny force succeeded in achieving its objective against the odds. The assault may have been helped by the presence of a number of Russian 'volunteers' among the 200 German defenders. They preferred a British POW camp to the German camp from which they had been released. (Most were to trade both for execution at the hands of the Soviet authorities when they were handed back without compunction in 1945.)

But the victory was a Pyrrhic one. Otway lost half of what remained of his force. Dowling, effectively his second-in-command by then, reported that the battery had been captured; saluting as he did so he fell dead at Otway's feet. Two of the guns were totally destroyed, the other two were put out of action temporarily. But the Allies had overestimated their size. They were only half as big as had been feared and were not nearly as grave a threat to the invasion as had been perceived. The yellow flare that Otway might have used to alert the gliders that the operation was to proceed was now put to a more important use in order to forestall a Royal Navy bombardment of the battery. The flare, fired from a Very pistol, was sent up with fifteen minutes to spare.

Otway's force had no instructions to hold or otherwise defend the battery, so what was left of the 9th Battalion of the Parachute Regiment withdrew. One hundred and seventy-eight Germans had been killed or wounded in the attack, only twenty-two prisoners had been taken. But Otway only had a force of eighty of his own men remaining after the engagement. The battery was subsequently retaken by the Germans and within forty-eight hours the two damaged guns were shelling the beaches of Juno, Gold and Sword. But at least they had been silenced for D-Day.

The 1st Battalion of the Royal Ulster Rifles did not succeed in taking its principal objective, Ste Honorine. But it did, at least, manage to survive the experience. While the Rifles waited to attack the village, they saw five Ferdinand 88-millimetre self-propelled cannon coming up to defend the target that had been relatively undefended only a while before. A belated assault took place under heavy machine-gun and cannon fire. Predictably the lightly armed airborne troops had no chance. They were repulsed with heavy losses; 150 men were killed or wounded, including many officers. The RUR withdrew to the nearby village of Longueval.

While fighting raged inland around a number of strategically important targets, thousands of troops, homesick and seasick, were anxiously heading for their first tilt at the German army. Rommel had put all his considerable logistical skill into organising the defences they would face. He was determined that the invading force would be stopped on the beaches and thrown back into the sea. If they were allowed to establish a bridgehead it would only be a matter of time before their inexorable march across France and into Germany itself would begin. Crucially for Rommel, and for the German war effort, the field marshal chose to be in Berlin with his wife (for her birthday) on 6 June. The weather had been so foul that he judged it highly unlikely that any invasion force would land while he was away. It may have been the vital straw that broke the German defensive operation.

According to the late Cornelius Ryan in his exhaustively researched *The Longest Day*, the tension of the occasion had been dissipated on at least one ship in the flotilla heading for Normandy by what can best be described as an Irish *ceili*. On board *HMS Ben Machree* there had been a hooley: recitations, jigs and reels. At one point it all became too much for an Irish sergeant, James Percival – 'Paddy' – de Lacy, 3rd Battalion,

King's Regiment, attached to 3rd Canadian Division. He was so overwhelmed by the strains of 'The Rose of Tralee' that he proposed a toast to de Valera for 'keepin' us out of the war'. The enormity of this flotilla of troopships will never be forgotten by anyone who saw it. It was like a huge shoal of fish of varied species, tightly packed together. Sub-Lieutenant Michael d'Alton of the Royal Navy, from Dalkey, County Dublin, remembers the ships as being 'so close together that no manoeuvre was possible'.

Almost every Irish veteran you speak to about D-Day (except those in the navy) mention the nauseating seasickness, particularly once they had climbed onto their landing crafts and headed for shore. The army had obligingly provided each man with an outlet for this nausea. It was listed on the loading sheets rather cryptically as 'bag, vomit, one'. However, a visit to the side of the ship or landing craft was about as far as most got. Some did not even have that luxury. Sub-Lieutenant Tony Brehony from Dunmanway in County Cork had an excellent view from the deck of the *HMS Emerald* (bombarding German positions near Omaha beach) of landing crafts containing soldiers, shoved together like sardines, 'getting sick on top of one another. They were so miserable, with miles to go before they reached the shore.' Dubliner William Gannon, now living in Dolphin's Barn, was a veteran of a number of amphibious assaults. Nonetheless, he 'thought that out of that ship I'd never get'. Once on board the landing craft, however, his mind wandered shorewards. 'You were always worried because the beaches would be full of mines. But there were no mines.' There had been, but by the time Gannon landed the 'funnies' had done their job well.

David McCaughey of the Royal Navy, sure of his own 'sea legs', might have been glad of some distracting regurgitation from his American charges as his ship headed for a temporary berth off of Omaha beach. Instead, he had to cope with the almost overwhelming enthusiasm of the green troops as they clustered around the bridge of the ship from which he would disembark to pilot a landing craft. 'There's a boyishness about Americans . . . they were disappointed that there were no aeroplanes bombing us, saying, "Gee skipper where are the aeroplanes?" They were kind of disappointed that they weren't able to have a pot at them.'

The infantrymen probably did not pay very much attention to the Royal Navy sailors and marines steering their landing craft ashore. But the pilots of these boats had a tough job to do which involved a lot more than just dumping riflemen in rough water and gratefully withdrawing to the safety of the officer's mess. Captain Michael Previty, a Galwayman from Moycullen and a Marine, had charge of twelve landing craft. Getting the troops onto the beaches and getting his craft off again was a delicate operation. 'You would approach it in such a way as not to run up the shore so that you couldn't get off again. Usually it was preferable to land on a slightly rising tide so that you could get off. If you were on a falling tide then of course if you did get stuck you were there for keeps, till the next tide came in.' Or until your craft was hit by a stray German shell!

But for Previty, who won a Croix de Guerre and was mentioned in despatches for his work on D-Day, the most alarming part of the entire operation was not the actual landing but the setting off. Being lowered from ship into water was a hair-raising experience. 'I suppose the waves must have been going up and down about ten or twelve feet, up and down the side of the ship. You would unhook, hopefully, both ends of the boat at the same time and then you would set off.' He was to discover the value of Eisenhower's decision to go in at low tide and expose the beach defences. 'There were a number of stakes stuck into the sand and I think some of these had little mines on the top of them. But we didn't know anything about these and if we had gone in at higher tide there could have been a few casualties.'

David McCaughey dried out on Omaha beach and had to wait for the tide to lift him off. As he withdrew a torpedo hit his landing craft amidships. 'The compass hit me in the chest and when I came to in the bridge I thought I was in the water. My one worry was that I had a pair of fur-lined boots on, air pilot boots. I wanted to get these off but in actual fact it was only three or four inches of water that had got blown up with the torpedo and into the bridge and lodged there.' He managed to stay afloat but soon after he was shelled five miles off the French coast. 'This was an American cruiser which decided to have a pot at us and then they decided to have a look at us. When they called me up to apologise I'm afraid my language wasn't very good. I didn't care if there was an admiral on board.'

Back on shore the 2nd Battalion of the Royal Ulster Rifles, attached to the 3rd Division, was landing on Sword beach, west of Ouistreham.

Charles Alexander from Lisburn, an officer with the Rifles, remembers his queasiness on the crossing and being able to empathise with the driver of the small armoured vehicle of which he was in charge. 'A very fine Dublinman by the name of Maher . . . I have a very vivid recollection of myself and Maher coming down from the LCT, down the ramp and the water came in over the front edge of the Bren-gun carrier and Maher had been so ill he was sitting there trying to drive with his head on the wheel and as soon as we touched the sand underneath this five foot or so of water he turned to me and he said, "Thank God for dry land, Sir." '

William Clarke from Clonsilla in Dublin, serving with a combined operations Sappers Unit, landed at Juno about two hours after the first wave of troops had come ashore. His job was to help build forward air bases. 'All I remember is shells screaming overhead and a lot of sniper fire. We got out of it fairly well because I didn't have to swim ashore. So we must have got right onto the beach.' Already a backlog had built up as the invading force had to claw its way off the beach. The scene was one of barely organised chaos. 'I saw a lot of tanks with their tracks off and a lot of dead bodies lying around.' Christopher Murphy from Pearse street in Dublin was with the Royal Scottish Fusiliers. He had already been required to clamber down a net and jump, in the dark, into his LCT. His memories of landing on the beach are fleeting. 'Anywhere you stopped there was no cover, and the sergeant was shouting, "Get off the beach, get off the beach."' He did, and spent the night in a slit trench listening to the cries of a wounded German who had died by the following morning.

Sergeant James Percival – 'Paddy' – de Lacy and Sergeant Paddy McQuaid, attached to the Canadian 3rd Division for the duration, also came ashore on Juno. Cornelius Ryan records that they had drunk ample supplies of Royal Navy rum. Prior to landing they contemptuously surveyed the group of mainly Englishmen under their command and McQuaid remarked to de Lacy, 'Don't you think that some of these boys seem a wee bit timid.' As their LCT made ready to beach de Lacy shouted to his men, 'All right, here we go, at the run.' Disembarking, McQuaid raced towards the shoreline roaring, 'Come out ye bastards and fight us now', then he disappeared under the water and emerged a few seconds later. De Lacy heard him cry fulsomely, 'Oh, the evil of it, trying to drown me before I even get up on the beach.'

The confusion which William Clarke witnessed on Juno was also evident on neighbouring Sword beach, to the east. By the time Lord Killanin landed, two days after D-Day, the situation was chaotic. He went up and down the promenade at Dives trying to find his unit's tanks. 'It had been heavily bombed and heavily shelled. There were these odd tanks here and there with unburied bodies. I remember I found one of our tanks . . . belonging to the 22nd Dragoons. It was my first contact with death. I looked in the tank and there I could see a little bit of a backbone melted in the commander's seat.'

General Sir Ian Harris (then a lieutenant colonel) from Tipperary was commander-in-chief of the 2nd Battalion of the Royal Ulster Rifles and came ashore on Sword beach. As well as leading the Rifles, he found himself assuming temporary command of his brigade after the brigadier was wounded. He remembers the confusion on Sword and what it meant in terms of the invading force achieving its primary objective, the taking of the town of Caen, fourteen kilometres to the south, on D-Day itself. 'There weren't enough beach exits and as the morning went on the tide was coming up; it got rougher and the wind was onshore and there was the most terrible congestion on the beach. As a result 185 Brigade, who were supposed to go dashing off up the main road towards Caen . . . didn't progress as it was hoped on D-Day.'

The Rifles had been supplied with folding bikes to speed up their progress towards Caen. It had been feared that they would not be able to keep pace with the armoured units which were to precede them. In the event, as Charles Alexander recalls, the cumbersome bikes were totally unnecessary. 'Coming ashore into five feet of water were small Irish lads, five-foot-three to five-foot-six with a bicycle over one shoulder, a rifle over the other shoulder, a great pack on their back, which contained a greatcoat or a blanket, and all their equipment, ammunition and so on.' He adds, tongue in cheek, 'Some of them didn't manage to bring their bicycles ashore. The remainder who got them ashore got rid of them as quickly as possible because there was no chance of us getting to Caen by bicycle.'

The Normandy landings, despite the disorder often verging on havoc on most beaches, have to be judged as an outstanding success. The lessons of Gallipoli had been well learned by the British army. Lives were not needlessly thrown away. The troops and their logistical support were well organised and well prepared. The obvious exception, however, was the experience of the American 1st Infantry Division on the infamous Omaha beach. Here the Americans suffered their private Gallipoli. At least one Irishman was an involuntary witness to the carnage of Omaha. David McCaughey had dried out on the beach. He remembers its imposing heights and its sound defences, 'Very high cliffs. . . . Stacks of mines that should have been done away with, that was on the cross pieces, the steel girder mines. When I dried out I don't really know how I dried out without hitting one. Something had gone wrong with the clearing of it.'

Something had indeed gone badly wrong, and not just with the disposal of mines. The German guns defending Omaha had not been silenced, they had survived an intense naval bombardment. In one defensive position alone, Strongpoint 62, unscathed German gunners would fire thousands and thousands of rounds of ammunition, raking the advancing American troops of the 1st Division and watching as they pitched forward until all the defenders could see was the number 1 on their helmets. Behind this carnage David McCaughey was busily saving the lives of Americans struggling in the water under the weight of huge packs. 'I don't want to be disparaging about the Americans, because we wouldn't have won the war without them, but . . . if they were dropped in more than three or four feet of water they were in a terrible state, they were drowning. We spent our time . . . chucking heaving lines out and hauling these fellows in.' He sometimes watched as the men he had fished out of the water advanced up the beach. 'You'd hear the sergeant major, or whoever, shouting "spread out, guys". And that instinct . . . this is where training comes in . . . that instinct to come together asserted itself; you could see them coming together, and then somebody stood on a mine and instead of one man going up or two men it was three or four.'

While McCaughey remained a prisoner of the tides on Omaha, Sub-Lieutenant Michael d'Alton from Dalkey was trying to land his cargo of six Sherman tanks and a command jeep from LC 796. The task was virtually impossible. Like so many bees waiting to get into their nest, landing crafts had begun to accumulate near Omaha, reluctant to share in the catastrophe taking place on the beach. LC 796's commander (d'Alton was second-in-command) eventually headed for high cliffs and beached his craft under heavy fire. The bow doors, d'Alton's responsibility, would not open. The reason was simple; they had been lowered onto a defensive stake on top of which was a Teller mine. LC 796 reversed away very gingerly.

The debacle at Omaha cost the Americans 2,500 dead, wounded or missing (many from the 29th Division which shared the beach with 1st Division). David McCaughey was a witness to this American 'Gallipoli'. Perhaps as an antidote to the scale of the tragedy, he remembers not just the death and destruction but something else besides, something both novel and bizarre. 'It was the first time I had ever seen polythene on rifles. In the Mediterranean the Eighth Army kept their rifles well over their heads, lifting them up with both arms. The Americans had polythene and they tore this off. The beach was chock-a-block with this stuff. I'd never seen it before, didn't know what it was.' Helmets, topped off with the number 1, piled up on a strand littered with the detritus of modern science: polythene, a substance far more permanent than the men who had been peeling it from their rifles as they went to their deaths.

After that crucial first day, and despite the two very different modes of transport conveying them to their fate, the experiences of the 1st and 2nd battalions of the Royal Ulster Rifles were not dissimilar. Just as the glider troops suffered their first reverse at Ste Honorine, those who had come ashore in the amphibious assault suffered heavy casualties at the small village of Cambes on 7 June. A number of RUR men were decorated after the action. Belfastman Captain Jim Montgomery received a Military Cross. Emphasising the cross-border nature of the battalion, Rifleman Deeney from Dublin and Rifleman Gilliland of Newtownards both were awarded Military Medals.

John Cooper, who was wounded in a Cambes attack, is one of the many members of the Rifles who has a story to tell about the battalion's Roman Catholic chaplain, Father Joe O'Brien. O'Brien was from County Mayo, five feet eleven inches in height, weighing about fifteen stone. He was 'built like a barn door', had no discernible neck and had boxed for Maynooth College. Cooper had taken bullets or shrapnel in each leg and was being treated by the battalion physician, Dr Wright, when Father O'Brien strolled up to inquire about his well being. 'Johnny, whatever happened to you?' he asked. Cooper drew the priest's attention to his legs and received the consoling response, 'You know that's the trouble. If someone doesn't tell them Jerries to put their sights up, sure they won't kill anybody.'

Between D-Day and the final taking of Caen in early July most of the RUR casualties occurred during skirmishes, fighting patrols or from shelling. A typical casualty was Rifleman Ryan, a Tipperary man like his battalion commander Lieutenant Colonel Harris. He had won the Military Medal in the First World War. A 'runner' for B Company, he shared with Harris an interest in horses. He sought shelter in a church near Cambes Wood during a bombardment. It took a direct hit. Harris, having been particularly fond of Ryan, found the letter of condolence to his wife (who lived in Birmingham) a particularly difficult one to write. 'I did write to the relatives of all the men who were killed and that I did find quite distressing, trying to give them encouragement and hope for the future.'

The Ulsters, like all other British army infantry units, would have been better served had they been better armed. One of the commonest weapons was the Sten gun, cheerfully loathed by most of those forced to use it. They were cheaply mass produced and had a tendency to jam. The story is told of a two-man RUR patrol which ran into a German unit. A sentry called on the soldiers to halt. The commanding officer of the patrol took aim to fire. He heard a mocking click as his gun jammed. His sergeant tried next, with exactly the same result. A third member of the patrol tried his gun and it too malfunctioned. The patrol beat a hasty retreat.

The 1st Battalion, on 6 June, were in Paddy Devlin's words 'still only tourists with guns'. Learning to keep their heads down, to survive, quickly turned them into soldiers. Devlin's own reaction to his first sight of a corpse and his later account of a casualty in Longueval provide a measure of this change in attitude. A dead German sat propped up, his back supported by a hedge, facing the slit trench Devlin shared with Corporal Bert Redmond. 'On guard at night-time it was a bit spooky looking at him. I eventually buried him on top of the ground by shovelling earth over him after I laid him out flat to stop his stench.'

Over a month after they were supposed to have cycled feverishly into Caen, the 2nd Battalion of the Royal Ulster Rifles moved in to take the city, or what was left of it. It had been reduced to rubble by an intense

RAF bombardment sufficient to make the ground shake around Paddy Devlin, with 1 RUR watching it miles off. Bulldozers had to clear a path for the battalion's vehicles. The assault on Caen took place on 9 July, beginning at 9.00 am. By 11.30 am 2 RUR were in the Boulevard des Allies. There, one of the first people they met was a Frenchman who was delighted to discover most of them were from Northern Ireland. He had spent many happy hours drinking in Mooney's, a Belfast pub.

They were welcomed by the French Resistance and, as Lieutenant Colonel Harris recalls, an RAF squadron leader who stepped out of a bar. 'He'd been shot down on D-Day and had been hidden by a French family. So he'd been at the receiving end of all the bombing that took place. . . . We pushed down to the canal and the River Orne; we had snipers to winkle out. There was an avocat, a barrister, who was one of the resistance who was most insistent that we come to his house. He wanted to celebrate our entry. He had buried some champagne in his garden. We had to go and dig it up.'

The Ulsters had to pick their way carefully and gingerly through the wreckage of Caen, seeking out any available cover. It was a pattern which was to be repeated right across Normandy and through the rest of France. Arbitrary death could come at any moment from three principal sources: German snipers, land mines or booby traps. Dubliner William Clarke, a Sapper, spent his time setting up landing strips in the fields of northern France. 'What frightened me were the mines. It was mostly orchards in Normandy and no matter where you saw *Achtung Minen* written up you weren't sure where there were mines.'

Michael J. Cavanaugh from Ballinrobe, County Mayo, was a lieutenant with the 44th Infantry Division who arrived in France several weeks after D-Day. He was involved in the breakout from Normandy. His great fear was the AP, the anti-personnel mine. 'It's sticking up out of the ground like you would be sticking a pencil out of the ground and if you step on it, naturally it explodes and it comes up from below and the first thing it hits is your stomach and it tears you all the way up. They're horrific. I saw my regimental commander, Colonel Nelson, right beside me, step on one and be blown to bits.'

The other great hazard, from determined, lonely and often courageous German snipers, may have had as much to do with laxity on the part of the Allies as it did with their own expertise. Paddy Devlin was a sniper with the 1st Battalion RUR. 'I used to go out on patrols and I'd never see a German soldier. The only reason I'd know there was somebody there was when I'd see a wisp of cigarette smoke coming up out of a hedge or something like that. I knew then that's where they were. Now when I turned around to come back in to our own lines I could have shot our own fellows right, left and centre. They were walking around as if they were miles behind the lines.'

For those with armoured units the narrow, twisting lanes and roads of Normandy could be extremely hazardous. Captain Patrick Jameson, a family member of the famous Dublin distillers, served with a tank regiment, the Westminster Dragoons. He was not impressed with the tank most commonly used by the Allied forces, the American Sherman. It was no match for the German Tiger. 'The Sherman was produced in big numbers because there was a shortage of tanks at the beginning of the war and the Americans concentrated more on production rather than armour plate. The Tiger had greater armament, greater fire power. We had the advantage of volume, of course. The Tigers were much fewer in numbers', as were the so-called Crocodiles. These were specially adapted flame-throwing tanks, more of Lord Killanin's 'funnies'. 'Those really flushed people. They weren't very nice. I remember seeing one in action on the road between Bayeux and Caen, a shot of Crocodile flame and out came Germans galore with their hands up.'

And what of the eccentric egotistical Irishman who commanded the British forces, General Bernard Montgomery? His idiosyncratic nature was borne out in his treatment of Lieutenant Colonel Ian Harris. Harris, after the RUR moved north of the Seine, met and married his French wife, Anne Marie. 'Monty' would have none of it; Harris was posted to the Far East, doubtless *pour encourager les autres*. Lord Michael Killanin would not have been aware of Colonel Harris's difficulties, but a *faux pas* on his part could be seen as poetic retribution on behalf of a fellow Irish officer. 'I saw a good deal of Montgomery. I have a picture of myself being introduced to him and he looks the other way. Luckily he didn't know me because one day shortly after the landings I was swanning round on my motor bike and I heard a siren. I saw two jeeps, one with Montgomery in it, and an officer asked me did I know the way to 2nd Army Headquarters, which I was looking for myself. Now I knew that you make up your mind quickly so I pointed down the road.' The cavalcade containing the brilliant but cantankerous general proceeded as advised. 'I suddenly realised when I got my map oriented on my handlebars that I'd sent General Montgomery straight into the German lines. So I laid low for several days.'

It is not possible to put a figure on Irish casualties in the Normandy campaign. They fought in too many different units in three separate national armies. The Royal Ulster Rifles lost nearly 200 killed in action between June and July 1944. Many of these men are buried in the airborne cemetery at Ranville. However, in the case of those who came from the Irish Free State there seems to exist a strange reluctance to acknowledge their sacrifice. *Irish Times* journalist and war historian Kevin Myers has wandered around the cemetery and seen the many Irish Catholic names on the grave markers. But in most cases when these names are looked up in the cemetery register there is no information available. The War Graves Commission would have asked the next of kin what details they wanted in the register about their dead son, husband or father. As Myers surmises: 'it's as if the family didn't want it known that their son had died in the service of the British army.'

The Rising Sun: The War Against the Japanese

The old soldier sits and talks haltingly. He is like a man confronted by a closed door who knows he will not like what he sees when he opens it. Jagged memories come flooding back with each sentence. Some are relayed, perhaps some are kept back to be mulled over privately. He breaks down, cannot continue, tears begin to come as he bitterly recalls humiliations, indignities, death. Some of the natural guilt of the survivor shows in his face and the cast of his sagging shoulders. Fifty years on and the memory of four years spent in Japanese prison camps will not go away.

The Irishman rarely finds himself fighting on familiar ground. As an emigré soldier he is equally comfortable (or profoundly uncomfortable) in desert, tundra or jungle. But he is hardly well suited for anything much beyond the temperate zones of his birth. He was certainly not adapted to the conditions he had to face in the war with Japan. To the great relief of Britain, the Japanese brought America into the war with their attack on Pearl Harbour on 7 December 1941. For the 'accidental tourist' Maurice Daly from Castleisland in Kerry, it meant another extraordinary forward thrust from the pinball machine which seemed to be dictating his life. Daly had gone to visit relatives in the US in 1939 and had been caught in America by the declaration of war in Europe. When his visa expired he was deported to Canada. It took him nearly two years to get back into the US. 'But I was only back into the States less than three months when Uncle Sam pointed a finger at me.'

William Hamilton, born in Tyrone in 1913, was already *in situ* when the Japanese attacked Singapore. He had joined the Royal Engineers in 1938. In anticipation of an attack, the causeway which linked Singapore to the mainland was mined. 'We were just about a week or so back on the island when we got ordered that the causeway was to be destroyed. We didn't make a very good job of it, I'm afraid . . . it delayed the advance, but only for a few days.' The battle for Singapore lasted just over a week. Hamilton was one of the victims of the relentless artillery pounding. Suddenly, on a Sunday night, it stopped. 'We were greatly relieved when the dead silence came. There was hardly a murmur. Even the birds had stopped singing.' What Hamilton did not know was that the lull, signalling an end to hostilities, would be followed by the much darker silence of captivity and forced labour.

George Berrill from Drogheda was one of Orde Wingate's Chindits, an elite unit which operated behind enemy lines in Burma in two operations whose military value has been questioned. 'I remember Wingate telling us he didn't want anyone over twenty-five; you start to think when you're that age, the younger the better . . . you had to be fairly fit and not afraid to die. You knew that if you got hit you were left and you had to make your own way out.' Despite being a member of the crack force commanded by the charismatic and unconventional Wingate, Berrill was as vulnerable to fear and terror as any other mortal. During his first enemy attack his instinct was to dive into the bottom of a trench. 'A corporal roared, "Get up you fucking bastard and shoot." I pissed myself, I was afraid [for] my life.'

Eric Dunlop, flying RAF missions over Burma, tended to be fatalistic about his chances of survival should he be shot down. 'With the Japs it was a bit unpredictable. They were pretty tough as an army, tough with their own people and tough with anybody else . . . between the jungle terrain and the fact that the Burmese didn't like us very much either meant that you didn't really have very much of a future if you went down.'

The great fear, aside from violent death, of those involved in the war against the Japanese was of being taken prisoner. Bill Mannion, from Boyle in County Roscommon, served with the 158th Field Royal Artillery in Burma. He was aware of what the Japanese often did to prisoners. 'Several times they used our fellows for bayonet practice. You'd much rather be killed than taken prisoner. They had no facilities, no lines of communication to send prisoners back, no hospitals. They moved in small units, very fast and mobile. They didn't want to take prisoners.' George Berrill did not want to get captured but ran a serious risk of being taken prisoner when operating with Wingate. 'I saw and heard a lot of what they did. They beheaded a lot of blokes, disembowelled them. I always kept one grenade on me. I'd have pulled the pin on myself.'

The Burma campaign was, according to Bill Mannion, the 'hind leg' of the British war effort. Conditions for the foot soldiers did not improve until the men at the top changed. 'When Mountbatten came things improved enormously.' Lord Louis Montbatten became supreme commander in Asia in October 1943. Equipment improved, the letter service became more regular and the little luxuries (cigarettes and alcohol) which oil any campaign became more plentiful. Eric Dunlop met Mountbatten in East Bengal early in 1944; morale was bad at the time and the new commander was visiting all units. 'I can remember him speaking to a few people before me, asking them, "Where do you come from?". . . . He came to me and I said "Dublin". He was a bit taken aback by that, he looked at me and said, "I congratulate you."'

There is admiration also among the Irish veterans for the leadership of Field Marshal Viscount Slim, one of the most brilliant and humane generals of the war. Bill Mannion believes that 'his tactics prove that he was a great general in the most difficult terrain and conditions'. Eric Dunlop agrees. 'He spotted straightaway that it was the welding of the Air Force and the Army and particularly the different branches of the Army all advancing together that would bring success.'

The Japanese probably did not account for nearly as many British or American army casualties as did the jungle. Malaria was the main killer. 'You were very lucky if you didn't catch it', explained Bill Mannion, who managed to stave it off until the end of the campaign. William Hamilton saw the after effects of cholera when he was a Japanese prisoner of war. He moved to a new camp, and 'Didn't we discover a mass grave. The doctor poked about at it and discovered they were all belonging to one regiment, the Manchester Regiment. The whole camp had been wiped out with cholera.'

If the diseases did not get the ill-adapted Europeans then there was a fair chance the animals or insects would. Bill Mannion had to contend with scorpion spiders. 'Before you went to bed at night you had a good look around to make sure that those fellows weren't in there.' Leeches were a particularly loathsome nuisance: 'They would get onto your skin, you didn't know they were there until you found there was lots of blood in your boot. The first reaction is to rub them off, but you mustn't do that. You either carry a little salt with you, and then they curl up and withdraw, or else a cigarette end.' The snakes tended to give humans a wide berth but the cobras, if cornered, would attack. Malnourished as a prisoner, William Hamilton treated the snakes as friends. Catching a snake or an iguana was a dietary bonus. He and a Yorkshire friend once spotted an iguana going into a hole. They waited for hours, as patiently as any wild animal, for it to re-emerge. When it was caught it was boiled and eaten.

The war in the Pacific came to a premature end when the Americans dropped the atomic bomb on the Japanese city of Hiroshima on 6 August 1945. The plane used for the mission, the *Enola Gay*, was based on the island of Tinian, where Kerryman Maurice Daly served with about 15,000 other US troops. All were completely unaware of the significance of the *Enola Gay*'s mission that day but when the news came through there was a rush of servicemen to have their pictures taken beside the plane. Daly did not bother, considering himself at the time a bit above the fuss that was going on among the Americans. 'I regret that today,' he observes ruefully, 'that I didn't have my picture taken with the *Enola Gay*.'

Memories linger, even with the passing of a half century. Bill Mannion lost many young friends in Burma.

> Rarely a day goes by when I don't think of them, particularly one fellow who volunteered to come with me when it wasn't his turn and he'd just come back from seven or eight days of a very hard trip. I was going out the next day and we were very good friends. I was looking for someone to operate the wireless set. He said he would, and he did. He got killed. I always have very sad feelings

about it. . . . I suppose as you get older you get more nostalgic. You think a lot about it really. They were very impressionable years and I suppose being young it sticks in your mind. Those experiences will always be with you.

George Berrill was one of only a few survivors in his unit of the Burma campaign. 'There was a roll call once and no one answered. They were gone.' He acknowledges similar feelings towards friends he saw killed, but says, 'you don't cry or anything, you knew what the game was all about. But you miss them.'

Irish Prisoners of War

Huge armies and large-scale campaigns inevitably led to thousands upon thousands of prisoners of war. How you were treated depended very much on who you were as well as where and when you were captured. For example, the probability was that if you were a British officer you would receive better treatment from the Germans than if you were a private in the Soviet Red Army. On the whole the Germans tended to treat British and American POWs better than did the Italians, who in their turn were far more solicitous than the Japanese.

William Shorten, an infantryman from Dundrum in Dublin, was captured by the Germans in the desert near Tobruk in November 1941 and handed over to the Italians. His company was forced to surrender to a German tank unit. 'And then, in perfect English – you'd think he was an Englishman – a German got up out of the turret and said, "Get up Tommies we won't shoot you." It was a relief really because I hadn't the stomach, no more than anyone else, to come to hand-to-hand fighting. We were given orders to just take the bolt out of our rifles and surrender.'

Shorten describes conditions in the Italian prisoner-of-war camp where he was incarcerated as atrocious. 'I swore that to my dying day I'd never forgive or forget them the way they treated the wounded. Any compassion shown towards us was by the Germans, believe it or not. You'd imagine they would have been a bit more lenient with the wounded.' After the collapse of Axis resistance in North Africa, Shorten was transported to Italy. 'Even in Italy itself they were bastards, that's the only way I can describe them.' This draconian attitude seems to have applied to the Italians who were in allied POW camps as well. Dr Andy Parsons from Athlone looked after POWs in a number of camps in North Africa. 'The Germans would not co-operate with the Italians, very wisely, I think, and any supplies that I could get for the camp the Germans took. The Italians were as indifferent to their own sick as they have always been to our wounded prisoners of war.'

William Shorten was aware of German attempts to get prisoners of war to augment their dwindling manpower, particularly on the Russian front, before the end of the war. In one camp in Germany where he was imprisoned he believes there were approximately 1,500 Irish POWs. Shorten was interrogated by an English-speaking German civilian on his arrival. The German, it was apparent from his detailed knowledge, had spent some time in Dublin. 'Now they didn't ask us to join up or anything but the rumour had it that they were recruiting what they called the Legion of St George and they were looking for non-British personnel to join up and fight only against the Russians, which I found out after the war they did do. One case I have in mind, a New Zealander, got fifteen years for doing it.'

Some might have been forgiven for choosing the dubious freedom of the Russian front over imprisonment. 'I heard of cases where they committed suicide. You didn't see the body but the camp leader informed you. Depression got a grip on them, which it could do. It never happened to me, I always felt that I'd be back here in Ireland.' Shorten was eventually released from a POW camp near Satzkorn by the Russians. The German guards had disappeared before their arrival. A long wait followed; after six weeks Shorten decided to take things into his own hands. With a fellow prisoner, an RAF man, he stole a bike in the nearest town and cycled to Wittenberg before being properly liberated by the Americans. 'My mates were still in the camp when I got home.'

Warrant Officer Denis Murnane was also a prisoner of the Germans but for a much shorter period of time. He was shot down in a bombing raid over Germany and succeeded in avoiding capture for two days. On the night of the second day he took refuge in a haystack. 'An hour after I'd gone to sleep I heard this shout of "Raus! Raus!" and there were two Luftwaffe ground staff who took me into custody.' The flight engineer on his bomber had also been captured. Their guards brought them through a village which had a rail depot and had been badly bombed. 'An attempt was made there by some of the villagers to lynch us, but the two guards stopped them. They took the safety catches off their guns and threatened the people.' Murnane was aware of reports of lynchings having taken place in cases where German townspeople had reached pilots before the army did.

Murnane was interrogated near Frankfurt. 'You'd remove your flying kit, go to bed and wake up a couple of hours later absolutely frozen. They'd turned on some sort of refrigeration system. So you'd get dressed in your flying kit and go to bed. You'd wake up a few hours later and the sweat would be pouring off you. But there was no physical ill treatment.' He ended up in a camp near the Swiss border, which allowed for easy access to Red Cross parcels. Food was basic and inadequate. The bread ration for the day was a two kilo loaf (just over two pounds) divided amongst forty men. Their daily 250 gram allowance of meat included bone so the rations were pooled and used for making soup. 'But the German guards didn't seem to fare much better with food.'

The first indication Murnane had that the war had ended came when the prison guards did not rouse the POWs from their huts one morning at 6.30 am. At 8.00 am someone broke down the door of one of the huts and discovered that there were no guards left in the camp other than an SS unit manning the main watchtower. The POWs could move freely around the camp but not out of it. The SS presence did not last very long. Three American Mustang fighters overflew the camp and the SS officer, inadvisedly, ordered his men to fire on them. One of the pilots returned and obliterated the tower. For ten days nobody came near the camp, then an American tank arrived. Clearly visible in the turret was a red-headed black soldier. Murnane was struck by this bizarre racial mixture. 'I looked at him coming in and I said, "I suppose your name's Murphy." He looked at me in astonishment and said, "How did you know?"'

After four months on board a prison ship in the South Atlantic, merchant seaman Timothy Ronan from Cork was landed in Bordeaux and transferred to a camp in the south of France 'where we lived mainly on dates and nettles for approximately three months'. It was the first of a series of moves. Once, while imprisoned in Berlin, the RAF attacked his camp, mistaking it for a nearby Afrika Corps base. 'They dropped incendiaries on our huts. These huts were made of wood and they caught fire.' He spent the freezing winter of 1944 in Poland, in a camp east of Cracow; the prison building was a disused mental hospital. 'We all had beards then and the intensity of the cold was such that our beards just became covered over with frost. Every stitch of clothes you had you wore.'

The advance of the Red Army forced the Germans to move the prisoners westwards into the Fatherland itself. 'Several prisoners were forced to walk. Many prisoners could not do this and they died of exhaustion or lack of food.' The westward movement meant that Ronan would be a witness to one of the most controversial and horrific episodes of the war, the firebombing of Dresden. The flight of thousands of refugees from the Soviet army had resulted in the movement of masses of people into the city. This meant Dresden had a huge transient population on the night of the bombing. Timothy Ronan was being held in a cattle truck just outside of the city. 'I was sure we would never get out of it. It seemed to go on for hour after hour . . . the sound was dreadful, the vibrations were frightening.'

Ronan's final destination was the Austrian town of Villach. There he ate cooked mule for the first time. His assessment of its culinary merits – 'the most succulent meat I ever tasted' – must be taken with a pinch of salt. It was, after all, quite a few steps up the food chain from nettles and dates. A poignant footnote to his four-and-a-half years in captivity came when the ship carrying him and many of his fellow prisoners back to England entered Liverpool Harbour. 'There was a chap on board who rolled over, fell into the sea and was lost. I thought that was very, very sad, to go through the whole war and die like that.'

William Hamilton, the Tyrone-born Sapper with the Royal Engineers, saw plenty of death. It was usually slow, painful, brutal and undignified. Hamilton had become a prisoner of the Japanese after the fall of Singapore. Fate frowned upon him and he was conscripted by his captors to work on the infamous Thailand-Burma railway line. The film *Bridge on the River Kwai* captures something of the hideous treatment meted out to the conscripts who worked on that project, but the real picture was much bleaker than anything which a cinema-going audience could ever be allowed to see. Hamilton is unambiguous in his judgement. 'Looking back on it now I wouldn't call it work, it was pure downright slavery.'

Japanese methods of discipline were peremptory and violent. 'They didn't really need weapons, just bamboo canes. You were stripped naked, except for a bit of a loincloth, because of the heat. After about twelve months your clothes had rotted. If they thought someone wasn't working hard enough they went down on him with the bamboos. It just wasn't a few taps with the bamboo, it was merciless.' One young Australian was punished by the Japanese for some minor infraction. The entire camp was required to witness his torture. 'They strung him up on a tree and lashed him with bamboos. We couldn't believe it, that one human being could do it to another. He died. They left him there till he was finished.'

Most of those who did not suffer from outright brutality, and few if any could avoid it, endured longer-term privation from the starvation rations issued by the Japanese. Hamilton befriended a young conscript soldier whom he calls Kibby. He had none of the toughness of the regular army types.

> He just wasn't fit for the work. I used to try and help him out as much as I could. But they weren't content . . . that I, or anyone else, could help him, they just wanted to punish him . . . they loved to torture and punish them as much as they could for no reason. It would have been much more sensible if they had allowed us to help each other. But they wouldn't, they were absolute monsters. He disintegrated so much, he was a little fat tubby lad, but he was really going downhill. You could see it every day. Eventually he was evacuated.

With the railroad nearly finished Hamilton was moved to a prison camp at a place called Chung Kai. Here he came across Kibby again. 'He was just an absolute skeleton. I felt very much for him, he was such a youngster you know. I used to go down most days to try and get him to eat something, I'd rub him down with a rag. He was so grateful for it. But he didn't last long.' Fifty years after the death of a boy he knew for only a few months, Hamilton still finds it hard to cope with the revival of this painful memory.

Night-time only further sharpens the vivid memories. 'I still dream about being a prisoner. The worst part of the dream is that I have a wife and family and that they are also prisoners. I say to myself in the dream,

"How in heaven's name did I let this happen?" after I swore to myself at the end of the war that I would never allow myself to become a prisoner again. That really gets me into a sweat.' By the end of the war Hamilton, a man of average height and build, weighed less than eight stone. 'I wasn't too bad. There was ones far, far worse, ones that had to be stretchered out. Some of them were what you might call walking skeletons, six- and seven-stone weight.' Having witnessed some of the worst atrocities that man can inflict upon his fellow beings, Hamilton has never been disposed to overlook or dismiss what he experienced at the hands of the Japanese. He cannot put it behind him or set it aside. 'I think it's bloody awful that they kow tow, all "Hail fellow well met" with them nowadays. . . . I don't forgive and I don't forget.'

With Malice Towards None

'De Valera was always wise enough to co-operate sufficiently with the Allies to ensure that they did not feel provoked into decisive action against Irish interests, even while his rhetoric satisfied national psychic needs by insisting on Ireland's equal independence from all belligerents.' So wrote Professor Joseph Lee in *Ireland 1912–1985*. The country was, indeed, neutral during the Emergency but it was in many ways a neutrality which exhibited some of the less admirable traits of the Irish character. It came close to being the dishonest neutrality of the 'wideboy' rather than that of the non-belligerent remaining aloof from a struggle that does not concern him.

It was a very partial, pragmatic neutrality. Britain was a much closer and more immediate threat to Ireland than was Germany, so neutrality was shaded in favour of the Allies. However, as Professor Lee points out, this could not be admitted by the government, for fear of upsetting the 'England's difficulty, Ireland's opportunity'-wing of Fianna Fail. Here de Valera had an ally in the bloody-minded prejudice of Winston Churchill. Every vindictive anti-Irish statement made by the British prime minister was another sizeable sum in the cash register of Fianna Fail's anti-British credentials.

Neutrality, furthermore, never extended as far as preventing Irish nationals from serving in the British Armed Forces. Aside from the familiar arguments about the freedom of movement in a democratic society, there was an economic imperative involved. Many of the Irishmen who joined the British army, like their forebears in 1914, could not afford the luxury of remaining neutral. They were forced to take the 'shilling' because their own country was unable to offer them any more attractive coinage. The philosophy of the 'blind eye' has stood Ireland in good stead over the years. Seldom has that eye been more tightly shut than in the regular passage of Irish members of the British Armed Forces back and forth between Holyhead and Dun Laoghaire. Provided that no one was foolish enough to actually wear British khaki while at home on leave, no questions were asked. Don Mooney always took advantage of the alternative access to the ferryboat granted to him and his peers. 'Going back at Dun Laoghaire there used to be a special gangway with a notice saying, "Forces This Way". I mean, we were always neutral against somebody.'

But what were these men doing in a conflict which their government had effectively told them did not concern them? All were volunteers, but some were more voluntary than others. The pathos of enforced Irish emigration is clearly not as profound in this instance as it was in the case of the US Civil War or even the First World War, but thousands of men had little choice but to join the Armed Forces. They either carried a rifle for the king or suffered economic deprivation. To most of them it was of little consequence that they were carrying that same rifle into battle against one of those periodic manifestations of pure evil, Nazism.

Chris Byrne, who found his way into the Royal Artillery, was a Dubliner, a plasterer by trade who had run out of walls to plaster and had no means of feeding his six sons and four daughters. 'We had no work, everything went wrong. Things went bad, the cement strike came off and we'd no other alternative but to join the army. . . . I'd a family. I had to go.' Sub-Lieutenant Tony Brehony of the Royal Navy watched the invasion of France in 1944 from a ship moored off the Normandy beaches. But he never would have been there if he could have worked in his native Dunmanway. 'I joined the navy as a job, pure and simple. I joined at eighteen. I knew Hitler was a baddie but essentially it was a job. A lot of us had the mercenary tag and to tell you the truth we were quite proud of it.' Jimmy Tallon from Whitehall in Dublin could earn more serving the King than he could in the Irish army. Thirteen shillings a week was all he got for protecting the Irish Free

State. The British army gave him twenty-two shillings a week for being a Sapper in the Royal Engineers. 'It was nothing to do with being anti-Hitler.'

Charles Alexander, 2nd Battalion RUR, remembers his fellow Irishmen — small, undernourished, with a hint of desperation — as they came across the border to join the Royal Ulster Rifles. 'Each day in Armagh there were three, four, five, six boys from the South of Ireland came over the border, some of them, literally, in their bare feet, because at that time there was very little work in the South and they came and joined up for two shillings per day.'

It was not desperation or poverty which drove all of the Southern Irish recruits northwards. Some were motivated by curiosity and the desire for adventure. Don Mooney could have stayed at home and continued studying engineering in Trinity. 'All the excitement started up about 1940 and fellows I was knocking around with talked about going. I think there was no great moral urge to go because of great problems over fascism or anything like that. It was just that we were a bunch of students. We didn't think very much about the depths of what was happening . . . we didn't want to be wasting all this excitement by sitting out in the Curragh or Gormanstown. . . . So a lot of us just went up to Belfast, signed on the dotted line and went.'

Denis Murnane might not have ended up in the RAF had his Irish been better. His family had their hearts set on Murnane becoming a barrister like his father, but he had other ideas, a yen for something more exciting than law. Joining the forces was a way out for him, an adventurous half-way house while he sorted out his life. 'So I tried to join the Irish Army Air Corps, but having failed Irish in my leaving certificate there wasn't much hope. I went up to Belfast and joined the RAF instead.' Eric Dunlop was already working there, a twenty-two-year-old clerk with a secure job in the Guinness organisation. His motives for joining the RAF were mixed. 'Apart from any definite sense of obligation to oppose and fight the Germans, I was still very young and instinctively keen to savour any adventure that might be open to me.'

There were many idealists who left Ireland because they saw evil about to triumph and did not wish to be included in the ranks of the good but silent. Kevin Gibney from Howth 'was conscious that Hitler was a threat to peace, not necessarily Germany'. The Spanish Civil War had influenced his thinking. His mother had been pro-Franco but despite this powerful influence he 'took an opposite view'. Lord Michael Killanin was a journalist working for the *Daily Mail*, just returned from China, when the lights began to go out, all over again, in different parts of Europe. He had been a pacifist at Cambridge during the Burgess-Maclean era. He happened to be in Downing Street covering Neville Chamberlain's return from Munich in 1938. 'I was standing beside an old left-wing journalist who shouted, "traitor, traitor, traitor" to Chamberlain. I suddently realised there was going to be a war and I felt very strongly anti-Nazi.'

For others the impetus came from old ties of kinship. Patrick Jameson had tradition on his side. His mother's and father's family both had long histories of military service. He had been at Wellington, a British public school which was very oriented towards the army. 'About a hundred out of 650 boys there were the sons of officers who got killed in action. On my mother's side, her brother was killed at Gallipoli and my father was gassed at the battle of Verdun.' Jameson might just as well have been a reservist, which of course many Irishmen were, both North and South. They were called back to the forces on the outbreak of war. The Free Staters were under no obligation to go, but many did.

The decisions of many thousands of Northerners to enlist obviously paralleled those of their Southern counterparts, except of course for the crucial element which made this conflict different, from an Irish perspective, from the Great War. Northern Ireland was now a part of the United Kingdom, so the fight was as much a Northern Irish one as it was Scottish, English or Welsh. Many of those who joined from Northern Ireland would have done so out of a sense of obligation to Britain rather than a simple desire to end the spread of fascism. Few from the Free State would have entered the British forces prompted by a similar motive!

How many answered the call? Because this is a subject which has had even less light shone upon it than that of Irish participation in the First World War there might be a tendency to underestimate the numbers of Irish who fought. Because there were no great Irish divisions, such as the 10th, 16th and 36th in the Great War, it is much more difficult to track down the individual participants. But the one compelling figure is the number of servicemen who gave Irish next-of-kin addresses; this amounted to 165,000 men. Add to this total the number of native-born Irish domiciled in Britain who joined up, and the numbers in the American and Commonwealth Forces, and the figure may not be far short of 200,000. Irishmen won eight VCs. As John P. Duggan suggests it in his excellent *Neutral Ireland and the Third Reich*, 'Ireland has nothing to be ashamed of in its crusading record to combat [Nazism]. . . . It was an extraordinary unsung contribution.'

However, it was different in nature to the Irish contribution in the Great War and was unsung because it was unco-ordinated. To a far greater extent than between 1914 and 1918, the Irish simply blended into British army units. Aside from Gough's ill-fated attempt to gather an Irish division and the subsequent establishment of an 'Irish Brigade' (which would have had a significant percentage of non-Irish personnel), no effort was made to filter Irishmen into distinct units. Neither does the Second World War have the same emotional impact. It was far better conducted from the Allies' point of view, and although there was tragic loss of life, the manner and the cause in which those lives were expended were altogether different to the 'death for death's sake' carnage of the First World War. As already mentioned, the Royal Ulster Rifles, which was at the sharp end of most of the fighting in the European 'theatre', post-Normandy, lost 382 killed from June 1944 to the end of the war. Although the lives of nearly 400 men are involved, it must be pointed out that First World War generals would routinely account for that many Irishmen before breakfast on some obscene offensive!

The attitude in the Free State towards Irishmen serving in the British forces was tolerant enough, many indeed becoming objects of awe or curiosity. But with the renewal of violence in Northern Ireland, Irish veterans of the Second World War tended to be less forthcoming about their service. Don Mooney, who still works with retired service personnel, has noticed this phenomenon. 'It's much more difficult to be open . . . about your past connections than it was in the earlier days shortly after the war finished. After 1968 and 1969, there developed, naturally enough, a kind of anti-Brit feeling and we were dragged into the net of that feeling, quite wrongly so.'

Even though he served in the British Armed Forces during the Second World War simply because he had no other prospect of employment, Chris Byrne is unambiguous about what he, and others like him, were defending. 'We were defending Ireland, because we had a bit of an incident with a Gerry coming over and discharging his bombs on Irish territory. No one fired on him, no one took him down. But we took him down and we fired on him.'

4

The Cold War

Korea 1950–1953

In the late 1940s and 1950s Ireland was a good country to get out of for all sorts of socio-economic reasons, and thousands did just that. Emigration stood at 30,000 a year for most of that period. The US was a popular destination for the economic refugees who post-dated the Famine emigrants by exactly a century. Britain was closer to hand and cheaper to get to, but the US promised a completely new start. For hundreds of Irishmen, however, that new start took a while to materialise. 'Uncle Sam' had first claim on their services. This is why Irish farmers and labourers swopped the harsh hills of Kerry and Donegal for the bleak and frigid mountains of Korea, and the mists of Connemara for the dust of Pusan.

Even by the standards of the peripatetic Irish soldier it was a remote conflict. A territorial dispute between an American-backed dictatorship and a Soviet-backed communist regime in distant Asia had little direct relevance to Ireland – even to a pious, conservative, rabidly anti-communist Ireland. Liberated from the Japanese, Korea had been partitioned in 1945 at the 38th parallel between the Soviets, advancing from the North, and the late arriving Americans coming from the South. The Soviets immediately set about establishing a client state in North Korea with a full-dress communist government. Had they been allowed to extend their influence south of the 38th parallel and had free elections taken place in 1945 it is entirely possible that a communist or quasi-communist regime would have been the result. After years of Japanese domination the Soviet message, part socialist, part nationalist, had considerable appeal. The Americans countered with support in the South for a regime almost as brutal as its Northern equivalent would become and one which was considerably more corrupt. This South Korean state was ruled by Dr Syngman Rhee.

Hostilities between North and South began on 25 June 1950. An unprovoked North Korean invasion was disguised as a response to a Southern border incursion. The attempt at subtlety fooled nobody. The United Nations Security Council, bereft of the support of the Soviet Union which was exercising a boycott at the time and was thus denied its veto power, approved a US proposal to send a UN force to repel the aggression of the People's Republic of Korea. Five days after the invasion, American President Harry Truman ordered US ground troops to Korea and enforced a naval blockade of the North Korean coast. On 7 July the great American hero of the Pacific war against the Japanese, General Douglas McArthur, was put in supreme command of the United Nations forces. General William Walker, commander of the Eighth Army, took control of the forces on the ground.

During the first weeks after the arrival of American troops it was an almost uninterrupted rout. They had come from occupation duties in Japan and were accustomed to 'Japanese girlfriends, plenty of beer and servants to shine their boots'. They were untrained for the conditions they would face and physically and mentally unprepared for combat. The Americans did not retreat, however. In official army-speak, they merely 'readjusted their lines'. Readjustment followed readjustment, none in a forward direction. But that early defensive force accomplished one primary objective. They retained control of the port city of Pusan, vital to UN supply lines. Six weeks after the war began Walker told his commanders that there were to be no more retreats or withdrawals. 'There are no lines behind which we can retreat. This is not going to be a Dunkirk or Bataan.' The so-called Pusan Perimeter became a *cordon sanitaire* around the port. The American Eighth Army held the line until help arrived.

When it came it was by means of a seaborne assault on the port of Inchon, near Seoul. The object was to recapture the capital city while landing a force behind the North Korean army, cutting its supply lines. Charles Dennehy today farms near Straffan in County Kildare. He had joined the 7th Infantry Division in Japan shortly after the outbreak of the war. His earlier training near Norfolk, Virginia, in amphibious landings would come in useful at Inchon. 'We got terrific aerial support and naval support as well. I think our firepower was by far superior to theirs. . . . I think they were taken by surprise. They had good defences set up there but the air force and navy took care of a lot of that.'

The Inchon landings in September 1950 were a success, and eleven days after X Corps came ashore Seoul fell. In the meantime, with the communists in disarray, the Eighth Army broke out from behind the Pusan perimeter and began to push northwards towards the 38th parallel. It was into this fluid situation that the first British troops were pitched. The decision to join the UN force had had traumatic consequences for some of the units selected to take part in the operation. The peace-time British army was an understandably depleted force when compared with its Second World War counterpart. Units were well short of fighting strength. The policy adopted to bring them back up to par was to call up reservists. Many of these men had fought in Second World War campaigns and felt they had 'done their bit'. Most had acquired families, jobs and businesses since their demobilisation. They had embarked on a life that was far from wars and armies.

Herbert Mayne, a Dubliner, was a regular. He had joined the Royal Ulster Rifles after the Second World War. Like the other members of his battalion he was expecting to be told he was going to the Sudan when the company commander summoned his unit to the parade ground. 'We already had our tropical kits issued for Khartoum, so we said, "This is it!" We got on parade and he got up and said, "You're going to K all right, but it's not Khartoum, its another K . . . Korea."'

Like Herbert Mayne, Henry O'Kane, a young Derryman, did not know much about Korea. His ignorance began with its exact location. O'Kane was an Inniskilling Fusilier who had been subsumed into the Rifles in 1947. Based in Colchester when news came through of the posting of the 1st Battalion of the Rifles, he found out what he could about the country from the barracks library. Captain (later Major General) James Majury and Captain Bill Anderson just went out and got deliriously drunk when they heard the news of their posting. Returning home they received a steely welcome from their respective wives, both of whom were nursing new-born babies.

Brigadier M. N. S. McCord was afraid he would not get to Korea in time. 'We were warned for Korea in July 1950 and were all afraid the war would be over before we got there.' Clearly, not everyone in the

Korea. A soldier of the Royal Ulster Rifles, wrapped up against the cold, looks out over a frozen landscape of hills and paddy fields.

Royal Ulster Rifles Museum.

A tank from C Squadron, 8th Irish Hussars, after the Battle of the River Imjin at which Henry O'Kane and other members of the Royal Ulster Regiment were taken prisoner.
Henry O'Kane.

Dubliner Herbert Mayne, of the Royal Ulster Rifles, on the North-South Korean border in 1951.
Herbert Mayne.

Officers and men of the Royal Ulster Rifles beside the memorial to those who died at 'Happy Valley' in January 1951.
Royal Ulster Rifles Museum.

Members of 1 Battalion of the Royal Australian Regiment in Vietnam. Ed Somers, from Wexford, is kneeling on the extreme right.
Collection of Ed Somers.

Illegally taken photograph by Ed Somers of the site, in Saigon, where weekly public executions took place by the South Vietnamese government.

Ed Somers with Sgt Walsh (Royal Australian Regiment) and two Viet Cong prisoners
taken near the Cambodian border. The man in the dark shirt is 'Colonel Ho', the local Viet
Cong commander. Within two hours of the Vietnamese insisting on the prisoners being
handed over, they were shot.

SACRED HEART OF JESUS
HAVE MERCY ON THE SOUL
OF
GEORGE NAGLE
33 BARRON PARK
KILLED IN ACTION IN VIETNAM
6TH JAN. 1969.
AGED 23 YEARS.
AND HIS MOTHER
ELLEN NAGLE
DIED 2ND MAY 1987.
AGED 78 YEARS.

R. I. P.

George Nagle was one of a number of Irishmen killed in Vietnam while serving with the US army.

Ulsters felt the same way. McCord recalls that 'as we set sail from Liverpool, amid scenes similar to the sailing for the Falklands, we spotted a deserter on the quayside waving goodbye. A snatch party had him on board before he knew what was happening.' His punishment is not recorded. Embarkation was a bittersweet occasion. Liverpool docks were crowded with well-wishers to see the Ulsters off. O'Kane remembers the 'warriors' for whom the whole thing was an adventure. 'The band played and one large Irish group of men and women danced about, waving the bottles they were sipping as they sang with the band the traditional songs of the Rifles.'

There were also the sullen. 'Another group stood apart silent, subdued and bewildered by it all. These friends, sweethearts and wives of the reservists, just stood around silently and must have wondered what was happening to them, that their men, torn from their homes, should be part of such a joyful gathering of wild Irish going to a war that was causing so much grief and hardship to so many reservists' families.' The fears of the 'warriors' about the war being over before they got there were not without some substance. McArthur had been having spectacular success against the retreating North Koreans. In October the UN forces had moved north of the 38th parallel. On 19 October the Eighth Army took the North Korean capital Pyongyang and pushed forward to the Yalu River, the border between Korea and China.

However, this was not a war that was about to end, just the honeymoon. Threatened by an American force on their south-eastern frontier, Mao Tse Tung ordered Chinese volunteers to 'resist the attacks of US imperialism'. Within days the Chinese army was directly involved in a shooting war with the Americans. The US forces, overwhelmed by the ferocity of the 'human wave' assaults by the cacophonous bugle-blowing Chinese, were forced into another headlong 'readjustment of their lines'. For Charles Dennehy, who had been with one of the first units to reach the Yalu, the Chinese offensive was a cruel shock. 'We'd thought it was all over. We felt great. We figured, "That's it, we've reached the borders of China." And then the Chinese came in.' They attacked, mostly at night, like swarms of bees. 'They blew a lot of bugles and a lot of whistles. They outnumbered us, I suppose, twenty to one at times. They suffered heavy casualties because they came in open waves and superior firepower always counteracts that.'

US army Captain Michael J. Cavanaugh from Westport, County Mayo, was shocked by the the blunt frontal Chinese approach. 'We'd just take our machine-guns and traverse them back and forth across the top of the hill and we'd go out a half an hour later and the bodies would be strewn all over the place. I always maintain they must have been drugged because sensible soldiers would not do it. It was absolute suicide what they were doing.' Corporal Joe Lavery, a soft-spoken Northerner serving with the Ulster Rifles, has similar recollections of his first encounters with the Chinese. 'It was just masses and masses of bodies. The front attacking ranks would have had rifles, Brens, machine-guns and small arms. The people behind would have maybe had a stick or nothing at all and took whatever they found on the battlefield, whether your weapon or the weapon of the chap in front of them that got killed.'

Their high casualty rates did not seem to perturb the Chinese commanders and the communist advance proceeded relentlessly southwards, pushing the Eighth Army and X Corps in front of them. At the Chosin reservoir elements of X Corps suffered horrendous casualties in a notorious rearguard action. It was at Chosin that Charles Dennehy was wounded by a Chinese grenade which killed three of his comrades. He was one of the fortunate ones; he was evacuated. Many of the victims of the various Chosin battles ended up as prisoners of war.

The other great enemy during the December retreat was the weather. 'General Winter', in theory, should have been neutral. But the Chinese troops were more inured to the kind of hardships of that frozen lunar landscape than were the UN forces. Korea experiences the same sort of extremes of heat and cold as China. The temperature often dropped to -20 degrees Fahrenheit and below. At that temperature a man's hand could stick to the barrel of his gun. The food he kept in his pocket froze solid. The water in his shaving cup did likewise. His gun might jam just when he needed it most, the lubricating oil having frozen. The same was often true of the moving parts of tanks or transport vehicles.

The British army was ill-equipped. Joe Lavery's footwear was typical. 'We had boots that had been made for the Norwegian campaign in 1940 and had been sitting in stock all those years being carefully looked after. They were issued to us and as soon as they got wet and dried off the soles came off. So you were standing there with uppers, heels but no soles, or vice versa and it was very hard to get replacements for them, unless you went scrounging with the Americans or something like that.'

'You couldn't wash because the water froze on your face', Herbert Mayne recalls of his Korean winter. 'You were lying in damp clothes all the time. But you got over it and you got your tot of rum at night-time to keep the heat in you.' Joe Lavery discovered an unusual source of warmth. 'The shock of actually wanting a drink of water and putting your bowl or your hand or something below ice and the running water feeling really roasting hot – I thought, first of all, I was dipping into a thermal stream until I realised it was that cold outside that the running water underneath the ice was so much warmer.' The Chinese suffered as well, but to a far lesser extent than Europeans who were accustomed to persistent clammy rainfall, overnight frost in winter and the occasional surprise snowstorm. 'They had padded suits, padded boots, a padded hat and a sort of sack of something that looked like muesli, and that was their food. They carried their rations, a little drop of that and a little drop of water. And with the padded clothes they could have lain down and slept on the snow and it wouldn't have fizzed on them. While we were running around freezing with our ultra modern clothing.'

'General Winter' and the Chinese onslaught invited comparison between McArthur and Napoleon on his retreat from Russia. There was evidence that the *'folie de grandeur'* of the two men was on a par. McArthur, a soldier with presidential pretensions and a military man's understanding of political realities, had been making pronouncements contrary to the prudent policies of Truman and Secretary of State Dean Acheson. But when he apparently proclaimed himself in favour of ending the Korean conflict by using nuclear weapons against Chinese troops, he had gone too far. Truman took the difficult and unpopular decision to dismiss him. In lowly Captain Michael J. Cavanaugh the president had an enthusiastic supporter. 'My brother served under him . . . but I should say that my brother would have shot him if he got the chance. I went into the Congress to listen to his speech when he addressed the joint session. I was there in the gallery that day to listen to him. He was a great orator, very brilliant, but as a tactician he was useless.'

In early 1951 the Royal Ulster Rifles suffered their highest casualties of the Korean War in two battles. The first, at the ironically nicknamed

'Happy Valley', was in defense of Seoul against a massive communist offensive. It was the first major engagement of the British 29th Brigade which had arrived from England in the wake of the 27th Brigade, based in Hong Kong. The Ulsters were left exposed by the withdrawal of American units which they were supposed to be supporting. Brigadier A. E. C. Bredin, in his book *A History of the Irish Soldier*, diplomatically refers to this as 'the premature retirement of an American division'. Max Hastings records the retreating Americans as shouting, 'You're going the wrong way, buddy' at the advancing tanks of the 8th Royal Irish Hussars. It was the Ulster's introduction to the phenomenon of 'bugging out', making yourself scarce in the face of the enemy.

Company Sergeant Major Sean Fitzsimmons, one of the Rifles' Southern recruits, had not been anticipating much action. 'In actual fact we were in reserve and we had set up camp. We were having ourselves a nice little time and then word came down that the Chinese had broken through and were heading right in our direction. We were the only brigade in front of them.' In fact the 29th Brigade was being called upon to defend an area more appropriate to a division, and the Rifles, a lone battalion, was covering positions which should have been the preserve of a brigade. In support of the Ulsters were the Cromwell tanks of the 8th Hussars commanded by Captain Donald Astley-Cooper's 'Cooper Force'. The small and manoeuvrable Cromwells were more appropriate to the terrain in Happy Valley.

O'Kane's Korea, the memoirs of Henry O'Kane, contains a graphic account of the fighting early in the morning of 3 January. One attack had already been dispersed when the Chinese returned.

> Their tactics this time were to crawl unobserved through the thick scrub to the crest of the hill; they then came in shouting, 'South Koreans. We surrender', blowing whistles and bugles. This attack started with fury, grenades followed up a mad charge, then another and another; this time the enemy did not call off his attack but kept on coming. It was not until the Chinese had overrun two platoons and made a deep impact that HQ became aware of the true situation, so swiftly did the attack take place. . . . The whole area seemed to be filled with smoke and fire, long looping curves of red tracer arched above us, our fighting blood was up, that brand of fatalism that only the infantryman knows had gripped us and true

to form the Battalion stood like a rock that the Chinese kept attempting to overcome. Soon after first light they were dispersed leaving their dead and wounded behind.

But despite having held their positions the Ulsters were ordered to withdraw. Late on the evening of 3 January the battalion started down an icy six-mile trail towards the main highway into Seoul. Sean Fitzsimmons's platoon was ordered to leave along with Cooper's tanks. 'We got aboard and we thought, "This is great, we're going to be out before the rest, just a doddle down the road." But it finished up we had every tank shot out from under us. They [the Chinese] completely surrounded us and blocked all the roads out. We lost every one of the tanks. So it was a matter of getting off our tanks with the tank crews, destroy them and then head for the hills.'

The column had been attacked within half an hour of the withdrawal and was 'exposed to severe machine-gun and mortar fire from the nearby hills where the 25th US Infantry Division should have been', says Henry O'Kane.

We were forced to scatter for what little cover there was by the side of the track, adopting firing positions, sensing the *mêlée* that was about to come. The leading vehicle was then hit and came to a halt, blocking any further movement forward. Confusion reigned. The Chinese came swarming down the sides of the cliffs then calling on us to surrender, shouting, blowing whistles and bugles, the noise echoing in the hills. The machine-guns and small arms mowed them down but they came relentlessly on as if drugged or drunk. They swarmed around the vehicles and carriers pulling men off and fighting at close quarters.

O'Kane was wounded in the fighting. He managed, along with some others, to escape in the darkness. Joe Lavery was not so fortunate. He was on the back of a transport vehicle when the attack came. 'We were flying towards the only way out of the valley, which was a sort of a fork, and the driver of the Bren-gun carrier ran straight into a haystack covered with snow which we thought was a road. Immediately we were surrounded by all these Chinese. Everybody jumped out and got behind this little house and started to try and put up a bit of a defence. I was trying to destroy my radio when I got pulled by the earphone cord onto the ground and practically killed. But I was taken prisoner. I made a couple of attempts to escape in the confusion through the night. But I ended up getting beaten over the head, had to stay there, and was just taken prisoner.'

M. N. S. McCord managed to escape and headed south towards the capital. 'We reached the bridge over the Han at Seoul moments before it was blown up to stop the Chinese. At the roll-call later the CIC, Major Blake, had been killed and ten officers and 280 men were missing, including Major General, then Captain, Majury. One officer asked by the BBC to describe his first action said with typical understatement: "It was very noisy with a lot of very unpleasant peasants about."' Another victim of the battle was captain Astley-Cooper, whose tanks had covered the evacuation of the Ulsters. His own tank cast a track and his crew managed to bail out and escape. However, their commander was never seen again. Worse was soon to follow for the depleted Ulsters — they had an appointment to meet at the Imjin River.

The Battle of the Imjin River began on 22 April 1951. The positions defended by the 29th Brigade were thirty miles north of Seoul in a hilly region. Once again the line was thinly spread. The brigade was expected to cover almost seven and a half miles of front. The intention was to initiate a big Allied push northwards so the Ulsters and other regiments in the brigade like the Northumberlands and Gloucesters were not dug in defensively. Small slit trenches had been created but the area had not been mined and air support was inadequate. In addition the 29th lay right in the path of any Chinese push southwards towards Seoul.

The Ulsters were in reserve when the action started. Despite intelligence reports indicating the presence of a large Chinese force, the atmosphere along the Imjin was relaxed. Sean Fitzsimmons recalls the first indication that all was not as it should have been. 'D Company in front of us, they got hit badly one night. That was the Chinese coming down again. It transpired it was the Chinese Nineteenth Army on its way, trying to take Seoul and to have their Mayday parade there. We thought it was just a few patrols that had hit us but it was a complete Chinese army.' The engagement which followed should probably never have been allowed to happen. The 29th Brigade was hopelessly overmatched, trying to hold out against two Chinese divisions. But the brigade was under a temporary American command which did not appreciate its critical position, though any assistance would have been meagre. The UN forces were facing the full brunt of a Chinese offensive.

The 29th's positions were, over a period of days, infiltrated and circumvented. The Gloucesters were left defending a hill which was surrounded by Chinese forces. The Ulsters were defending positions in sight of the highest mountain in the area, Kamak San. It was to the south and it was held by the Chinese. A withdrawal, covered by the tanks of the 8th Hussars, began. It was directed towards the town of Uijongbu, north of Seoul. But to the dismay of the acting commanding officer, Major Gerald Rickord, the Ulsters were ordered to abandon their defences on high ground and withdraw along the mountain valleys below. This order came on the night of 24 and 25 April, after a fatigued battalion had been fighting for close on seventy-two hours. As the Chinese, who now had the high ground, pursued the retreating Ulsters the withdrawal became, in the words of Major Henry Huth of the Hussars, 'one long bloody ambush'.

During the battle Henry O'Kane was hit and climbed aboard a Centurion tank. 'It was a wild, swaying, bouncing ride on the Centurion. It didn't last long – but I shall never forget it. The dust, the rattle of the tracks, the Besa machine-gun, the screams of wounded men as we were repeatedly hit.' The tank lost its track and slewed off into a paddy field. 'I was covered in blood, my nose and ears were bleeding from concussion. I had lost my rifle – it was the only thing at that particular moment that worried me. The Chinese by now were darting across the road and the paddy fields in hot pursuit of the battalion. They passed us by without a glance. . . . Three Chinese in shoddy cotton uniforms suddenly appeared and handed us safe conduct passes. One, who spoke a little English and appeared to be of fairly high rank, said "good fight" and "for you the war is over" and then disarmed our group. With our hands on our heads we were marched down the road and across to our old positions. Wounded who were unable to walk were left behind. They were never seen again.'

Altogether the 29th Brigade had over 1,000 casualties. The Gloucesters, with more than 500 of their number taken prisoner, suffered most but the Ulsters lost 186 dead, wounded and captured. It was some consolation that the rearguard action they fought took much of the steam out of the Chinese offensive. Although the communists got to within five miles of Seoul they were unable to penetrate the UN defenses along the Han River. The offensive petered out. For Henry O'Kane and dozens of other members of the Royal Ulster Rifles it was the end of the shooting war and the introduction to a regime which would place far greater physical and psychological pressures upon them than those posed by combat.

The brutishness and oppression which awaited them were already being experienced by some of their former comrades who had been captured at Happy Valley. The ultimate destination of most of the Irish troops taken prisoner in Korea was either Camp One, Chongsong, or Camp Five, Pyoktong. They were on or near the Yalu River on the Korean-Chinese border. Joe Lavery, suffering from pneumonia, was dropped half-way, at a camp forty miles south east of Pyongyang, the North Korean capital. 'We called it the Bean Camp because that was the only thing we got to eat, boiled beans. The Chinese, we found out, were using it as a staging post for their troops and their ammunition. So the Americans knew this and they were bombing and rapid machine-gunning night, noon and morn. The prisoners suffered a lot from that end. But most of them were just dying of starvation, cold, disease, wounds or whatever.'

Henry O'Kane and the other members of the Ulsters captured with him assumed that they would be summarily shot; rather than waste good tobacco they sat down and smoked their entire ration while they waited for a bullet in the back of the neck. It never came and they would regret their precipitate action in smoking the last of their cigarettes many times in the weeks that followed. Before they were marched across bare hills to North Korea they were given slim green branches from a type of fir tree. During the day when aircraft were heard overhead they would be ordered to sink to their knees and cover their heads. They were not, obviously, instructed to pray for their own deliverance but they did. Allied aircraft, on seeing a column of Chinese moving below, would not stop to investigate whether the enemy was accompanied by prisoners before strafing.

One of the great psychological hardships among prisoners, particu-larly the wounded in the days immediately after their capture, was apathy. Joe Lavery witnessed lassitude and despair gripping many of his injured comrades at the Bean Camp.

I got on my feet, I wasn't fit but I was probably fitter than anything else which was lying around the place. So I got the job of going and looking for the food for the sick, bringing it back to them and getting them on their feet. Well, I was putting these bowls of sorghum in front of them and they wouldn't eat it. They were just lying there, defecating in their clothes and peeing and all the rest of it and I ended up – it was probably a bit of psychology – kicking them and fighting them and trying to make them that raging mad that they'd get up and kick me, with the purpose that they'd get up and fight for themselves. It worked in some cases but one or two just didn't give a damn, they wouldn't even get up and fight with you to try and save their lives.

Prisoners were routinely interrogated even before they got to the camps where they would play out the remainder of the war. Henry O'Kane treated his inquisitor to the history of the Royal Ulster Rifles and was instructed to draw a map of Europe clearly marking the unknown political entity of Ireland. This drew a lecture from the Chinese interrogator. 'Soon he was tirading me about being a tool of the warmongering American imperialists. I had apparently been duped by the Duponts and Rockerfellers of Wall Street. He also went on to inform me that I had been duped by the British imperialists as well, but went on to say that soon I would be taken to a safe area where, with the help of the lenient policy, I would learn the truth from the peace loving people.'

O'Kane pointed out the inconsistency of a lenient policy which did not seem to cover the treatment of wounded prisoners. He indicated his wounded leg and bandaged head. Unlike hundreds of less fortunate prisoners he won his point. 'A Chinese doctor and two male nurses removed some shrapnel from my leg, plastered me with a black ointment and replaced the old bandages. I truly believed the black ointment that smelled like Stockholm Tar was the same as was used for horses back home, and at that moment I began to feel very pessimistic indeed about the so-called "lenient policy" treatment. However, I was lucky – my wounds healed well.'

The practice of taking prisoners (which seemed almost alien to the North Koreans) was the public face of what the Chinese called their lenient policy. Keeping enemy soldiers alive rather than shooting them may have been genuinely regarded as an indulgence by the communists, but this front-line approach was not matched by the treatment the prisoners received when they reached their detention camps. The Americans seemed to suffer most. They lost 2,701 of 7,140 men taken prisoner. Fifty of the 1,188 Irish, British, Australian and Canadian prisoners died in captivity.

Henry O'Kane ended up in Chong Song, or Camp One. A number of Americans were also incarcerated there, among them Irishman Mairtin 'Korea' McDonnachadha, a native Irish speaker from the small Gaeltacht area of Rathcarn in County Meath. He remembers the squalor of their surroundings. 'You just ate and slept in the one place. The conditions were bad. They were dying at the rate of twenty a day in it. I often went to twenty funerals, and there was a little graveyard, we used to call it Boot Hill. I think over 700 died in that camp.'

Food was inadequate. Prisoners received rough, unpalatable maize or millet twice a day. Rice was a rare luxury. The Chinese adopted a feeding technique which Henry O'Kane called the whistle stop. 'We would line up with our tins, bowls or hats, or whatever container we had grabbed on our way north. We would then sit around with our food until everyone was served – a great ordeal for starving men. The whistle was blown and everyone started eating, most with their hands. Those that finished their first helping rushed back for more, that is if there was anything left. When the allotted time was up the Chinese guard blew the whistle again and everyone had to stop. Woe betide the man who tried to eat later.'

The Chinese, in addition to physical privations, subjected their 'guests' to indoctrination and 're-education'. One of O'Kane's political instructors was a Chinese called Su, known to his pupils as 'Machine Gun' because of his staccato delivery of English. He was from a rich land-owning family and had been an astronomy lecturer in Peking. His tedious political lectures, when they took place out of doors, could often be sidetracked by prisoners who engaged him in a conversation about the canopy of stars above their heads. Another instructor was nicknamed 'Pagliacci' – he would wander around the camp singing snatches from Western and Oriental operas; the 'Hedgehog' had a sparse beard, unusual for a Chinese. Hedgehog was a graduate of City College, New York.

Despite their best efforts (up to eight hours a day, seven days a week) the Chinese had few takers, as Mairtin McDonnachadha recalls. 'I believe some of the fellows stayed back. I didn't know anyone personally that stayed on but they never came out with us anyway. There were supposed to have been twelve in our camp. Whatever became of them I don't know.' He himself was given an opportunity to take advantage of a less rigorous regime in Camp One when he was discovered to be Irish. But he refused. 'I didn't bother with them. But they brought me several times and questioned me about how was it that I was an Irishman in the American army.'

Unlike the British or American prisoners, he was able to turn the tables on his Chinese captors in at least one .respect. His fluent Irish proved useful when the Ulsters arrived, with a sizeable contingent of Southerners in tow. 'There was a fellow there from Offaly. He was a fluent Irish speaker.' Even the English-speaking Chinese were perplexed at the peculiar dialect which emanated from conversations between the US and the British army privates.

Attempts at escape were unusual and unprofitable. The camps were 300 miles from the 38th parallel. The height of the escaped prisoners alone, whatever Oriental disguise they might adopt, was a complete giveaway. The North Korean people were the 'eyes and ears' of the Chinese and of their own armed forces. There were no safe houses en route back to the front lines. Joe Lavery was in another enlisted mens' camp, Pyoktong, Camp Five. (The officers, NCOs and enlisted men were strictly segregated into different camps; leadership was discouraged.)

> There were escape bids. It wasn't a very profitable exercise. Where would you go, what would you eat? And the country, every crossroads, every little road was chock-a-block with Chinese. People made attempts to escape and were soon brought back after a week or so. Then they were thrown into the 'hole' which was our name for a little jail they made out of an old safe. I don't think, to the best of my knowledge that there was ever a successful escape.

The same was true of Camp One. Mairtin McDonnachadha on one occasion noticed two unusually tall Koreans. 'They were dressed like

Koreans and I thought they were two Koreans but I found out after that they were two British soldiers. Someone told me afterwards that they didn't make it either.'

British and American servicemen got a close look at how their respective forces fought wars in the First World War and again in the Second World War. Once again the two countries were allied in the Korean War. But it would not be true to say that a universal sense of mutual admiration existed between members of both armies. To put it bluntly, the British serviceman had a healthy disrespect (often bordering on lofty contempt) for his American counterpart. This is reflected in the views of Irishmen who fought with both forces. 'We used to sing a little song about them', George Berrill from Drogheda remembers with cynical relish. '"Listen to the clatter of the tiny feet/ Here's the Cav in full retreat." That was our opinion of them. The First American Cavalry ran like fuck. They left us in the shit one night. We were running short of ammunition. The Chinese were running through our positions and the Yanks – I didn't know which was chasing which – were all running the one way, back. There was only us left in the front. We were only brigade strength and they just told us, "You'll have to stay, hold the line."'

Joe Lavery agrees. 'I wasn't greatly impressed, to tell you the truth, because they didn't seem to have a sort of command structure like ours. A platoon would have had about three or four sergeants and to me they weren't one patch on the backside of a lance corporal in the British army. Their discipline left a lot to be desired and they took a decision among themselves. They had a famous phrase, "let's bug out of here" – which means "let's retreat" and they didn't wait for an order; if they wanted they took the decision themselves, which you wouldn't have done in the British army, I can assure you.'

US army Sergeant Charles Dennehy disputes these claims. 'They always think that about American soldiers. But the American soldiers have proved themselves over and over again. They've beaten the best that the Japanese and the Germans put out. People have the wrong idea about the American soldier. I'm an Irishman, born in Ireland and at heart I'm an Irishman, but don't ever underestimate the American soldier, never.' Henry O'Kane's assessment of the Americans is somewhat more charitable. 'Well, in the early days I didn't have much good to say for them. They didn't seem to want to stand and fight. . . .

They'd gone soft. All they wanted was to get back to their soft billets in Japan. Whereas as the war went on more and more troops came from America and they were trained and had a different attitude towards the war.'

Herbert Mayne's opinions are an interesting presentiment of criticisms later made of US methods in Vietnam. 'The Americans, they'd pound everything before they'd go and have a look. They'd no retaliation from air power there. They had the whole run of the skies with the Meteor jets. They'd go in with napalm bombs and they'd go on like this for days before the ground troops got near a target at all. And when they'd go in there was nothing left, no resistance.' All of this made sound military sense, according to Charles Dennehy. 'That way you'd save the lives of your own men. I don't know why they should complain about that. Because I think myself they were damn glad to get American firepower to back them up there, artillery and aerial support. I'm surprised really. Any good infantryman is only delighted to get good support like that.'

The Korean conflict was short and vicious. It produced, for example, as many American dead as did ten years of the subsequent Vietnam conflict. But not all the true casualties came home in body bags. Much of what they experienced and what they saw as relatively young men was to remain with Ireland's Korean war veterans. Shortly after the Inchon landings Charles Dennehy was a witness to the savagery of a struggle which was based as much on ideology as on territory. The North Koreans, while occupying Seoul, had systematically liquidated political opponents. 'They wiped out whole South Korean families. We found the bodies in swamps. They were bound, their hands and feet, with wire, shot in the head and thrown into these rice fields.'

It was a gruesome image but not so difficult to shake as memories of a phobia he developed during the fighting. 'I had nightmares about snakes for a while. There were snakes in Korea. You'd go into a fox hole at night and a regiment would be defending a hill and they'd lose it and we'd be sent up that night to retake it. Well they had their foxholes already dug and you'd have to go into their foxholes. I always thought there'd be a snake in the bottom of the foxhole and it's dark, you can't see. Or sometimes I'd dream that I was walking along a road and suddenly I'd run into hundreds of Chinese soldiers and they'd open fire on me.'

Henry O'Kane found it difficult to settle down after coming home. The evidence of his ordeal in Camp One shows clearly in photographs of the cheerful, lighthearted soldier who embarked for Korea and the haunted, emaciated veteran who returned home. 'In my wandering years that followed I have often been aware of a smiling Chinese interrogator, sitting by my bed in some hazy awakening moment. On others, the bad ones . . . have been climbing in the windows, but that is all gone now.'

Survivors, like George Berrill, still harbour misgivings about making it home safely while others didn't. His last memory of Korea is of a battle patrol; then he woke up in a hospital in Japan. 'We went out looking for trouble and must have bit off more than we could chew. I was told we were blown up, the platoon was wiped out. The psychiatrist was telling me that in Tenno in Japan. I said, "None of the fellows are around." He said, "You won't get them around, they're dead." I just remember being on patrol and coming back myself . . . I'd no weapons so I must have run back. I must have skipped. They stayed and got the works.'

US army Captain Michael J. Cavanaugh's nemesis was a hill nicknamed 'Jane Russell' because of its unusual contours. '1,100 of us attacked it and 400 of us came back.' After a second frontal assault he rebelled, refusing to take his men on a third attack. He remonstrated with his colonel and was slapped down. 'My nerves were beginning to crack and I was taken off the line altogether. I was sent back to get a few days' rest because I just wasn't able to take it.'

Two years as a prisoner of war, subjected to physical deprivation and psychological overkill, had a predictable effect on Joe Lavery. 'My wife said I was daft when I came home. From being a very cheerful, happy person she said I was moody. Many's a time she said she woke me up when I was having a fight in the middle of the night, when I was asleep.' He experienced the frustration of alienation. 'People would say to you, "What was it like?" and that was the sum of their interest. You could have talked for a fortnight but they weren't really interested, so you withdrew from that and you didn't talk about it.'

For many Korean War veterans the first renewal of their acquaintance with the state which emerged in 1953 was the TV presentation of the Seoul Olympics. When Sean Fitzsimmons, late of the Royal Ulster Rifles, saw the modernised and restored city which he had last seen in ruins he felt some sense of mission, of having achieved something. But few would care to repeat the experience. Joe Lavery would 'find some way to make sure I didn't go through that. The hunger when you had nothing to eat didn't seem as bad as hunger when you had a little to eat every now and again. And the pains and the waiting for the next bite to come. And how could we get a bit of heat . . . the cold, oh my goodness. I've lain and cried myself to sleep with the misery of it many's a time.' For Charles Dennehy this is a memory best left undisturbed. 'To me it's away in the distant past now. It's like looking through a fog. You can't. Sometimes the fog would just clear for a moment and then it comes back again. It's blotted out of my memory.'

Paddy Fields: The Irish in Vietnam

T. K. Whitaker can probably take some of the credit for the fact that relatively few Irishmen took any part in one of the major military tragedies of the Cold War period, America's ill-advised and ruinous misadventure in Vietnam. Ireland's economic prosperity in the 1960s (for which Whitaker and Sean Lemass must take much of the kudos) kept thousands at home who would otherwise have emigrated to the US.

Many of those Irish who did serve in Vietnam migrated to the US with their families in the 1950s. The decade was a time of high unemployment (although percentages were much lower than in the 1990s) and inadequate social welfare payments. It is highly likely, though not verifiable, that a minority of those who served in the Vietnam War were only recently 'off the boat'. Sean McGovern from Belfast moved to New York with his family as a thirteen-year old in 1961. He joined the air force, volunteered to go overseas and served in Cam Ranh Bay and Ton San Nhut in 1971 and 1972. His younger brother joined the navy and did a stint in Vietnam as well. McGovern now works in the Lord Mayor's office in New York City.

Seamus Gallagher, a Leitrim man, had come to the US with his family the previous year. Once he finished high school he decided to get his military service over with. Rather than wait to be drafted, he joined up. Five months later he was stationed in Vietnam. He saw a lot of comrades die in action but a decade after the building of the cathartic

Vietnam Veterans Memorial in Washington he has not 'taken time or found the courage to pay tribute to some friends there'. He now lives in upstate New York.

Seamus McWilliams settled in Philadelphia. His family had moved from Maghera in County Derry in October 1955. He is still quite reticent about his service in South-East Asia where he was in the Marine Corps between September 1968 and October 1969. He was based north of the ancient city of Hue which had seen some of the worst fighting of the crucial Tet offensive six months before his arrival. Like most who fought in South-East Asia, Jim Garvey remained in the US afterwards. He now lives in Columbus, Ohio. He served three tours in Vietnam, two with the elite Special Forces, the Green Berets, who spent much of their time behind enemy lines (insofar as 'lines' existed in Vietnam). His third tour was as adviser to the Vietnamese Airborne Division. He is struck by the interest among Irish people in his Vietnam experience. 'In the spring of 1990 I visited Ireland and at one point, in Cork, found that I was discussing Vietnam with several people.'

Many of the Irish who served in the US forces in Vietnam died there. Most are buried in the US though some chose Ireland as their last resting place. The Pentagon has no figures for Irish enlistment in the their armed forces from 1963 to 1973, when the Vietnam War was at its height. Neither does it, nor any of the other agencies associated with military statistics, such as the Veterans Administration, have any idea how many Irish soldiers died there. Some, of course, died with the Australian army as well. The Aussies, who sent troops to South Vietnam in 1965, helped provide some sort of fig leaf for the Americans (as did the South Korean units), who could claim that the fight for 'democracy' in Vietnam was not solely their concern. Dan Danaher, a short, stocky, fast-talking, likeable man, originally from Tipperary, joined the Australian army for adventure. A charitable recruiting officer stretched a point and defied centuries of Irish history by defining Tipperary as part of the United Kingdom on the basis that it was located in the British Isles. Danaher would otherwise not have been allowed to enlist as he was neither an Australian nor a British subject. He was assigned to the 1st Battalion, Royal Australian Regiment.

There was more than one Irishman in 1 RAR. Edward Somers from Enniscorthy, County Wexford, had emigrated to Australia in 1962. He had already chalked up three years of experience in the British army, driving trucks for the Royal Army Service Corps in Cyprus. Like Dan Danaher, with whom he became friendly (they're still good friends), Somers went to Vietnam because he wanted to. 'It sounded like an exciting place to be.' He enlisted in the tiny Australian army and was posted to Vietnam in May 1965. His fourteen-month stint was spent, along with the rest of B Company, at Bien Hoa airbase, thirty miles north-east of Saigon. 1 RAR became part of the 173rd Airborne Brigade, along with two American regiments.

An out-of-the-way farm in Roscommon little resembles the perilous jungles of South-East Asia. However, Gerard Duignan eventually made his way back home after four years in Vietnam. Outwardly, at least, he does not appear to have left his youth behind him there. Slight and dark he looks ten years younger than his actual age. He was working on Wall Street in the early 1960s, a time when Vietnam was moving from the status of an American preoccupation to an obsession. He had gone to New York straight from school in Roscommon. At the time, he was curious about the war and unlike his friends, who were keen to avoid the draft, sought out the company of men who had been there. He went to a recruiting office to volunteer for the air force where he was told that he needed to set about becoming a US citizen first. Once in the air force, which he entered on 25 July 1965, he volunteered for overseas duty and, as an alien, had to subject himself to an FBI investigation. He ended up having almost as tough a struggle to get to Vietnam as thousands of young Americans were enduring to stay away.

The military draft claimed a twenty-three-year-old Dubliner, John Kennedy, in 1965. He was an emigrant working for a bus company in New York. 'I could have run home but I didn't. I know a lot of Irish guys who headed for the hills and came back to Ireland. But I was young and Vietnam sounded like the sort of country I wouldn't get to otherwise. It wasn't until I got there in 1966 that I realised this wasn't war games, this was the real McCoy.' Kennedy was with A Company of the 32nd Infantry, stationed outside the massive Da Nang airbase.

Canice Wolohan, a soft-spoken and articulate Dubliner, began the process of enlistment in the US navy in Ireland itself. His objective on leaving school was to see as much of the world as possible; visiting the US Embassy as an eighteen-year old in 1963 he was told he would have to go to the States if he wanted to join up. Using his aunt's address in Cleveland and having begun the naturalisation process he was accepted by the navy in December of that year. He did his basic training in San Diego and was sent to Vietnam in June of 1964 as an 'adviser', just after a force of Marines, the first American ground-combat troops, landed at Da Nang and the US troop escalation began.

By the time Gerard Duignan arrived in Vietnam in January 1968 his training had transformed him from enthusiastic amateur to a gung-ho professional soldier. But he still experienced an apprehensive lurch in the pit of his stomach when landing at Cam Ranh Bay on his first tour of duty. He had been warned to expect extreme heat, 'but when we landed at Cam Ranh Bay it was upwards of 120 degrees and steamy. But that wasn't the problem; it was the smell, the squalor and the dirt. In all our training you came home in the evening-time to a clean bed, clean room, a shower and good food. You got up next morning ready to go again. But this was filth.'

Duignan's fastidiousness was put to a severe test in his first transit camp. This was a large tented village with open-field toilet facilities 'which we had been taught to make in training but which we never used. These were half-cut barrels and there was no privacy.' Duignan picked himself out a tent with a spare bed and went for a shower, having sought directions from the only occupant of his new billet. To his dismay the showers were from the same architectural school as the toilets. 'There were people walking up and down including Vietnamese women, maids working on the base.' With a becoming Irish coyness and modesty Duignan decided against giving scandal to others and returned to his tent. He was forced to lie when asked if he had found the showers and was escorted back to them by his obliging colleague. Running out of choices, he gritted his teeth and got on with his sanitary 'initiation'. 'That was the hardest thing; once you got used to it, that didn't bother you any more, but it bothered me an awful lot that first day.' Arriving, as he did, a few short weeks before the VC and NVA 'Tet' offensive of 1968, Duignan would have more to worry about than his modesty before he left Vietnam.

To eighteen-year-old Canice Wolohan, Vietnam was 'a tremendous adventure, a great opportunity and I was dying to grab it'. The first time it struck him that he might be going to a place which was not altogether safe was when landing in Saigon. 'The plane itself was a standard Pan American Boeing 707. Coming into land the pilot advised the passengers, who were all military people like myself, that we better brace ourselves because we were going to have to come down in a very steep dive.' Planes had been strafed by Viet Cong before, so the pilot was taking no chances. The landing was a rough one for Wolohan but he got down in one piece.

The 1968 'Tet' (Vietnamese New Year) offensive was a well-planned co-ordinated military operation which shocked the military and the home front in the US out of a complacent feeling that the Viet Cong and the North Vietnamese were only capable of mounting small-scale offensives or guerrilla-type operations. The Viet Cong had perfected the latter years before. One of their most conspicuous successes had been an attack on Christmas Eve 1964 on the Brinks Hotel in central Saigon. The hotel housed a number of American military personnel and the bar was much frequented by US and Vietnamese officers. The Viet Cong managed to get a huge car bomb into the hotel parking lot which went off at 5.45 pm. Canice Wolohan was a transport officer for the 'Bob Hope Show' that Christmas and was driving past the area shortly after the bomb went off. 'Even though things happened right beside me on occasions, I think that was probably the most frightening. There was mass hysteria, bits of people lying all over the place, both military and civilian.'

Close to Bien Hoa airbase was an area notorious for Viet Cong and North Vietnamese army activity known as the 'Iron Triangle'; it consisted of four villages and, unknown to the Americans and Australians, it was a mass of secret tunnels fashioned by the Viet Cong, some created, in fact, by the Viet Minh twenty years before, during their war with the French. Periodic attempts were made to clear it of communists, most notably with Operation Cedar Falls in 1967. But the previous year, on 6 January 1966, the 173rd Airborne had gone into part of the Iron Triangle, called Hobo Woods, to flush out the VC. They succeeded, but at great cost to themselves. A so-called 'free fire zone' was created by the evacuation of villagers, and the peppering of Hobo Woods by artillery and aircraft followed.

1 RAR were helicoptered into Hobo Woods at 5.00 am on the morning of 6 January. Their first casualties were from friendly fire – an American artillery unit which did not know they were there. They fought their way into a village and set up a defensive perimeter. Ed Somers was puzzled at the time by the ease with which VC, apparently cornered, would manage to get away. 'We wondered where the enemy

would disappear to. We thought they were just lucky.' The puzzlement turned to outright confusion that night as the Viet Cong consistently penetrated the circular perimeter set up by the regiment around the village. Australian riflemen, responding to bursts of automatic fire from within the village itself, would fire back and frequently hit their comrades on the far side of the perimeter.

One Aussie, Private Penn, hit by friendly fire, was dragged in by Somers under a hail of bullets coming from all directions. He had been hit in the shoulder and seriously hurt. Somers's bravery counted for nothing, however, as Penn died shortly after he was hoisted onto a 'dust off' (evacuation helicopter). Sorting through the dead man's effects the following day, Somers found a letter from Penn's mother covered in his blood. Penn had died on his way to a field hospital but, in Somers's opinion, dozens of others were saved that night by the courage of the helicopter pilots who ferried the wounded away from danger. 'The real heroes that night were the "dust-off" pilots. They were coming down in the dark not knowing what was on the ground. We only had torches to guide them in. We might just as easily have been Viet Cong, that was a trick they tried now and again.'

It soon became clear to the Australians that there were tunnels leading into and out of the village. The following morning two American engineers arrived with a generator and began pumping smoke and CS gas into some of the tunnel openings to make them un-inhabitable. Two Australian engineers decided to go down and take a look for themselves. However, the tunnels were extraordinarily narrow, barely two feet across, wide enough to accommodate the frame of a tiny Vietnamese but not a muscular Australian. One of the engineers, Dan Danaher recalls, got stuck in a bend. One after another, twelve volunteers climbed down to try and pull him out; one after another they returned to the surface retching and twitching from the effects of the gas. All insisted, however, that the trapped engineer was still breathing. As he was only about twenty feet underground a decision was taken to dig down to him directly from the surface. 'They started to dig straight down. It took about two hours to dig the hole and by the time they got down to him, put a rope around his leg and pulled him out he was dead.'

On the second day of the operation, 7 January, 1 RAR moved out of the village; as they crossed a clearing in Hobo Woods a sniper opened fire and hit an Irish-Australian, Private Delaney, in the lung. Ed Somers watched as a medic ran to help Delaney and was shot with deadly accuracy in the skull. A second ran forward and was killed in precisely the same way. The sniper was spotted shooting from behind a large ant hill. In order to blow away his cover a disposable anti-tank weapon, called a LAW, was used. This was effective in destroying the ant hill but there was no sign of the sniper when the dust cleared. He had managed to dive into yet another tunnel system, a huge network. Dogs were brought in and sent down the tunnels to locate the Vietnamese. The dogs never came back. The soldiers refused to follow them. 'We wouldn't go underground. We were too big for one thing, the tunnels were very narrow.' Finally all the ammunition captured in the operation was gathered together; a bulldozer was brought in to excavate one of the tunnels, the ammunition was placed in it and the entire cache was exploded. 'We were hoping to collapse the whole tunnel system that way. There was quite a shock wave from the explosion.'

Gradually, as the war progressed, the Viet Cong developed the capability of taking the battle, in numbers, into the heart of Saigon itself. They demonstrated this graphically with the attack on the US Embassy during Tet on 31 January 1968. It was that attack, right to the symbolic heart of American power in South-East Asia and filmed by a US network TV, which began the Vietnam endgame. But Gerard Duignan was not greatly concerned with the travails of the Marine guards trying to keep a Viet Cong 'suicide' squad out of the ambassador's drinks cabinet. He was having his own problems on the perimeter of Phu Cat airbase. Warning sirens had gone off in the late night and early morning and a sleepy Duignan was roused, crammed into a lorry and dumped into a foxhole on the edge of the base. Half an hour later 'all hell broke loose behind us, tracers, machine-gun fire, everything'. Viet Cong Sappers had been placing explosives on the planes when one of them strayed across a trip wire and alerted the defenders; a vicious fire fight broke out and the Viet Cong withdrew. They had already taken the nearby town of Dap Da. This was then used as the platform for further attacks on the base. However, by this time the whole country was in chaos after the first wave of Tet attacks, and the base defenders were well prepared. The First Cavalry Division arrived in force from Quinhon and retook Dap Da with the aid of a large force of tanks.

I remember that for three days we didn't sleep at all. When we went down to the town, where they had supposedly killed 214 North Vietnamese, there were bodies stacked everywhere just like you'd stack bags of flour on top of each other. You had some fellows there taking photographs of the bodies . . . taking close-up shots. That's the way you'd be, your mind would be that way inclined. You could sit on one of them, eat your dinner and it wouldn't upset you. You'd just get up and complain that it wasn't comfortable enough, or something like that. That was the mentality.

Part of the outlying area around Phu Cat airbase was turned into what the Americans called a 'free fire zone'. This meant that all the inhabitants of an area were ordered out and resettled. From then on anyone found in such a sector was assumed to be Viet Cong and could be shot on sight. In theory the indigenous Vietnamese should have stayed well away from the homes and villages from where they had been evacuated, but they did not subscribe to the theory. What they did subscribe to was a reverence for the place of their birth, their livelihood and the resting place of their ancestors. Many strayed back into free-fire zones and were killed.

One night Gerard Duignan, who was not normally assigned to such tasks, asked to be allowed to accompany an armoured patrol into the bush. Shortly after they left the base they came under fire, replied, and killed one Viet Cong. The patrol continued on to sweep its designated area, unnerved by the attack. Movement was spotted in an abandoned hamlet and the three personnel carriers in the patrol opened up on the huts. Fire was returned but it soon petered out under the hail of American ordnance. When the patrol went in to examine their handiwork they discovered that they had wiped out a twenty-five member South Vietnamese unit. 'Because of the fact that I wasn't listed on the patrol,' says Duignan, 'I remained at Phu Cat. Everybody else was shipped out of there within twenty-four hours.'

The determination of those legally dissenting Vietnamese, opposed to their own government and the US forces, was a constant reminder to the Americans of what they were up against. The well-publicised self-immolations staged by Buddhist monks protesting against the repressive policies of the minority Catholic-dominated government were an indication of the desire of the Southern Vietnamese to see real democracy in Vietnam; they would not support high-handed puppets whose strings were pulled by the US Embassy. During his tour, Canice Wolohan once saw a crowd running towards something in the streets of Saigon which he could not immediately identify. 'In Vietnam crowds generally ran *away* from an area rather than [towards] it.' They decided to investigate and then watched as a Buddhist monk knelt in the street, poured petrol over himself and lit a match. 'He stayed squatting there, praying, while he burnt to death. None of us could do anything about it, he just went up into a ball of flame. As he did this the Buddhists were chanting around him. . . . I couldn't understand why somebody would inflict something like that on themselves. I didn't think the situation was as bad as all that.'

The Geneva Convention somehow seemed superfluous and irrelevant in Vietnam. Both sides were guilty of flagrant abuses of common humanity. The massacre of Vietnamese villagers in My Lai by American troops in 1968 and the systematic murder of collaborators by the communists in Hue during the same year are the two most egregrious examples of the sheer brutality of the war. Some of the worst savagery was meted out by the South Vietnamese to their own. Five poles in a market square in Saigon were the pockmarked witnesses to hundreds of executions which took place on a weekly basis. The area was restricted, but Ed Somers passed through in an American truck and, struck by these poles, took a number of slides. It did not take him long to figure out exactly what it was he was photographing. 'There was sand on the ground to hide the blood and poles were rough and chipped away by bullets.' This was the place where the American-backed South Vietnamese government disposed of its undesirables, anyone from black marketeers to political dissidents. Somers found out about the methods of execution later. A proper military firing squad should consist of ten armed men. The prisoner, in these circumstances, would be killed instantly. 'But these prisoners had one soldier each to execute them. They were using 30-calibre carbines and many of those troopers were nervous. Often, instead of killing a man outright, they might shoot him in the stomach and leave him in agony.'

'In country' there was a different kind of war going on. It was a vicious guerrilla war with no front lines and no rear echelon. If you were an American or Australian soldier you could die just as easily in a Saigon bar from a grenade thrown by a passing cyclist as you could at the hands of a North Vietnamese regular south of the ironically named demilitarised zone (DMZ). This knowledge bred a callousness in the American troops which resulted in the consistent flouting of the Geneva Convention during the interrogation of prisoners of war. 'How many wounded Viet Cong ended up in hospital?' asked one Irish veteran. On at least half a dozen occasions he saw enemy injured shot dead where they lay. 'Admittedly, some of them would have been pretty far gone. They had the sort of wounds where you die slowly and in agony. You were doing them a favour.' He no longer attempts to justify that sort of treatment and admits that many Viet Cong, who were not *in extremis*, were nevertheless despatched.

The first and last months of the normal twelve-month tour were the most risky, according to Canice Wolohan. During the introductory month, valuable experience was acquired which could then be put to good use for the next eleven, assuming, that is, the 'raw meat' (as the rookies were often elegantly called) made a few minor mistakes and not that first fatal one. 'In the last month people tended to become a little bit too "*flaithulach*", saying: "Nothing can happen to me now." This system of one year rotations is often seen as one of the principal contributors to the American defeat. 'It was a one-year stint. The basic objective of every fellow going to Vietnam was to survive over there for one year. It wasn't to win a war, it wasn't to carry out any particular objective. It was basically to survive for one year and go home.'

The attitude of combat troops towards the Vietnamese, while regrettable, was in many respects understandable. You never knew your enemy in Vietnam, particularly in rural areas where more Vietnamese than was ever admitted by the Americans or the Saigon government were part of the so-called VCI (Viet Cong Infrastructure). The 'grunt' on the ground knew, often from bitter experience, what the officer briefing the Saigon Press Corps at the so-called 'Five O'Clock Follies' did not care to acknowledge. This explained, without necessarily excusing, his frequent displays of hostility to the native population. Dan Danaher was taught a number of Vietnamese phrases but only really used one which translated roughly as 'get lost'. John Kennedy, serving in Da Nang, thought of them as 'human beings like the rest of us but you were suspicious of them, you always had to be slightly wary'.

Gerard Duignan, partly because he chose to spend four years in Vietnam, became more involved with the Vietnamese. Both he and a colleague, Sergeant di Pepe, gave English lessons in a local village. Their classes were popular and packed out every week. On the base no one in authority was told about these classes. 'They would be suspicious that you were working the black market or that you were doing something illegal.' The area in which the lessons were conducted was a known Viet Cong sphere of operation. After about eight months di Pepe came back from class one day carrying a letter. He and Duignan read it. It was a request not to conduct any more classes for the time being as their safety could not be guaranteed. It was signed by the local Viet Cong commander!

When Ed Somers fought in Vietnam during 1965 and 1966, the typical American soldier serving there was a career regular. It was only after 1966, when the American commitment escalated, that non-volunteer GIs, caught by the draft, began to arrive in large numbers. Even so, Somers was struck by the naivety of some of the battle-hardened regulars in the 173rd Airborne Brigade. Unlike subsequent drafts of so-called airborne troops in Vietnam (whose only claim to being airborne was that they were transported by helicopter), the men of, for example, the 503rd Regiment, who formed part of the 173rd Brigade, were tough paratroopers. Yet Somers recalls an incident in which the neglect of everything they had learned in basic training cost lives.

The 503rd were moving through an area of jungle when the 'point man' came across a twelve-inch-high wooden sign hanging from a tree. The lettering was in red, the background white. The front men in the column stopped to look at this strange sign and slowly a crowd began to gather as they assembled beneath the tree, attempting to decipher the inscription. Few were ever to realise that it read: 'Anybody who looks at this sign is about to die'; the Viet Cong detonated a huge bomb underneath the tree, killing more than twenty GIs and wounding many more. The first Somers knew about this incident was when the 'dust offs' flew back to Bien Hoa with the casualties and he, along with many of 1 RAR, gave blood to help save more lives. His candidly proffered opinion is that 'though they were brave, they were extremely foolhardy and pretty clumsy people in the bush'.

While there were unquestionably more Irishmen fighting in Vietnam than Vietnamese in the Irish Civil War, it remains true that Irishmen in the American or Australian army in South-East Asia were not numerous. But there was still room, even in remote Phu Cat, for traditional Irish rivalries to be played out. Gerard Duignan remembers a Protestant Belfast-born former professional footballer, Sergeant Reed, and a Belfast Catholic named Evans, also a proficient soccer player, trading republican and unionist songs in a rare victory celebration after a match against a Vietnamese unit. They were performing before a bar full of bemused Americans. Duignan met quite a number of other Irishmen during his four-year stint. He even has a photograph from the *Roscommon Herald* taken in Tan Son Nhut air base of three Roscommon men, in uniform, sitting on a bench reading a copy of the *Roscommon Herald*. The other two men, both from Boyle, were Chaplain (Captain) Patrick Feely, who was based at Tan Son Nhut, and Sergeant Michael Noone who was stationed at Binh Thuy.

Leaving Vietnam was something nearly three million Americans did at one time or another. Leaving Vietnam behind was an entirely different matter. Dan Danaher's metaphor, offered by way of explanation for the behaviour of some veterans, post war, is an accessible one. 'If you have a little puppy dog and he's sitting by the fire, he's comfortable and he's friendly, and you keep going up to him and bursting a paper bag beside his ear, sooner or later that dog is going to get jumpy and probably bite you.' The syndrome has been identified as Post Traumatic Stress Disorder; in wars gone by it was probably called battle fatigue or shell shock. It is a mechanism devised by the psyche for telling somebody that they have seen one horror too many.

Even though Gerard Duignan spent four years in Vietnam of his own volition he still found it hard to adapt to the pace and priorities of a life spent a safe distance away from the edge of a physical and psychological precipice. 'You take death as a part of living. To turn round and kill somebody or to see somebody dead has no effect on you. You just turn them over with your boot. You get that callousness in you and it means that you're afraid you could actually do something like that to somebody else, even though it mightn't be in a war. . . . I could easily understand how fellows would blow their tops.' His work with Vietnamese orphans and refugees, he reckons, kept him from plunging over his own self-made precipice. And leaving Vietnam meant going home, which, in the case of Irish veterans, involved a return to the United States. But for most it was a very different America to the one they had left. Twelve months had wrought changes in the attitude of the American people to this ugly, inglorious war. Canice Wolohan was under no illusions as to the dwindling popularity of the war by the time he returned Stateside. 'And, in fact, it grew worse. Even when I was in the forces subsequently, I recall where troops were literally spat upon when they got back to America. They didn't receive the sort of heroes' welcome awaiting troops from the Second World War, the First World War or even the Korean War. It was not a popular war. Guys going over there subsequently realised this before they left and therefore they didn't go into it with any great enthusiasm.'

The contrast between the departure of 1 RAR from Sydney and its return fourteen months later was noted ruefully by Dan Danaher. They had received a stirring send-off but their return, and their street parade, had a mixed reception. They marched in columns six deep, Danaher nearest the kerb in his line. The battalion had been instructed, in the event of any protesters getting among the ranks, not to break stride but to simply push them out of the way. The commander of B Company, which also included Ed Somers, was marching about ten yards in front of the leading column of soldiers. Suddenly a woman broke away from the spectators on the pavement, dashed out onto the street and poured the contents of a tin of red paint over the CO. 'The officer kept his salute. He just ignored her even though she was hanging onto him and he had red paint all over him.'

John Kennedy, who joined the New York Police Department after his Vietnam experience, is to this day supportive of the war in South-East Asia. In common with many American veterans he feels a war which had been undeniably lost could have been won. 'The Americans had the equipment to win that war, equipment which wasn't being used. The military had their hands tied behind their backs. Look at the Gulf War. If Vietnam had been approached in the same way the result would have been the same.'

However, an inescapable sense of sadness and loss pervades the conversation of most Irish Vietnam veterans. It reflects more then the sense of waste which most soldiers carry home from a war. Perhaps for some it is a vague sense of guilt at having been there in the first place. Canice Wolohan talks about the enormous loss of Vietnamese life. 'At the end of the day, it's very hard to see what it has all achieved. I don't think the Vietnamese people themselves are really happy today. So from their point of view I don't know whether the war really did achieve anything either.' Gerard Duignan made some good Vietnamese friends. 'I never met a family that hadn't lost a brother, a sister, a father or a mother, be it at the hands of the Viet Cong or the Americans. They accepted it then, but I don't think now that it need ever have happened.'

Epilogue: And So It Goes On

It may be a trickle but the source has not dried up. In April 1982 three Irish members of the secretive British SAS (Special Air Services) were killed in the Falklands, one from Northern Ireland, one from Donegal and the other from Tipperary. Their Sea King helicopter crashed, killing eighteen members of the SAS, a regiment which two Irishmen, Colonel Blair Mayne (a former rugby international) and Ambrose McGonigal (a future High Court judge) helped found.

In the 1991 Gulf War, Operation Desert Storm, the British element of the Task Force included the 600 members of the Queen's Royal Irish Hussars, a tank regiment in the 7th Armoured Brigade (the Desert Rats). Only about 30 per cent of the regiment was actually Irish, about 120 from Northern Ireland and sixty from the Republic. Isolated individuals served in the US Armed Forces. Gerard Murran from Slane and Ciaran Allison from nearby Drogheda were part of the elite 82nd Airborne. Paul Carr from Clondalkin in Dublin served with the 22nd Airborne. Colum Kearns from Bantry in Cork reached the rank of sergeant with the Special Forces Airborne Group and was due to leave the army on 10 January 1991 when he was sent to Saudi Arabia.

More recently, when Yugoslavia began to feed on its own organs Western reporters simultaneously began to run across the epitome of the 'universal soldier'. Shane McCormick from Athlone in County Westmeath is a stocky five foot two inches bullet-headed mercenary with experience in the British army and the French Foreign Legion. His father is a Second World War veteran who landed in Normandy on D-Day. Shane was fighting with the right-wing Croatian 'private' army HOS, an elite unit which offered fierce resistance to the Serbian invasion of Eastern Croatia in the winter of 1991 and 1992. He probably became involved in fighting for HOS through a Croatian friend who was a Legionaire. McCormick was enthusiastic about his work, which involved killing 'Chetniks' (pejorative slang for Serbian militia). Sitting in a Zagreb restaurant looking out at the rain, he was quoted in one paper as saying, 'great weather for fighting – when it's raining like this you get a bunch of Chetniks huddled in a bunker, you lob in a grenade and bang — all out in one go.'

Just over a year later Irish newspapers carried reports of a twenty-two-year-old Dubliner, Ivan Farina from Killiney, losing an eye in a landmine explosion while on an operation for HOS in Croatian-occupied Bosnia. He spent several weeks in a coma before his family evacuated him to Dublin. Doubtless, Farina and McCormick are not the only Irish who became involved in the internecine carnage of the imploding Yugoslavia.

A civil war of a different kind brought Austin Empey to Somalia with the American Operation Restore Hope. It was a far cry from his army posting in Alaska for the young Dubliner, whose father is a Church of Ireland canon and whose uncle is the Bishop of Meath.

And so it goes on . . .